The Econon

D0725256

POCKET WORLD IN FIGURES

2018 Edition

Published by
Profile Books Ltd
3 Holford Yard
Bevin Way
London WC1X 9HD

This special paperback edition produced in association
with and exclusively for The Economist

Published under exclusive licence from
The Economist by Profile Books, 2017

Copyright © The Economist Newspaper Ltd, 1991, 1992,
1993, 1994, 1995, 1996, 1997, 1998, 1999, 2000, 2001,
2002, 2003, 2004, 2005, 2006, 2007, 2008, 2009,
2010, 2011, 2012, 2013, 2014, 2015, 2016, 2017

Material researched by
Andrea Burgess, Lisa Davies, Graham Douglas, Mark Doyle,
Ian Emery, Conrad Heine, Carol Howard, David McKelvey,
Georgina McKelvey, Guy Scriven, Christopher Wilson

All rights reserved. Without limiting the rights under copyright
reserved above, no part of this publication may be reproduced,
stored in or introduced into a retrieval system, or transmitted, in
any form or by any means (electronic, mechanical, photocopying,
recording or otherwise), without the prior written permission of
both the copyright owner and the above publisher of this book.

The greatest care has been taken in compiling this book. However,
no responsibility can be accepted by the publishers or compilers
for the accuracy of the information presented.

Typeset in Econ Sans Condensed by MacGuru Ltd

Printed in the United States

A CIP catalogue record for this book is available
from the British Library

ISBN 978 1 78125 889 7

Contents

7 Introduction
8 Notes

11 Part I World rankings

Geography and demographics

12 **Countries: *natural facts***
Countries: the largest Largest exclusive economic zones
Mountains: the highest Rivers: the longest
Deserts: the largest non-polar Lakes: the largest

14 **Population: *size and growth***
Largest populations, 2015 Largest populations, 2030
Fastest-growing populations Slowest-growing populations

16 **Population: *matters of breeding and sex***
Total births Teenage births Highest and lowest fertility rates
Highest and lowest contraception rates

18 **Population: *age***
Median age biggest change over 50 years
Oldest and youngest populations

19 **City living**
Biggest cities Fastest- and slowest-growing cities
Biggest urban populations Highest and lowest urban growth
Highest and lowest rural growth City liveability index
Tallest buildings

22 **Migrants, refugees and asylum seekers**
Biggest migrant populations Biggest destination country for migrants
Refugees by country of origin
Countries with largest refugee populations
Origin of asylum applications to industrialised countries
Countries where asylum applications were lodged

Economics

24 **The world economy**
Biggest economies Biggest economies by purchasing power
Regional GDP Regional purchasing power
Regional population Regional international trade

26 **Living standards**
Highest and lowest GDP per person
Highest and lowest purchasing power

28 **The quality of life**
Highest and lowest human development index
Inequality-adjusted human development index
Highest and lowest Gini coefficient

30 **Economic growth**
Highest economic growth Lowest economic growth
Highest services growth Lowest services growth

32 Trading places
Biggest exporters Most and least trade-dependent
Biggest traders of goods Biggest earners from services and income

34 Balance of payments: *current account*
Largest surpluses Largest deficits
Largest surpluses as % of GDP Largest deficits as % of GDP
Official reserves Official gold reserves Workers' remittances

37 Exchange rates
The Economist's Big Mac index

38 Inflation
Highest and lowest consumer-price inflation
Commodity prices: change House prices: change

40 Debt
Highest foreign debt Highest foreign debt burden
Highest debt and debt service ratios Household debt

42 Aid
Largest recipients Largest donors Biggest changes to aid

44 Industry and services
Largest industrial output
Highest and lowest growth in industrial output
Largest manufacturing output Largest services output

46 Agriculture and fisheries
Largest agricultural output Most and least economically dependent
Fisheries and aquaculture production
Biggest producers: cereals, meat, fruit, vegetables, roots and tubers

48 Commodities
Leading producers and consumers of: wheat, rice, sugar, coarse grains, tea, coffee, cocoa, orange juice, copper, lead, zinc, tin, nickel, aluminium, precious metals, rubber, cotton, major oil seeds and vegetable oils, oil, natural gas, coal Top proved oil reserves

54 Energy
Largest producers Largest consumers
Most and least energy-efficient
Highest and lowest net energy importers
Largest consumption per person Sources of electricity

56 Labour markets
Highest and lowest labour-force participation
Most male and female workforces Highest rate of unemployment
Highest rate of youth unemployment Minimum wage
Average hours worked Poverty pay

Business

59 Business costs and foreign direct investment
Office rents Foreign direct investment

60 Business creativity and research
Entrepreneurial activity Brain drains
R&D expenditure Innovation index

62 Businesses and banks
Largest non-financial companies Largest banks
Largest sovereign-wealth funds

64 Stockmarkets
Largest market capitalisation
Largest gains and losses in global stockmarkets
Largest value traded Number of listed companies

Politics and society

66 Public finance
Government debt Government spending Tax revenue

67 Democracy
Most and least democratic Most and fewest parliamentary seats
Women in parliament

68 Education
Highest and lowest primary enrolment
Highest secondary enrolment Highest tertiary enrolment
Least literate Highest and lowest education spending

70 Marriage and divorce
Highest marriage rates Lowest marriage rates
Highest divorce rates Lowest divorce rates
Youngest and oldest mean age of women at first marriage

72 Households, living costs and giving
Biggest number of households Average household size
Highest and lowest cost of living World Giving Index

74 Transport: *roads and cars*
Longest road networks Densest road networks
Most crowded road networks Most road deaths
Fastest-growing car ownership Slowest-growing car ownership
Car production Cars sold

78 Transport: *planes and trains*
Most air travel Busiest airports Longest railway networks
Most rail passengers Most rail freight

80 Transport: *shipping*
Largest merchant fleets by country of domicile and country of registration

81 Crime and punishment
Murders Robberies Prisoners

82 War and terrorism
Defence spending Armed forces Arms traders
Terrorist attacks

84 Space and peace
Space missions Orbital launches Global Peace Index

85 Environment
Biggest emitters of carbon dioxide
Largest amount of carbon dioxide emitted per person
Most polluted capital cities Lowest access to improved sanitation
Lowest access to electricity Largest forests Most forested

Biggest decrease and increase in forestation Most dams
Largest reservoirs Slums Environmental Performance Index
Worst natural catastrophes

Health and welfare

90 Life expectancy
Highest life expectancy Highest male life expectancy
Highest female life expectancy Lowest life expectancy
Lowest male life expectancy Lowest female life expectancy

92 Death rates and infant mortality
Highest death rates Highest infant mortality
Lowest death rates Lowest infant mortality

94 Death and disease
Diabetes Cardiovascular disease
Chronic respiratory diseases Tuberculosis
Measles and DPT immunisation HIV/AIDS prevalence and deaths

96 Health
Highest health spending Lowest health spending
Highest and lowest population per doctor Obesity
Highest and lowest food deficits

Culture and entertainment

98 Telephones and the internet
Mobile telephones Landline telephones Internet users
Broadband

100 Arts and entertainment
Music sales Book publishing
Cinema attendances Oscar nominations by ethnicity

102 The press
Daily newspapers Press freedom

103 Nobel prize winners
Peace Medicine Literature Economics Physics Chemistry
Total wins by country of birth

104 Sports champions and cheats
World Cup winners and finalists: men's and women's football, cricket,
Davis Cup winners Summer Olympics, athletes sent per gold medal
Anti-doping rule violations

106 Vices
Beer drinkers Smokers Gambling losses

107 Tourism
Most tourist arrivals Biggest tourist spenders
Largest tourist receipts

109 Part II Country profiles

242 WORLD RANKINGS QUIZ
248 Glossary
250 List of countries
254 Sources

Introduction

This 2018 edition of *The Economist Pocket World in Figures* presents and analyses data about the world in two sections:

The **world rankings** consider and rank the performance of 185 countries against a range of indicators in six sections: geography and demographics, economics, business, politics and society, health and welfare, and culture and entertainment. The countries included are those which had (in 2015) a population of at least 1m or a GDP of at least $3bn; they are listed on pages 250–53. New rankings this year include topics as diverse as the average number of births, biggest destination countries for migrants, largest merchant fleets by flags of convenience, terrorist attacks, dams, reservoirs and countries with most urban population living in slums. Some of the rankings data are shown as charts and graphs.

The **country profiles** look in detail at 64 major countries, listed on page 109, plus profiles of the euro area and the world.

Test your *Pocket World in Figures* knowledge with our **World Rankings Quiz** on pages 242–7. Answers can be found in the corresponding world rankings section.

Notes

The extent and quality of the statistics available vary from country to country. Every care has been taken to specify the broad definitions on which the data are based and to indicate cases where data quality or technical difficulties are such that interpretation of the figures is likely to be seriously affected. Nevertheless, figures from individual countries may differ from standard international statistical definitions. The term "country" can also refer to territories or economic entities.

Definitions of the statistics shown are given on the relevant page or in the glossary on pages 248–9. Figures may not add exactly to totals, or percentages to 100, because of rounding or, in the case of GDP, statistical adjustment. Sums of money have generally been converted to US dollars at the official exchange rate ruling at the time to which the figures refer.

Some country definitions

Macedonia is officially known as the Former Yugoslav Republic of Macedonia. Data for Cyprus normally refer to Greek Cyprus only. Data for China do not include Hong Kong or Macau. For countries such as Morocco they exclude disputed areas. Congo-Kinshasa refers to the Democratic Republic of Congo, formerly known as Zaire. Congo-Brazzaville refers to the other Congo. Euro area data normally refer to the 19 members that had adopted the euro as at December 31 2016: Austria, Belgium, Cyprus, Estonia, Finland, France, Germany, Greece, Ireland, Italy, Latvia, Lithuania, Luxembourg, Malta, Netherlands, Portugal, Slovakia, Slovenia and Spain. Euro area (18) excludes Lithuania, which adopted the euro on January 1 2015. Euro area (15) refers to the 15 countries in the euro area that are members of the OECD. Data referring to the European Union include the UK, which in June 2016 voted in a referendum to leave the EU. Negotiations over the country's departure will take some time. For more information about the EU, euro area and OECD see the glossary on pages 248–9.

Statistical basis

The all-important factor in a book of this kind is to be able to make reliable comparisons between countries. Although this is never quite possible for the reasons stated above, the best route, which this book takes, is to compare data for the same year or period and to use actual, not estimated, figures wherever possible. In some cases, only OECD members are considered. Where a country's data are excessively out of date, they are excluded. The research for this edition was carried out in 2017 using the latest available sources that present data on an internationally comparable basis.

Data in the country profiles, unless otherwise indicated, refer to the year ending December 31 2015. Life expectancy, crude birth, death and fertility rates are based on 2015–20 estimated averages; energy data are for 2014 and religion data for 2010; marriage and divorce, employment, health and education, consumer goods and services data refer to the latest year for which figures are available.

Other definitions

Data shown in country profiles may not always be consistent with those shown in the world rankings because the definitions or years covered can differ.

Statistics for principal exports and principal imports are normally based on customs statistics. These are generally compiled on different definitions to the visible exports and imports figures shown in the balance of payments section.

Energy-consumption data are not always reliable, particularly for the major oil-producing countries; consumption per person data may therefore be higher than in reality. Energy exports can exceed production and imports can exceed consumption if transit operations distort trade data or oil is imported for refining and re-exported.

Abbreviations and conventions

(see also glossary on pages 248–9)

bn billion (one thousand million)
EU European Union
GDP gross domestic product
GNI gross national income
ha hectare
kg kilogram
km kilometre
m million
PPP purchasing power parity
TOE tonnes of oil equivalent
trn trillion (one thousand billion)
... not available

World rankings

Countries: natural facts

Countries: the largest[a]

'000 sq km

1	Russia	17,098
2	Canada	9,985
3	United States	9,832
4	China	9,563
5	Brazil	8,516
6	Australia	7,741
7	India	3,287
8	Argentina	2,780
9	Kazakhstan	2,725
10	Algeria	2,382
11	Congo-Kinshasa	2,345
12	Saudi Arabia	2,150
13	Mexico	1,964
14	Indonesia	1,911
15	Sudan	1,879
16	Libya	1,760
17	Iran	1,745
18	Mongolia	1,564
19	Peru	1,285
20	Chad	1,284
21	Niger	1,267
22	Angola	1,247
23	Mali	1,240
24	South Africa	1,219
25	Colombia	1,142
26	Ethiopia	1,104
27	Bolivia	1,099
28	Mauritania	1,031
29	Egypt	1,001
30	Tanzania	947
31	Nigeria	924
32	Venezuela	912
33	Namibia	824
34	Mozambique	799
35	Pakistan	796
36	Turkey	785
37	Chile	756
38	Zambia	753
39	Myanmar	677
40	Afghanistan	653
41	South Sudan	644
42	Somalia	638
43	Central African Rep.	623
44	Ukraine	604
45	Madagascar	587
46	Botswana	582
47	Kenya	580
48	France	549
49	Yemen	528
50	Thailand	513
51	Spain	506
52	Turkmenistan	488
53	Cameroon	475
54	Papua New Guinea	463
55	Morocco	447
	Sweden	447
	Uzbekistan	447
58	Iraq	435
59	Paraguay	407
60	Zimbabwe	391
61	Norway	385
62	Japan	378
63	Germany	357
64	Congo-Brazzaville	342
65	Finland	338
66	Malaysia	331
	Vietnam	331
68	Ivory Coast	322

Largest exclusive economic zones[b]

Million sq km

		Marine territory	*Land area*
1	United States	11.4	9.832
2	France	11.0	0.549
3	Australia	8.5	7.741
4	Russia	7.6	17.098
5	United Kingdom	6.8	0.244
6	New Zealand	6.7	0.268
7	Indonesia	6.2	1.911
8	Canada	5.6	9.985
9	Japan	4.5	0.378
10	Brazil	3.7	8.516
	Chile	3.7	0.756
12	Mexico	3.2	1.964
13	Denmark	2.5	0.043
14	Norway	2.4	0.385
	Papua New Guinea	2.4	0.463
16	India	2.3	3.287
17	Portugal	1.7	0.092

a Includes freshwater. b Area extending 200 nautical miles (370km) from the coast.

Mountains: the highest[a]

		Location	*Height (m)*
1	Everest	China–Nepal	8,848
2	K2 (Godwin Austen)	China–Pakistan	8,611
3	Kangchenjunga	India–Nepal	8,586
4	Lhotse	China–Nepal	8,516
5	Makalu	China–Nepal	8,463
6	Cho Oyu	China–Nepal	8,201
7	Dhaulagiri	Nepal	8,167
8	Manaslu	Nepal	8,163
9	Nanga Parbat	Pakistan	8,126
10	Annapurna I	Nepal	8,091

Rivers: the longest

		Location	*Length (km)*
1	Nile	Africa	6,695
2	Amazon	South America	6,516
3	Yangtze (Chang Jiang)	Asia	6,380
4	Mississippi–Missouri system	North America	5,959
5	Ob'-Irtysh	Asia	5,568
6	Yenisey–Angara–Selanga	Asia	5,550
7	Yellow (Huang He)	Asia	5,464
8	Congo	Africa	4,667

Deserts: the largest non-polar

		Location	*Area ('000 sq km)*
1	Sahara	Northern Africa	8,600
2	Arabian	South-western Asia	2,300
3	Gobi	Mongolia/China	1,300
4	Patagonian	Argentina	673
5	Syrian	Middle East	520
6	Great Basin	South-western United States	490
7	Great Victoria	Western and Southern Australia	419
8	Great Sandy	Western Australia	395

Lakes: the largest

		Location	*Area ('000 sq km)*
1	Caspian Sea	Central Asia	371
2	Superior	Canada/United States	82
3	Victoria	East Africa	69
4	Huron	Canada/United States	60
5	Michigan	United States	58
6	Tanganyika	East Africa	33
7	Baikal	Russia	31
	Great Bear	Canada	31

a Includes separate peaks which are part of the same massif.

Notes: Estimates of the lengths of rivers vary widely depending on, eg, the path to take through a delta. The definition of a desert is normally a mean annual precipitation value equal to 250ml or less.

Population: size and growth

Largest populations

m, 2015

1	China	1,376.0
2	India	1,311.1
3	United States	321.8
4	Indonesia	257.6
5	Brazil	207.8
6	Pakistan	188.9
7	Nigeria	182.2
8	Bangladesh	161.0
9	Russia	143.5
10	Mexico	127.0
11	Japan	126.6
12	Philippines	100.7
13	Ethiopia	99.4
14	Vietnam	93.4
15	Egypt	91.5
16	Germany	80.7
17	Iran	79.1
18	Turkey	78.7
19	Congo-Kinshasa	77.3
20	Thailand	68.0
21	United Kingdom	64.7
22	France	64.4
23	Italy	59.8
24	South Africa	54.5
25	Myanmar	53.9
26	Tanzania	53.5
27	South Korea	50.3
28	Colombia	48.2
29	Kenya	46.1
	Spain	46.1
31	Ukraine	44.8
32	Argentina	43.4
33	Sudan	40.2
34	Algeria	39.7
35	Uganda	39.0
36	Poland	38.6
37	Iraq	36.4
38	Canada	35.9
39	Morocco	34.4
40	Afghanistan	32.5
41	Saudi Arabia	31.5
42	Peru	31.4
43	Venezuela	31.1
44	Malaysia	30.3
45	Uzbekistan	29.9
46	Nepal	28.5
47	Mozambique	28.0
48	Ghana	27.4
49	Yemen	26.8
50	North Korea	25.2
51	Angola	25.0
52	Madagascar	24.2
53	Australia	24.0
54	Taiwan	23.4
55	Cameroon	23.3
56	Ivory Coast	22.7
57	Sri Lanka	20.7
58	Niger	19.9
59	Romania	19.5
60	Syria	18.5
61	Burkina Faso	18.1
62	Chile	17.9
63	Kazakhstan	17.6
	Mali	17.6
65	Malawi	17.2
66	Netherlands	16.9
67	Guatemala	16.3
68	Zambia	16.2
69	Ecuador	16.1
70	Cambodia	15.6
	Zimbabwe	15.6
72	Senegal	15.1

Largest populations

m, 2030

1	India	1,527.7
2	China	1,415.5
3	United States	355.8
4	Indonesia	295.5
5	Nigeria	262.6
6	Pakistan	244.9
7	Brazil	228.7
8	Bangladesh	186.5
9	Mexico	148.1
10	Russia	138.7
11	Ethiopia	138.3
12	Philippines	123.6
13	Congo-Kinshasa	120.3
14	Japan	120.1
15	Egypt	117.1
16	Vietnam	105.2
17	Iran	88.5
18	Turkey	87.7
19	Tanzania	82.9
20	Germany	79.3

Note: Populations include migrant workers.

Fastest-growing populations

Total % change, 2010–20

1	Oman	63.6
2	Niger	49.2
3	Kuwait	41.1
4	South Sudan	40.4
5	Qatar	38.8
6	Burundi	38.7
7	Uganda	38.3
8	Chad	38.1
9	Angola	37.8
10	Gambia, The	37.4
11	Congo-Kinshasa	36.7
12	Tanzania	36.4
13	Iraq	36.0
14	Lebanon	35.8
15	Zambia	35.7
16	Malawi	35.6
17	Senegal	35.0
18	Mali	34.9
19	Burkina Faso	33.5
20	Equatorial Guinea	33.2
21	Madagascar	31.9
22	Mozambique	31.5
23	West Bank & Gaza	31.1
24	Guinea	30.4
25	Afghanistan	30.3
26	Benin	30.0
27	French Guiana	29.9
28	Togo	29.8
29	Nigeria	29.7
30	Somalia	29.6
31	Congo-Brazzaville	29.4
	Kenya	29.4
33	Liberia	28.6
34	Cameroon	27.9
	Ethiopia	27.9
36	Mauritania	27.3
	Yemen	27.3
38	Ivory Coast	27.0
39	Guinea-Bissau	26.6
40	Rwanda	26.3
41	Eritrea	25.6
42	Ghana	25.5
	Sudan	25.5
44	Jordan	25.3
45	Zimbabwe	25.0
46	Namibia	24.5

Slowest-growing populations

Total % change, 2010–20

1	Andorra	-16.7
2	Lithuania	-10.5
3	Latvia	-8.2
4	Bulgaria	-7.1
	Romania	-7.1
6	Georgia	-6.4
7	Bermuda	-4.7
8	Ukraine	-4.3
9	Serbia	-4.2
10	Portugal	-4.0
11	Croatia	-3.6
12	Hungary	-3.3
13	Greece	-3.2
14	Estonia	-2.8
15	Bosnia & Herz.	-2.0
16	Japan	-1.8
17	Moldova	-1.5
18	Belarus	-1.3
19	Puerto Rico	-0.9
	Spain	-0.9
21	Poland	-0.4
22	Russia	-0.2
23	Germany	-0.1
24	Martinique	0.0
25	Italy	0.3
26	Cuba	0.5
	Slovakia	0.5
28	Czech Republic	0.6
	Montenegro	0.6
30	Virgin Islands (US)	0.9
31	Albania	1.1
	Slovenia	1.1
33	Macedonia	1.3
	Syria	1.3
35	Taiwan	2.1
36	Armenia	2.5
37	Malta	2.7
	Monaco	2.7
39	Thailand	2.8
40	Barbados	2.9
41	Austria	3.1
42	El Salvador	3.2
43	Netherlands	3.3
44	Mauritius	3.4
45	Jamaica	3.6
	Uruguay	3.6
47	Trinidad & Tobago	3.8
48	Finland	4.0
49	Denmark	4.1

Population: matters of breeding and sex

Total births

Average annual number, m, 2015–20

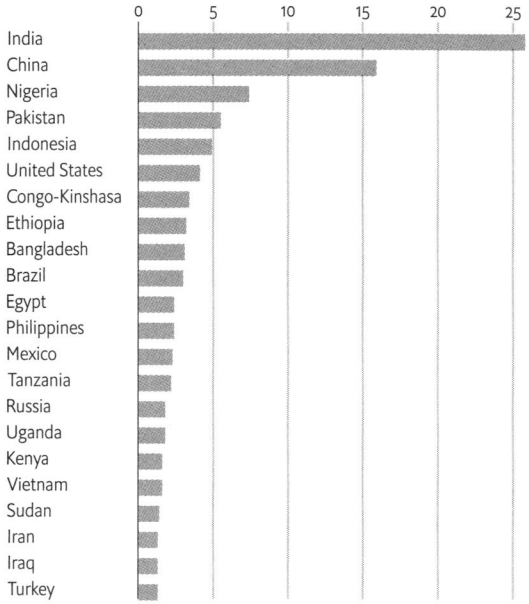

Teenage births

Births per 1,000 women aged 15–19, 2015–20

Highest

1	Niger	196.3
2	Mali	170.3
3	Angola	152.6
4	Ivory Coast	136.0
5	Guinea	135.4
6	Malawi	132.1
7	Mozambique	125.7
8	Congo-Kinshasa	120.9
9	Chad	114.9
10	Tanzania	114.4
11	Sierra Leone	111.0
12	Gambia, The	110.2
13	Congo-Brazzaville	109.9
14	Madagascar	109.5
15	Zimbabwe	106.0
16	Nigeria	104.1
17	Equatorial Guinea	103.0
18	Burkina Faso	101.6

Lowest

1	North Korea	0.4
2	South Korea	1.4
3	Switzerland	2.4
4	Hong Kong	2.9
	Macau	2.9
6	Slovenia	3.1
7	Netherlands	3.5
8	Denmark	3.6
	Japan	3.6
10	Singapore	3.7
11	Iceland	4.0
12	Maldives	4.1
13	Cyprus	4.5
14	Luxembourg	4.9
15	Germany	5.4
16	Oman	5.5
17	Austria	5.6
	Italy	5.6

Fertility rates

Average number of children per woman, 2015

Highest

1	Niger	6.8
2	Burundi	6.1
	Mali	6.1
4	Somalia	6.0
5	Burkina Faso	5.9
	Uganda	5.9
7	Zambia	5.7
8	Malawi	5.6
9	Angola	5.4
10	Afghanistan	5.3
	South Sudan	5.3
12	Ethiopia	5.2
	Mozambique	5.2
	Nigeria	5.2
15	Benin	5.0
	Timor-Leste	5.0
17	Guinea	4.9
	Tanzania	4.9
19	Cameroon	4.8
	Sierra Leone	4.8
21	Congo-Brazzaville	4.7
	Congo-Kinshasa	4.7
	Liberia	4.7
24	Chad	4.6
	Equatorial Guinea	4.6
26	Gabon	4.5
	Rwanda	4.5
	Togo	4.5

Lowest

1	Macau	1.0
	Singapore	1.0
3	Taiwan	1.1
4	Hong Kong	1.2
5	Bosnia & Herz.	1.3
	Poland	1.3
	Romania	1.3
	Slovenia	1.3
	South Korea	1.3
10	Andorra	1.4
	Czech Republic	1.4
	Germany	1.4
	Greece	1.4
	Hungary	1.4
	Italy	1.4
	Japan	1.4
	Serbia	1.4
	Slovakia	1.4

Women[a] who use modern methods of contraception

2015 or latest, %

Highest

1	China	82.5
2	United Kingdom	80.0
3	Thailand	76.5
4	Costa Rica	75.7
5	Nicaragua	75.4
6	Brazil	75.2
7	Hong Kong	75.1
8	Uruguay	73.8
9	Cuba	72.3
10	Finland	72.2
	France	72.2
	Switzerland	72.2
13	Colombia	71.7
14	Norway	71.5
15	Canada	71.1

Lowest

1	South Sudan	2.6
2	Chad	2.9
3	Guinea	4.6
4	Somalia	5.8
5	Congo-Kinshasa	8.5
6	Gambia, The	9.8
	Niger	9.8
8	Montenegro	10.2
9	Benin	10.4
10	Equatorial Guinea	10.6
11	Nigeria	10.8
12	Mali	11.4
13	Mauritania	12.5
14	Angola	12.6
	Central African Rep.	12.6

a Married women aged 15–49; excludes traditional methods of contraception, such as the rhythm method.

Population: age

Median age[a]

Biggest increase over 50 years

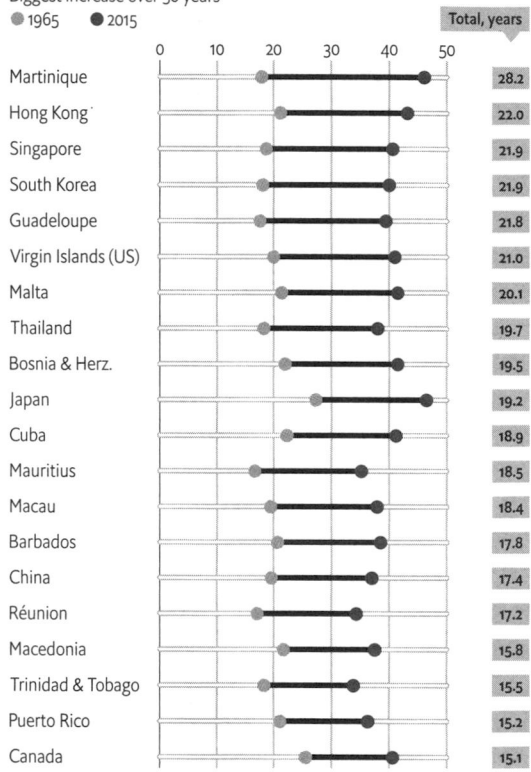

Most old people

% of population aged 70 or over, 2015

1	Monaco	22.9
2	Japan	18.9
3	Italy	16.3
4	Germany	16.1
5	Greece	15.4
6	Portugal	15.0
7	Latvia	14.5
8	Lithuania	14.3
9	Estonia	13.8
10	Austria	13.7
	Spain	13.7
12	Sweden	13.4

Most young people

% of population aged 0–24, 2015

1	Uganda	68.4
2	Niger	68.3
3	Chad	68.0
4	Angola	67.1
5	Mali	66.7
6	Somalia	66.6
7	Zambia	66.0
8	Gambia, The	65.8
	Malawi	65.8
10	Burkina Faso	65.5
	Congo-Kinshasa	65.5
12	Mozambique	65.3

a Age at which there is an equal number of people above and below.

City living

Biggest cities[a]

Population, m, 2016

1	Tokyo, Japan	38.1
2	Delhi, India	26.5
3	Shanghai, China	24.5
4	Mumbai, India	21.4
5	São Paulo, Brazil	21.3
6	Beijing, China	21.2
	Mexico City, Mexico	21.2
8	Osaka, Japan	20.3
9	Cairo, Egypt	19.1
10	New York, US	18.6
11	Dhaka, Bangladesh	18.2
12	Karachi, Pakistan	17.1
13	Buenos Aires, Argentina	15.3
14	Kolkata, India	15.0
15	Istanbul, Turkey	14.4
16	Chongqing, China	13.7
	Lagos, Nigeria	13.7
18	Guangzhou, China	13.1
	Manila, Philippines	13.1
20	Rio de Janeiro, Brazil	13.0
21	Los Angeles, US	12.3
	Moscow, Russia	12.3
23	Kinshasa, Congo-Kinshasa	12.1
24	Tianjin, China	11.6
25	Paris, France	10.9
26	Shenzhen, China	10.8
27	Bangalore, India	10.5
	Jakarta, Indonesia	10.5
29	London, UK	10.4
30	Chennai, India	10.2
31	Lima, Peru	10.1
32	Bogotá, Colombia	10.0
33	Seoul, South Korea	9.8
34	Johannesburg, South Africa	9.6
35	Bangkok, Thailand	9.4
	Nagoya, Japan	9.4
37	Hyderabad, India	9.2
38	Lahore, Pakistan	9.0
39	Chicago, US	8.8
40	Tehran, Iran	8.5
41	Wuhan, China	8.0
42	Chengdu, China	7.8
43	Nanjing, China	7.6
	Ahmadabad, India	7.6
45	Ho Chi Minh City, Vietnam	7.5
	Dongguan, China	7.5
47	Hong Kong	7.4
48	Foshan, China	7.1
49	Kuala Lumpur, Malaysia	7.0
50	Baghdad, Iraq	6.8

City growth[b]

Total % change, 2010–20

Fastest

1	Samut Prakan, Thailand	134.0
2	Batam, Indonesia	103.9
3	Mogadishu, Somalia	95.1
4	Ouagadougou, Burkina Faso	93.1
6	Xiamen, China	90.8
7	Yinchuan, China	80.8
8	Denpasar, Indonesia	80.4
9	Abuja, Nigeria	77.0
10	Can Tho, Vietnam	74.6
11	Dar es Salaam, Tanzania	73.8
12	Zhongshan, China	73.7
13	Kannur, India	73.3
14	Suqian, China	72.5
15	Suzhou, China	72.0
16	Malappuram, India	71.7
17	Hama, Syria	70.9
18	Bamako, Mali	69.2
19	Huambo, Angola	68.2

Slowest

1	Dnipropetrovsk, Ukraine	-9.3
2	Sendai, Japan	-7.8
3	Nizhniy Novgorod, Russia	-7.7
4	Saratov, Russia	-6.9
5	Donetsk, Ukraine	-6.5
6	Zaporizhia, Ukraine	-5.8
7	Khulna, Bangladesh	-5.4
8	Pusan, South Korea	-4.7
9	Yerevan, Armenia	-3.9
10	Detroit, US	-3.3
11	Perm, Russia	-3.0
12	Thessaloniki, Greece	-2.9
13	Buffalo, US	-2.8
14	Havana, Cuba	-2.6
15	Changwon, South Korea	-2.0
	Kitakyushu, Japan	-2.0
17	Kharkiv, Ukraine	-1.9
18	Sapporo, Japan	-1.6
19	Daegu, South Korea	-1.5

a Urban agglomerations. Data may change from year to year based on reassessments of agglomeration boundaries.

b Cities with a population of at least 750,000 in 2010.

Urban populations

% 2020

Highest

1	Bermuda	100.0
	Hong Kong	100.0
	Macau	100.0
	Monaco	100.0
	Singapore	100.0
6	Qatar	99.5
7	Guadeloupe	98.5
8	Kuwait	98.4
9	Belgium	98.0
10	Uruguay	96.0
11	Malta	95.9
	Virgin Islands (US)	95.9
13	Réunion	95.6
14	Japan	95.3

Lowest

1	Trinidad & Tobago	8.1
2	Papua New Guinea	13.3
3	Burundi	13.6
4	Liechtenstein	14.4
5	Malawi	17.3
6	Uganda	17.9
7	Sri Lanka	18.8
8	South Sudan	20.1
9	Niger	20.3
10	Nepal	20.6
11	Swaziland	21.5
12	Ethiopia	21.8
13	Cambodia	22.0
14	Chad	23.4

Urban growth

Total % change, 2010–20

Highest

1	Rwanda	82.4
2	Burkina Faso	74.8
3	Burundi	74.6
4	Uganda	71.0
5	Oman	70.8
6	Niger	70.2
7	Tanzania	67.8
8	Mali	65.3
9	Eritrea	63.5
10	Angola	61.4
11	Ethiopia	61.1
12	Madagascar	58.1
13	Laos	57.3

Lowest

1	Trinidad & Tobago	-9.9
2	Latvia	-5.9
3	Moldova	-5.3
4	Lithuania	-4.2
5	Estonia	-4.0
6	Bulgaria	-3.5
7	Ukraine	-3.3
8	Serbia	-3.1
9	Slovakia	-2.0
10	Russia	-1.4
11	Puerto Rico	-1.2
12	Armenia	-1.1
13	Georgia	-0.9

Rural growth

Total % change, 2010–20

Highest

1	Andorra	55.6
2	Niger	42.5
3	South Sudan	35.6
4	Uganda	33.0
5	Zimbabwe	32.9
6	Chad	31.8
7	Burundi	31.7
8	Oman	31.5
9	Malawi	29.7
10	Zambia	27.9
11	Eritrea	27.1
12	Equatorial Guinea	27.0
13	Iraq	26.6
14	Senegal	24.5

Lowest

1	Japan	-50.8
2	Qatar	-50.0
3	Netherlands	-42.7
4	Virgin Islands (US)	-33.3
5	Dominican Rep.	-26.3
6	Uruguay	-25.5
7	Costa Rica	-22.2
8	Malta	-21.7
9	Réunion	-19.6
10	Belarus	-19.3
	Thailand	-19.3
12	China	-19.1
13	Bulgaria	-18.3
14	Albania	-18.1

City liveability[a]

100 = ideal, 0 = intolerable, 2016

Best

1	Melbourne, Australia	97.5
2	Vienna, Austria	97.4
3	Vancouver, Canada	97.3
4	Toronto, Canada	97.2
5	Adelaide, Australia	96.6
	Calgary, Canada	96.6
7	Perth, Australia	95.9
8	Auckland, New Zealand	95.7
9	Helsinki, Finland	95.6
10	Hamburg, Germany	95.0
11	Sydney, Australia	94.9
12	Montreal, Canada	94.8
13	Tokyo, Japan	94.7
14	Osaka, Japan	94.5
15	Zurich, Switzerland	94.3

Worst

1	Damascus, Syria	30.2
2	Tripoli, Libya	35.9
3	Lagos, Nigeria	36.0
4	Dhaka, Bangladesh	38.7
5	Port Moresby, Papua New Guinea	38.9
6	Algiers, Algeria	40.9
	Karachi, Pakistan	40.9
8	Harare, Zimbabwe	42.6
9	Douala, Cameroon	44.0
10	Kiev, Ukraine	47.8
11	Dakar, Senegal	48.3
12	Abidjan, Ivory Coast	49.7
13	Tehran, Iran	50.8

Tallest buildings[b]

Height, metres

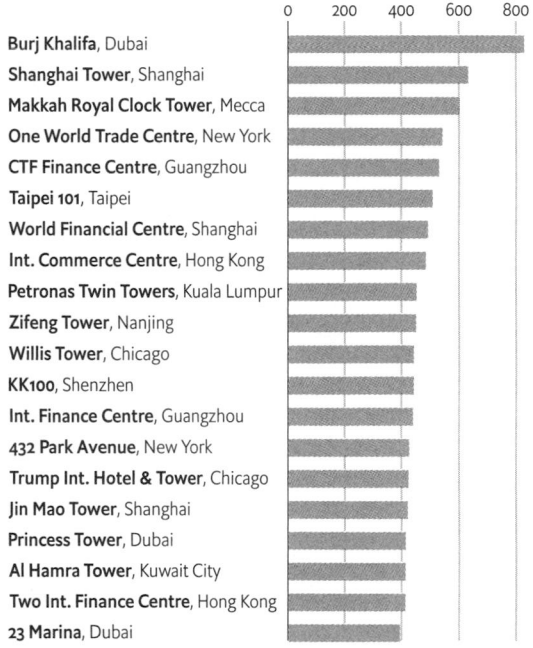

a EIU liveability index, based on a range of factors including stability, health care, culture, education, infrastructure. b Completed.

Migrants, refugees and asylum seekers

Migrants[a] by country of origin

m, 2015

1	India	15.6
2	Mexico	12.3
3	Russia	10.6
4	China	9.5
5	Bangladesh	7.2
6	Pakistan	5.9
7	Ukraine	5.8
8	Philippines	5.3
9	Syria	5.0
10	United Kingdom	4.9
11	Afghanistan	4.8
12	Poland	4.4
13	Kazakhstan	4.1
14	Germany	4.0
15	Indonesia	3.9
16	West Bank & Gaza	3.6
17	Romania	3.4
18	Egypt	3.3
19	Turkey	3.1
20	United States	3.0
21	Italy	2.9
	Myanmar	2.9
23	Morocco	2.8
24	Colombia	2.6
	Vietnam	2.6
26	Portugal	2.3
	South Korea	2.3
28	France	2.1
29	Somalia	2.0
	Uzbekistan	2.0
31	Sudan	1.9
32	Algeria	1.8
	Malaysia	1.8
	Puerto Rico	1.8
35	Bosnia & Herz.	1.7
36	Nepal	1.6
	Sri Lanka	1.6
38	Belarus	1.5
	Brazil	1.5
	Burkina Faso	1.5
	Iraq	1.5
42	Congo-Kinshasa	1.4
	Cuba	1.4
	El Salvador	1.4
	Peru	1.4
46	Canada	1.3
	Dominican Republic	1.3
	Laos	1.3
	Spain	1.3
50	Bulgaria	1.2
	Cambodia	1.2
	Haiti	1.2

Biggest destination country for migrant groups

'000, 2015

1	Mexico	12,050.0	United States
2	India	3,499.3	United Arab Emirates
3	Russia	3,276.8	Ukraine
4	Ukraine	3,270.0	Russia
5	Bangladesh	3,171.0	India
6	Kazakhstan	2,560.3	Russia
7	Afghanistan	2,348.4	Iran
8	China	2,307.8	Hong Kong
9	West Bank & Gaza	2,142.8	Jordan
10	Myanmar	1,978.3	Thailand
11	Poland	1,930.1	Germany
12	Philippines	1,896.0	United States
13	Puerto Rico	1,744.4	United States
14	Turkey	1,656.0	Germany
15	Syria	1,568.5	Turkey
16	Algeria	1,430.7	France
17	Vietnam	1,302.9	United States
18	Burkina Faso	1,294.3	Ivory Coast
19	Indonesia	1,294.0	Saudi Arabia
20	United Kingdom	1,289.4	Australia

a Living outside their country of birth.

Refugees[a] by country of origin

'000, 2015

1	Syria	4,872.6	**11**	Ukraine	321.3
2	Afghanistan	2,666.3	**12**	Vietnam	313.2
3	Somalia	1,123.1	**13**	Pakistan	297.8
4	South Sudan	778.7	**14**	Burundi	292.8
5	Sudan	628.8	**15**	Rwanda	286.4
6	Congo-Kinshasa	541.5	**16**	Iraq	264.1
7	Central African Rep.	471.1	**17**	China	212.9
8	Myanmar	451.8	**18**	Nigeria	168.0
9	Eritrea	411.3	**19**	Mali	154.2
10	Colombia	340.2	**20**	Sri Lanka	121.4

Countries with largest refugee[a] populations

'000, 2015

1	Turkey	2,541.4	**11**	Cameroon	343.0
2	Pakistan	1,561.2	**12**	Germany	316.1
3	Lebanon	1,070.9	**13**	Russia	314.5
4	Iran	979.4	**14**	Sudan	309.6
5	Ethiopia	736.1	**15**	China	301.1
6	Jordan	664.1	**16**	Iraq	277.7
7	Kenya	553.9	**17**	United States	273.2
8	Uganda	477.2	**18**	France	273.1
9	Congo-Kinshasa	383.1	**19**	Yemen	267.2
10	Chad	369.5	**20**	South Sudan	263.0

Applications for asylum by country of origin

'000, 2015

1	Syria	782.3	**11**	Nigeria	55.8
2	Afghanistan	486.7	**12**	Somalia	44.2
3	Iraq	300.6	**13**	Bangladesh	42.8
4	Ukraine	177.7	**14**	Ethiopia	36.9
5	Serbia[b]	133.6	**15**	Zimbabwe	36.3
6	Pakistan	92.8	**16**	China	30.7
7	Albania	74.2	**17**	Russia	28.7
8	Congo-Kinshasa	66.3	**18**	Sudan	27.9
9	Eritrea	62.9	**19**	Myanmar	24.9
10	Iran	60.5	**20**	El Salvador	22.9

Countries where asylum applications were lodged

'000, 2015

1	Serbia[b]	578.1	**11**	Italy	83.2
2	Germany	476.6	**12**	United Kingdom	53.3
3	Hungary	351.6	**13**	Belgium	49.3
4	Sweden	173.8	**14**	Netherlands	45.1
5	Russia	152.5	**15**	Switzerland	39.5
6	United States	136.0	**16**	Norway	36.7
7	Turkey	134.8	**17**	Uganda	35.9
8	South Africa	120.5	**18**	Finland	29.5
9	France	118.5	**19**	Egypt	23.1
10	Austria	89.9	**20**	Denmark	22.7

a According to UNHCR. Includes people in "refugee-like situations".
b Includes Kosovo.

The world economy

Biggest economies

GDP, $bn, 2015

1	United States	18,037
2	China	11,226
3	Japan	4,382
4	Germany	3,365
5	United Kingdom	2,863
6	France[a]	2,420
7	India	2,088
8	Italy	1,826
9	Brazil	1,801
10	Canada	1,553
11	South Korea	1,383
12	Russia	1,366
13	Australia	1,230
14	Spain	1,194
15	Mexico	1,151
16	Indonesia	861
17	Turkey	859
18	Netherlands	751
19	Switzerland	671
20	Saudi Arabia	652
21	Argentina	632
22	Taiwan	525
23	Sweden	496
24	Nigeria	494
25	Poland	477
26	Belgium	455
27	Thailand	399
28	Norway	387
29	Austria	377
30	Iran	374
31	United Arab Emirates	370
32	Egypt	332
33	South Africa	315
34	Hong Kong	309
35	Denmark	301
36	Israel	299
37	Singapore	297
38	Malaysia	296
39	Colombia	292
	Philippines	292
41	Ireland	283
42	Pakistan	271
43	Venezuela	260
44	Chile	243

Biggest economies by purchasing power

GDP PPP, $bn, 2015

1	China	19,696
2	United States	18,037
3	India	8,003
4	Japan	5,119
5	Germany	3,860
6	Russia	3,760
7	Brazil	3,216
8	Indonesia	2,850
9	United Kingdom	2,701
10	France[a]	2,666
11	Mexico	2,234
12	Italy	2,186
13	Turkey	1,908
14	South Korea	1,856
15	Saudi Arabia	1,704
16	Canada	1,637
17	Spain	1,613
18	Iran	1,347
19	Australia	1,144
20	Thailand	1,114
21	Taiwan	1,102
22	Nigeria	1,094
23	Egypt	1,072
24	Poland	1,012
25	Pakistan	932
26	Argentina	883
27	Netherlands	840
28	Malaysia	817
29	Philippines	744
30	South Africa	728
31	Colombia	667
32	United Arab Emirates	643
33	Algeria	580
	Bangladesh	580
	Iraq	580
36	Vietnam	553
37	Venezuela	514
38	Belgium	497
39	Switzerland	483
40	Singapore	477
41	Sweden	476
42	Kazakhstan	441
43	Chile	426
44	Hong Kong	416
	Romania	416
46	Austria	406

Note: For a list of 185 countries with their GDPs, see pages 250–53. "Advanced economies" refers to 39 countries as defined by the IMF.

a Includes overseas territories. b IMF coverage.

Regional GDP

$bn, 2016	
World	75,278
Advanced economies	46,076
G7	35,447
Euro area (19)	11,879
Other Asia	16,107
Latin America & Caribbean	5,003
Other Europe & CIS	3,571
Middle East, N. Africa, Afghanistan & Pakistan	3,110
Sub-Saharan Africa	1,412

% annual growth 2011–17	
World	3.4
Advanced economies	1.7
G7	1.6
Euro area (19)	0.9
Other Asia	6.7
Latin America & Caribbean	1.2
Other Europe & CIS	2.3
Middle East, N. Africa, Afghanistan & Pakistan	3.3
Sub-Saharan Africa	3.7

Regional purchasing power

GDP, % of total, 2016	
World	100
Advanced economies	41.9
G7	31.0
Euro area (19)	11.8
Other Asia	31.6
Latin America & Caribbean	7.9
Other Europe & CIS	8.0
Middle East, N. Africa, Afghanistan & Pakistan	7.6
Sub-Saharan Africa	3.0

$ per person, 2016	
World	16,439
Advanced economies	47,383
G7	48,978
Euro area (19)	41,672
Other Asia	10,675
Latin America & Caribbean	15,358
Other Europe & CIS	20,875
Middle East, N. Africa, Afghanistan & Pakistan	13,702
Sub-Saharan Africa	3,837

Regional population

% of total (7.3bn), 2016	
World	100.0
Advanced economies	16.7
G7	10.4
Euro area (19)	4.6
Other Asia	48.7
Latin America & Caribbean	8.4
Other Europe & CIS	6.3
Middle East, N. Africa, Afghanistan & Pakistan	9.0
Sub-Saharan Africa	13.0

No. of countries[b], 2016	
World	190
Advanced economies	23
G7	7
Euro area (19)	19
Other Asia	30
Latin America & Caribbean	32
Other Europe & CIS	24
Middle East, N. Africa, Afghanistan & Pakistan	22
Sub-Saharan Africa	45

Regional international trade

Exports of goods & services % of total, 2016	
World	100.0
Advanced economies	64.4
G7	34.7
Euro area (19)	26.3
Other Asia	17.9
Latin America & Caribbean	5.0
Other Europe & CIS	5.9
Middle East, N. Africa, Afghanistan & Pakistan	5.2
Sub-Saharan Africa	1.5

Current-account balances $bn, 2016	
World	286
Advanced economies	375
G7	-138
Euro area (19)	400
Other Asia	217
Latin America & Caribbean	-107
Other Europe & CIS	-37
Middle East, N. Africa, Afghanistan & Pakistan	-105
Sub-Saharan Africa	-56

Living standards

Highest GDP per person

$, 2015

1	Liechtenstein	159,030
2	Monaco	156,462
3	Bermuda	97,553
4	Luxembourg	94,718
5	Switzerland	80,802
6	Macau	76,963
7	Qatar	74,837
8	Norway	74,342
9	Ireland	60,303
10	Channel Islands[a]	51,166
11	United States	56,049
12	Iceland	55,947
13	Singapore	53,006
14	Denmark	52,861
15	Australia	51,238
16	Sweden	50,581
17	Netherlands	44,420
18	United Kingdom	44,255
19	Austria	43,855
20	Canada	43,254
21	Hong Kong	42,384
22	Finland	42,269
23	Germany	41,701
24	Belgium	40,295
25	United Arab Emirates	40,250
26	Andorra	40,166
27	New Zealand	38,501
28	Virgin Islands (US)[b]	37,650
29	France[c]	37,580
30	Israel	36,965
31	Japan	34,616
32	Brunei	32,328
33	Italy	30,532
34	Martinique	30,000
35	New Caledonia	29,790
36	Kuwait	29,251
37	Guam	28,670
38	Puerto Rico	27,812
39	South Korea	27,490
40	Spain	25,891
41	Malta	25,733
42	Réunion	24,444
43	Guadeloupe	24,000
44	Taiwan	22,446
45	Bahrain	22,228
46	Bahamas	22,135
47	Saudi Arabia	20,691
48	Slovenia	20,380
49	Portugal	19,342
50	Greece	17,723
51	Czech Republic	17,634
52	Estonia	17,286
53	Equatorial Guinea	17,274
54	French Polynesia	17,118
55	Trinidad & Tobago	16,828
56	French Guiana	16,667
57	Cyprus	16,308
58	Slovakia	16,169
59	Uruguay	15,620
60	Oman	15,518

Lowest GDP per person

$, 2015

1	Burundi	268
2	Central African Rep.	325
3	Niger	361
4	Malawi	373
5	Madagascar	403
6	Gambia, The	446
7	Liberia	453
8	Congo-Kinshasa	498
9	Mozambique	529
10	Guinea	535
11	Somalia	549
12	Togo	571
13	Guinea-Bissau	578
14	Afghanistan	606
15	Burkina Faso	614
16	Uganda	644
17	North Korea	646
18	Ethiopia	651
19	Sierra Leone	699
20	Rwanda	714
21	Mali	745
22	Nepal	748
23	Benin	761
24	Chad	782
25	Haiti	810
26	Tanzania	853
27	Eritrea	880
28	Senegal	905
29	Zimbabwe	908
30	Tajikistan	924
31	South Sudan	1,007
32	Myanmar	1,105

a 2010 b 2004 c Includes overseas territories.

Highest purchasing power

GDP per person in PPP (US = 100), 2015

1	Monaco	302.9
2	Qatar	256.6
3	Macau	191.2
4	Luxembourg	169.2
5	Singapore	151.9
6	Brunei	147.9
7	Liechtenstein	142.7
8	Kuwait	133.8
9	United Arab Emirates	124.6
10	Norway	122.2
11	Ireland	115.7
12	Switzerland	103.9
13	Channel Islands	102.6
14	Hong Kong	101.7
15	Bermuda	101.4
16	United States	100.0
17	Saudi Arabia	96.5
18	Iceland	90.5
19	Netherlands	88.7
20	Sweden	86.6
21	Germany	85.3
22	Australia	85.0
23	Austria	84.2
24	Taiwan	84.0
25	Denmark	83.7
26	Bahrain	81.8
27	Canada	81.4
28	Andorra	80.6
29	Belgium	78.4
30	Equatorial Guinea	77.6
31	United Kingdom	74.5
32	France	73.9
33	Finland	73.1
34	Malta	72.5
35	Japan	72.1
36	Oman	70.2
37	Virgin Islands (US)	67.7
38	New Zealand	66.6
39	South Korea	65.8
40	Italy	65.2
41	Puerto Rico	63.5
42	Israel	62.8
43	Spain	62.4
44	Trinidad & Tobago	57.7
45	Czech Republic	57.4
46	Martinique	56.3
47	Slovenia	54.2
48	Slovakia	53.7
49	New Caledonia	52.1
50	Estonia	51.3
51	Lithuania	51.1
52	Portugal	50.4
53	Malaysia	48.1
54	Hungary	47.1
55	Poland	46.8
56	Russia	46.7
57	Greece	46.3
58	Guadeloupe	45.6
59	Kazakhstan	44.7
60	Latvia	43.7
61	Guam	43.6
	Réunion	43.6
63	Turkey	43.2
64	Chile	42.5
	French Polynesia	42.5
66	Cyprus	42.3
67	Panama	40.0
68	Cuba	39.9

Lowest purchasing power

GDP per person in PPP (US = 100), 2015

1	Somalia	0.73
2	Central African Rep.	1.10
3	Burundi	1.25
4	Congo-Kinshasa	1.45
5	Liberia	1.49
6	Niger	1.70
7	Malawi	2.12
8	Guinea	2.13
	Mozambique	2.13
10	Madagascar	2.62
11	Togo	2.67
12	Guinea-Bissau	2.68
13	Sierra Leone	2.78
14	North Korea	2.83
15	Ethiopia	2.91
16	Eritrea	2.94
17	Gambia, The	2.95
18	Burkina Faso	3.03
19	Haiti	3.14
20	Zimbabwe	3.21
21	Rwanda	3.27
22	Afghanistan	3.40
23	South Sudan	3.41
24	Mali	3.62
25	Benin	3.66
26	Uganda	3.67
27	Chad	3.89
28	Senegal	4.34

The quality of life

Human development index[a]

Highest, 2015

1	Norway	94.9
2	Australia	93.9
	Switzerland	93.9
4	Germany	92.6
5	Denmark	92.5
	Singapore	92.5
7	Netherlands	92.4
8	Ireland	92.3
9	Iceland	92.1
10	Canada	92.0
	United States	92.0
12	Hong Kong	91.7
13	New Zealand	91.5
14	Sweden	91.3
15	Liechtenstein	91.2
16	United Kingdom	90.9
17	Japan	90.3
18	South Korea	90.1
19	Israel	89.9
20	Luxembourg	89.8
21	France	89.7
22	Belgium	89.6
23	Finland	89.5
24	Austria	89.3
25	Slovenia	89.0
26	Italy	88.7
27	Spain	88.4
28	Czech Republic	87.8
29	Greece	86.6
30	Brunei	86.5
	Estonia	86.5
32	Andorra	85.8
33	Cyprus	85.6
	Malta	85.6
	Qatar	85.6
36	Poland	85.5
37	Lithuania	84.8
38	Chile	84.7
	Saudi Arabia	84.7
40	Slovakia	84.5
41	Portugal	84.3
42	United Arab Emirates	84.0
43	Hungary	83.6
44	Latvia	83.0
45	Argentina	82.7
	Croatia	82.7
47	Bahrain	82.4
48	Montenegro	80.7
49	Russia	80.4
50	Romania	80.2
51	Kuwait	80.0
52	Belarus	79.6
	Oman	79.6
54	Barbados	79.5
	Uruguay	79.5
56	Bulgaria	79.4
	Kazakhstan	79.4
58	Bahamas	79.2
59	Malaysia	78.9
60	Panama	78.8
61	Mauritius	78.1
62	Trinidad & Tobago	78.0

Human development index[a]

Lowest, 2015

1	Central African Rep.	35.2
2	Niger	35.3
3	Chad	39.6
4	Burkina Faso	40.2
5	Burundi	40.4
6	Guinea	41.4
7	Mozambique	41.8
	South Sudan	41.8
9	Eritrea	42.0
	Sierra Leone	42.0
11	Guinea-Bissau	42.4
12	Liberia	42.7
13	Congo-Kinshasa	43.5
14	Mali	44.2
15	Ethiopia	44.8
16	Gambia, The	45.2
17	Ivory Coast	47.4
18	Malawi	47.6
19	Afghanistan	47.9
20	Yemen	48.2
21	Benin	48.5
22	Togo	48.7

a GDP or GDP per person is often taken as a measure of how developed a country is, but its usefulness is limited as it refers only to economic welfare. The UN Development Programme combines statistics on average and expected years of schooling and life expectancy with income levels (now GNI per person, valued in PPP US$). The HDI is shown here scaled from 0 to 100; countries scoring over 80 are considered to have very high human development, 70–79 high, 55–69 medium and those under 55 low.

Inequality-adjusted human development index[a]

Highest, 2015

1	Norway	89.8
2	Iceland	86.8
3	Australia	86.1
	Netherlands	86.1
5	Germany	85.9
	Switzerland	85.9
7	Denmark	85.8
8	Sweden	85.1
9	Ireland	85.0
10	Finland	84.3
11	Canada	83.9
12	Slovenia	83.8
13	United Kingdom	83.6
14	Czech Republic	83.0
15	Luxembourg	82.7
16	Belgium	82.1
17	Austria	81.5
18	France	81.3
19	United States	79.6
20	Slovakia	79.3
21	Japan	79.1
	Spain	79.1
23	Estonia	78.8
24	Malta	78.6
25	Italy	78.4
26	Israel	77.8
27	Poland	77.4
28	Hungary	77.1
29	Cyprus	76.2
30	Lithuania	75.9
31	Greece	75.8
32	Portugal	75.5
33	South Korea	75.3
34	Croatia	75.2
35	Belarus	74.5
36	Latvia	74.2
37	Montenegro	73.6
38	Russia	72.5
39	Kazakhstan	71.4
	Romania	71.4

Gini coefficient[b]

Highest, 2010–15

1	South Africa	63.4
2	Namibia	61.0
3	Haiti	60.8
4	Botswana	60.5
5	Central African Rep.	56.2
6	Zambia	55.6
7	Lesotho	54.2
8	Colombia	53.5
9	Paraguay	51.7
10	Brazil	51.5
	Swaziland	51.5
12	Guinea-Bissau	50.7
	Panama	50.7
14	Honduras	50.6
15	Chile	50.5
16	Rwanda	50.4
17	Congo-Brazzaville	48.9
18	Guatemala	48.7
19	Costa Rica	48.5
	Kenya	48.5

Lowest, 2010–15

1	Ukraine	24.1
2	Slovenia	25.6
3	Norway	25.9
4	Czech Republic	26.1
	Slovakia	26.1
6	Kazakhstan	26.3
7	Kyrgyzstan	26.8
	Moldova	26.8
9	Iceland	26.9
10	Finland	27.1
11	Belarus	27.2
12	Sweden	27.3
13	Romania	27.5
14	Belgium	27.6
15	Netherlands	28.0
16	Albania	29.0
17	Denmark	29.1
	Serbia	29.1
19	Germany	30.1
20	Austria	30.5

a Where there is inequality in the distribution of health, education and income, the IHDI of an average person in society is less than the ordinary HDI.

b The lower its value, the more equally household income is distributed.

Economic growth

Economic growth

Average annual % increase in real GDP, 2005–15

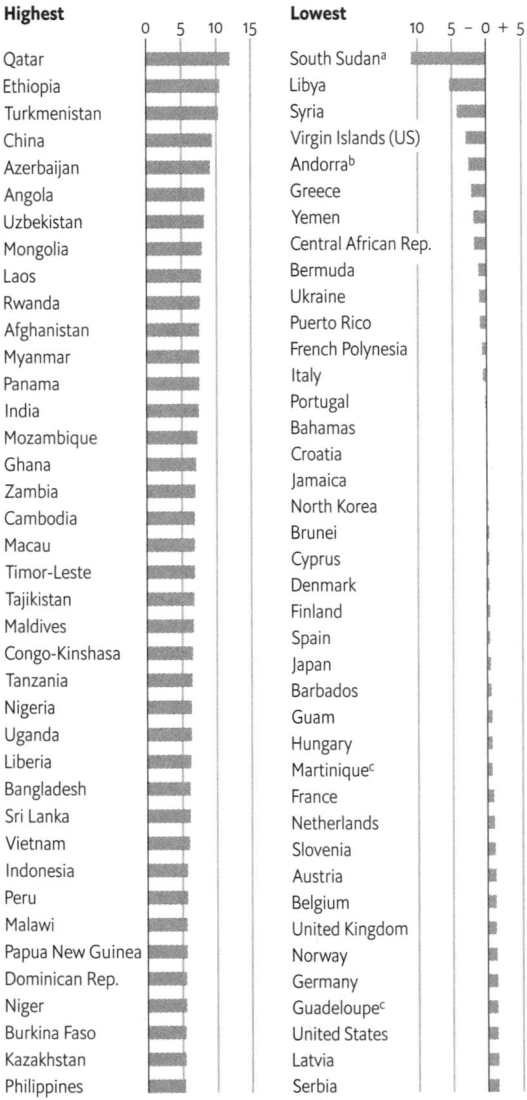

a 2011–15 b 2005–13 c 2005–14

Highest economic growth

Average annual % increase in real GDP, 1995–2005

1	Equatorial Guinea	45.3	**11**	Armenia	8.6
2	Iraq[a]	16.5		Chad	8.6
3	Sudan	15.5		Sierra Leone	8.6
4	Myanmar[b]	11.8	**14**	Cambodia	8.3
5	Mozambique	10.2	**15**	Angola	8.2
6	Turkmenistan	9.9	**16**	Bosnia & Herz.[c]	8.0
7	Qatar	9.7		West Bank & Gaza	8.0
8	Azerbaijan	9.5	**18**	Trinidad & Tobago	7.9
9	China	9.2	**19**	Maldives	7.8
10	Rwanda	8.7	**20**	Ireland	7.6

Lowest economic growth

Average annual % change in real GDP, 1995–2005

1	Zimbabwe[a]	-6.5		Japan	1.0
2	Congo-Kinshasa	-0.8	**12**	Germany	1.2
3	Central African Rep.	0.4		Paraguay	1.2
4	Togo	0.5		Uruguay	1.2
5	Channel Islands[a]	0.6	**15**	Burundi	1.4
	Gabon	0.6	**16**	Italy	1.5
7	Jamaica	0.7		Papua New Guinea	1.5
8	North Korea	0.8	**18**	Guyana	1.6
9	Guinea-Bissau	1.0		Venezuela	1.6
	Haiti	1.0	**20**	Brunei	1.7

Highest services growth

Average annual % increase in real terms, 2007–15

1	Mali	13.3	**10**	Angola[d]	8.7
2	Ethiopia	12.8	**11**	Zambia	8.6
3	Myanmar	10.1	**12**	Mongolia	8.5
	Qatar	10.1		Mozambique	8.5
5	Afghanistan	10.0		Tajikistan	8.5
6	Zimbabwe	9.7	**15**	Nigeria	8.3
7	India	9.4	**16**	Congo-Kinshasa	8.1
8	China	9.0	**17**	Uzbekistan	8.0
9	Rwanda	8.8	**18**	Timor-Leste[a]	7.9

Lowest services growth

Average annual % change in real terms, 2007–15

1	Greece	-2.9		Portugal	0.1
2	Ukraine	-2.1	**11**	Central African Rep.	0.2
3	Estonia	-0.6		Denmark	0.2
4	Bahamas	-0.5		Latvia	0.2
5	Italy	-0.4	**14**	Serbia	0.5
6	Croatia	-0.3	**15**	Iceland[e]	0.7
7	Jamaica	0.0		Slovenia	0.7
	Japan[d]	0.0	**17**	Cyprus	0.8
9	Finland	0.1		Germany	0.8

a 1998–2005 b 1997–2005 c 1996–2005 d 2007–14 e 2007–13

Note: Rankings of highest and lowest industrial growth 2007–15 can be found on page 44.

Trading places

Biggest exporters

% of total world exports (goods, services and income), 2015

1	Euro area (19)	16.28
2	United States	12.72
3	China	11.10
4	Germany	7.46
5	Japan	4.29
6	United Kingdom	4.16
7	France	3.89
8	Netherlands	3.62
9	South Korea	2.78
10	Italy	2.53
11	Switzerland	2.39
12	Canada	2.35
13	Spain	1.90
14	India	1.85
15	Russia	1.80
16	Ireland	1.76
17	Belgium	1.75
18	Mexico	1.72
19	United Arab Emirates	1.58
20	Taiwan	1.55
21	Singapore	1.54
22	Luxembourg	1.40
23	Thailand	1.17
24	Australia	1.15
	Hong Kong	1.15
26	Sweden	1.14
27	Poland	1.04
28	Saudi Arabia	1.02
29	Brazil	0.99
30	Austria	0.97
31	Malaysia	0.93
32	Turkey	0.85
33	Denmark	0.82
34	Norway	0.78
35	Vietnam	0.73
36	Indonesia	0.72
37	Czech Republic	0.67
38	Hungary	0.51
39	South Africa	0.44
40	Finland	0.43
41	Israel	0.42
	Qatar	0.42

Trade dependency

Trade[a] as % of GDP, 2015

Most

1	Slovakia	83.2
2	Vietnam	82.7
3	Hungary	71.2
4	United Arab Emirates	70.8
5	Czech Republic	68.5
6	Lesotho	65.7
7	Lithuania	62.7
8	Libya[b]	60.6
9	Slovenia	60.3
10	Puerto Rico	58.7
11	Netherlands	57.5
12	Belgium	55.8
13	Estonia	55.1
14	Ireland	54.8
15	Malaysia	54.6
16	Cambodia[c]	54.0
17	Bulgaria	52.6
18	Bahrain[c]	51.0
19	Thailand	50.8
20	Belarus	49.9
21	Singapore	49.5

Least

1	Sudan	6.0
2	Bermuda	8.1
3	Argentina	9.0
4	Brazil	10.1
5	Hong Kong	10.2
	Nigeria	10.2
7	Yemen	10.4
8	Egypt	10.5
	United States	10.5
10	Timor-Leste	10.8
11	Pakistan	11.4
12	Burundi	12.5
13	Cuba[b]	13.2
14	Venezuela	14.2
15	Central African Rep.[c]	14.3
16	Iran	14.9
17	Uganda	15.0
18	Japan	15.1
19	Colombia	15.4
20	French Polynesia	15.8

Notes: The figures are drawn wherever possible from balance of payment statistics, so have differing definitions from statistics taken from customs or similar sources. For Hong Kong and Singapore, only domestic exports and retained imports are used. Euro area data exclude intra-euro area trade.

a Average of imports plus exports of goods. b 2013 c 2014

Biggest traders of goods[a]

% of world, 2016

Biggest earners from services and income

% of world exports of services and income, 2015

1	Euro area (19)	18.26
2	United States	18.03
3	United Kingdom	6.53
4	China	6.05
5	Germany	5.65
6	France	4.94
7	Japan	4.76
8	Netherlands	4.61
9	Luxembourg	3.74
10	Hong Kong	3.16
	Switzerland	3.15
12	Ireland	2.49
13	Singapore	2.39
14	Spain	2.07
15	India	2.01
16	Belgium	1.93
17	Italy	1.85
18	Canada	1.78
19	South Korea	1.43
	Sweden	1.43
21	Denmark	1.09
22	Austria	1.06
23	Russia	1.05
24	Australia	1.03
25	Taiwan	1.02
26	Norway	0.98
27	United Arab Emirates	0.92
28	Thailand	0.78
29	Poland	0.68
30	Turkey	0.60
31	Malaysia	0.56
32	Brazil	0.54
33	Israel	0.53
34	Finland	0.49
35	Saudi Arabia	0.47
36	Greece	0.46

a Individual countries only. b Estimate.

Balance of payments: current account

Largest surpluses

$m, 2015

1	Euro area (19)	358,322
2	China	330,602
3	Germany	279,969
4	Japan	135,608
5	South Korea	105,940
6	Switzerland	77,378
7	Taiwan	76,165
8	Russia	69,000
9	Netherlands	65,129
10	Singapore	53,757
11	Norway	33,746
12	Thailand	32,149
13	Italy	29,348
14	Ireland	28,967
15	Denmark	27,582
16	Sweden	23,250
17	United Arab Emirates	17,253
18	Spain	16,208
19	Qatar	13,751
20	Israel	13,642
21	Macau	11,557
22	Hong Kong	10,264
23	Iran	9,016
24	Malaysia	8,960
25	Kuwait	8,584
26	Philippines	7,266
27	Austria	7,020
28	Puerto Rico	6,331
29	Papua New Guinea	5,326
30	Iraq	4,121
31	Hungary	3,946
32	Luxembourg	2,962
33	Bangladesh	2,687
34	Croatia	2,492
35	Nepal	2,447
36	Slovenia	2,216
37	Brunei	2,071
38	Belgium	1,936
39	Cuba[a]	1,850
40	Czech Republic	1,683
41	Bahrain[b]	1,124
42	Botswana	1,120
43	Trinidad & Tobago	957
44	Vietnam	906
45	Bermuda	886
46	Iceland	854
47	Malta	539
48	Estonia	493
49	French Polynesia	348
50	Swaziland	281

Largest deficits

$m, 2015

1	United States	-462,961
2	United Kingdom	-122,571
3	Brazil	-58,882
4	Australia	-58,280
5	Saudi Arabia	-56,724
6	Canada	-53,083
7	Mexico	-33,347
8	Turkey	-32,118
9	Algeria	-27,229
10	India	-22,457
11	Venezuela	-20,360
12	Colombia	-18,922
13	Indonesia	-17,586
14	Argentina	-16,806
15	Egypt	-16,787
16	Nigeria	-15,763
17	South Africa	-13,644
18	Oman	-10,807
19	Angola	-10,273
20	Peru	-9,210
21	Lebanon	-8,146
22	Sudan	-5,933
23	Mozambique	-5,833
24	New Zealand	-5,501
25	Kazakhstan	-5,464
26	Afghanistan	-5,121
27	France	-4,861
28	Chile	-4,761
29	Kenya	-4,038
30	Myanmar	-3,921
31	Tunisia	-3,850
32	Panama	-3,377
33	Jordan	-3,332
34	Tanzania	-3,312
35	Yemen	-3,026
36	Poland	-2,932
37	Ghana	-2,809
38	Costa Rica	-2,493
39	Uganda	-2,353
40	Laos	-2,264
41	Ecuador	-2,201
42	Morocco	-2,161

Note: Euro area data exclude intra-euro area trade.
a 2013 b 2014

Largest surpluses as % of GDP

$m, 2015

1	Papua New Guinea	25.1
2	Macau	25.0
3	Singapore	18.1
4	Brunei	16.0
5	Bermuda	14.9
6	Taiwan	14.5
7	Nepal	11.5
	Switzerland	11.5
9	Ireland	10.2
10	Denmark	9.2
11	Netherlands	8.7
	Norway	8.7
13	Qatar	8.4
14	Germany	8.3
15	Thailand	8.1
16	Botswana	7.8
17	South Korea	7.7
	Timor-Leste	7.7
19	Kuwait	7.2
20	Swaziland	7.0
21	Puerto Rico	6.2
22	French Polynesia	5.7
23	Malta	5.5
24	Slovenia	5.2
25	Croatia	5.1
	Iceland	5.1
	Luxembourg	5.1
28	Russia	5.0
29	Sweden	4.7
	United Arab Emirates	4.7
31	Israel	4.6
32	Trinidad & Tobago	3.7
33	Bahrain[a]	3.4
34	Hong Kong	3.3
	Hungary	3.3
36	Euro area (19)	3.1
	Japan	3.1
38	China	3.0
	Malaysia	3.0
40	Philippines	2.5
41	Cuba[b]	2.4
	Iran	2.4
43	Iraq	2.3
44	Estonia	2.2
45	Guinea-Bissau	2.1
46	Austria	1.9
47	Italy	1.6
48	Spain	1.4
49	Bangladesh	1.3
50	Czech Republic	0.9

Largest deficits as % of GDP

$m, 2015

1	Liberia	-41.9
2	Mozambique	-39.4
3	Afghanistan	-26.5
4	Sierra Leone[a]	-26.3
5	Niger	-20.8
6	Mauritania	-19.2
7	Laos	-18.3
8	Guinea[a]	-17.9
9	Oman	-16.9
10	Algeria	-16.5
	Lebanon	-16.5
12	Bahamas	-15.9
13	Suriname	-15.6
14	Kyrgyzstan	-14.9
15	Namibia	-14.8
16	Rwanda	-13.6
17	West Bank & Gaza	-13.5
18	Montenegro	-13.2
19	Burundi	-13.1
20	Georgia	-12.7
21	Chad	-12.4
22	Togo	-11.3
23	Malawi	-11.0
24	Gambia, The	-10.8
25	Albania	-10.7
	Zimbabwe	-10.7
27	Angola	-10.0
28	Cambodia[a]	-9.9
29	Uganda	-9.3
30	Benin	-9.0
31	Jordan	-8.9
	Tunisia	-8.9
33	Saudi Arabia	-8.7
34	Lesotho	-8.6
35	Burkina Faso	-8.4
36	Haiti	-8.3
37	Nicaragua	-8.2
38	Mongolia	-8.1
39	Yemen	-8.0
40	Venezuela	-7.8
41	Ghana	-7.5
42	Tanzania	-7.3

a 2014 b 2013

Official reserves[a]

$m, end-2016

1	China	3,097,955	**16**	Thailand	171,797
2	Japan	1,216,642	**17**	France	146,258
3	Euro area (19)	743,548	**18**	Italy	135,527
4	Switzerland	679,077	**19**	United Kingdom	134,982
5	Saudi Arabia	547,313	**20**	Algeria	120,816
6	Taiwan	449,879	**21**	Indonesia	116,382
7	United States	407,250	**22**	Poland	114,345
8	Hong Kong	386,241	**23**	Turkey	106,006
9	Russia	377,312	**24**	Israel	98,447
10	South Korea	370,171	**25**	Malaysia	94,487
11	Brazil	364,995	**26**	Czech Republic	85,727
12	India	361,784	**27**	United Arab Emirates	85,392
13	Singapore	251,079	**28**	Canada	82,718
14	Germany	184,574	**29**	Philippines	80,698
15	Mexico	177,993	**30**	Libya[b]	74,112

Official gold reserves

Market prices, $m, end-2016

1	Euro area (19)	399,111	**14**	Turkey	13,952
2	United States	300,959	**15**	Saudi Arabia	11,948
3	Germany	124,992	**16**	United Kingdom	11,481
4	Italy	90,724	**17**	Lebanon	10,614
5	France	90,133	**18**	Spain	10,419
6	China	68,179	**19**	Austria	10,360
7	Russia	59,767	**20**	Kazakhstan	9,549
8	Switzerland	38,482	**21**	Belgium	8,414
9	Japan	28,315	**22**	Philippines	7,265
10	Netherlands	22,662	**23**	Algeria	6,425
11	India	20,639	**24**	Thailand	5,639
12	Taiwan	15,675	**25**	Singapore	4,714
13	Portugal	14,153	**26**	Sweden	4,652

Workers' remittances

Inflows, $m, 2015

1	India	68,910	**16**	Lebanon	7,481
2	China	63,938	**17**	United States	7,069
3	Philippines	28,483	**18**	Sri Lanka	6,980
4	Mexico	26,233	**19**	Morocco	6,904
5	France	23,352	**20**	Russia	6,870
6	Nigeria	21,060	**21**	Poland	6,783
7	Pakistan	19,306	**22**	Nepal	6,730
8	Egypt	18,325	**23**	Guatemala	6,573
9	Bangladesh	15,388	**24**	South Korea	6,454
10	Germany	15,362	**25**	Thailand	5,895
11	Vietnam	13,000	**26**	Ukraine	5,845
12	Spain	10,281	**27**	Jordan	5,348
13	Belgium	9,790	**28**	Dominican Rep.	5,196
14	Indonesia	9,659	**29**	United Kingdom	5,003
15	Italy	9,517	**30**	Colombia	4,680

a Foreign exchange, SDRs, IMF position and gold at market prices. b End-September.

Exchange rates

The Economist's Big Mac index

Local currency under(-)/over(+) valuation against $[a], %
January 2017

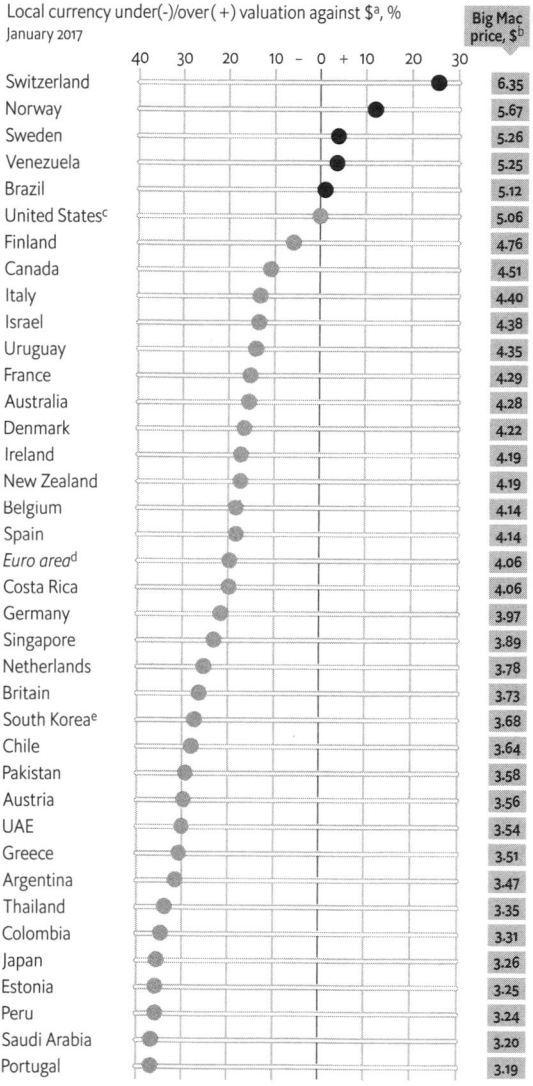

a Based on purchasing-power parity: local price of a Big Mac burger divided by United States price. b At market exchange rates. c Average of four cities. d Weighted average of prices in euro area. e Average of five cities.

Inflation

Consumer-price inflation

Highest, 2016, %

1	South Sudan[a]	379.8
2	Venezuela	254.9
3	Suriname	55.5
4	Angola[a]	32.4
5	Libya[a]	27.1
6	Congo-Kinshasa[a]	22.4
7	Malawi[a]	21.7
8	Mozambique	19.2
9	Zambia	17.9
10	Sudan[a]	17.8
11	Ghana[a]	17.5
12	Nigeria	15.7
13	Kazakhstan	14.6
14	Ukraine	13.9
15	Haiti	13.4
16	Azerbaijan[a]	12.4
17	Belarus[a]	11.8
18	Sierra Leone	11.3
19	Argentina	10.6
20	Egypt	10.2
21	Nepal	9.9
22	Uruguay	9.6

Lowest, 2016, %

1	Mali	-1.8
2	Romania	-1.6
	Zimbabwe	-1.6
4	Armenia[a]	-1.4
5	Bulgaria	-1.3
	Timor-Leste	-1.3
7	Cyprus	-1.2
8	Bosnia & Herz.	-1.1
	Chad[a]	-1.1
	Croatia[a]	-1.1
11	Benin	-0.8
	Jordan	-0.8
	Lebanon	-0.8
14	Brunei	-0.7
15	Poland	-0.6
16	Israel	-0.5
	Singapore	-0.5
	Slovakia[a]	-0.5
19	Montenegro	-0.4
	Switzerland	-0.4

Highest average annual consumer-price inflation, 2011–16, %

1	Venezuela[a]	85.1
2	South Sudan[a]	61
3	Sudan[a]	28.3
4	Malawi[a]	23.4
5	Belarus	23.1
6	Iran	19.9
7	Yemen[a]	14.1
8	Ghana[a]	13.7
	Ukraine	13.7
10	Angola[a]	13.4
11	Suriname	13.0
12	Ethiopia	11.2
13	Nigeria	10.7
14	Guinea[a]	10.6
15	Argentina	10.5
16	Sierra Leone	10.4
17	Uzbekistan[a]	9.8
	Zambia	9.8
19	Egypt	9.4
20	Libya[a]	9.3
21	Nepal	8.9
22	Uruguay	8.8
23	Mongolia	8.5

Lowest average annual consumer-price inflation, 2011–16, %

1	Greece	-0.5
	Switzerland	-0.5
3	Bulgaria	-0.3
4	Bosnia & Herz.[a]	-0.2
5	Brunei	-0.2
6	Cyprus	0.1
7	Zimbabwe	0.2
8	Senegal	0.4
9	Ireland	0.5
	Israel	0.5
	Puerto Rico	0.5
12	Poland	0.6
	Spain	0.6
14	El Salvador	0.7
	Japan	0.7
	Latvia	0.7
	Sweden	0.7
18	Croatia[a]	0.8
	France	0.8
	Niger	0.8
	Portugal	0.8
	Slovakia[a]	0.8
	Slovenia[a]	0.8

a Estimate.

Commodity prices

End 2016, % change on a year earlier

1	Rubber	44.1
2	Coconut oil	43.3
3	Tea	29.2
4	Wool (Aus)	28.0
5	Sugar	22.0
6	Zinc	20.9
7	Lead	15.0
	Palm oil	15.0
9	Cotton	12.8
10	Tin	11.9
11	Soya oil	5.2
12	Lamb	0.0
13	Oil[a]	-3.4
14	Soyabeans	-4.7
15	Aluminium	-5.2
16	Gold	-6.0
17	Timber	-9.0
18	Rice	-10.1
19	Coffee	-10.8
20	Copper	-13.4
21	Corn	-14.9
22	Soya meal	-16.6
23	Wool (NZ)	-20.7
24	Beef (Aus)	-24.0
25	Beef (US)	-24.8
26	Cocoa	-25.2

2011–16, % change

1	Zinc	40.1
2	Timber	19.0
3	Coconut oil	17.0
4	Wool (Aus)	14.0
5	Tin	9.5
6	Lead	5.0
7	Hides	4.0
8	Cocoa	0.8
9	Soya meal	0.1
10	Beef (Aus)	-1.8
11	Beef (US)	-2.4
12	Tea	-6.5
13	Lamb	-10.5
14	Aluminium	-12.6
15	Cotton	-14.9
16	Soyabeans	-17.6
17	Sugar	-21.0
18	Palm oil	-22.2
19	Rubber	-22.9
20	Copper	-27.8
21	Gold	-29.5
	Wool (NZ)	-29.5
23	Coffee	-31.2
24	Soya oil	-33.3
25	Rice	-36.1
26	Wheat	-39.0

The Economist's house prices

Q3 2016[b], % change on a year earlier

1	China	14.3
2	Turkey	14.0
3	New Zealand	12.6
4	Hungary	11.6
5	Canada	11.4
6	Colombia	10.8
	Latvia	10.8
8	Iceland	10.2
9	Israel	8.2
10	India	8.1
11	Norway	7.9
12	Portugal	7.6
	Slovakia	7.6
14	Estonia	7.4
	United Kingdom	7.4
16	Sweden	7.1
17	Ireland	7.0
18	Czech Republic	6.9
19	Mexica	6.7
20	Germany	6.2

Q3 2010–Q3 2016[b], % change

1	India	136.3
2	Turkey	117.1
3	Brazil	89.8
4	Hong Kong	87.2
5	Colombia	78.2
6	Estonia	62.9
7	New Zealand	60.2
8	Iceland	54.2
9	Israel	51.0
10	Sweden	47.5
11	Indonesia	42.3
12	Chile	41.4
	Norway	41.4
14	South Africa	40.0
15	Germany	39.1
	Latvia	39.1
17	Canada	38.6
18	Austria	38.4
19	China	36.9
20	Mexico	35.6

a West Texas Intermediate. b Or latest.

Debt

Highest foreign debt[a]

$bn, 2015

1	China	1,418.3
2	Brazil	543.4
3	Hong Kong	491.9
4	India	479.6
5	Russia	467.7
6	Singapore	465.5
7	Mexico	426.3
8	Turkey	397.7
9	South Korea	376.6
10	Poland	331.4
11	Indonesia	308.5
12	United Arab Emirates	203.3
13	Malaysia	191.0
14	Saudi Arabia	171.5
15	Argentina	159.7
16	Taiwan	159.0
17	Chile	156.2
18	Kazakhstan	154.3
19	Qatar	143.4
20	South Africa	137.9
21	Thailand	129.7
22	Hungary	127.4
23	Czech Republic	126.3
24	Venezuela	123.7
25	Ukraine	122.8
26	Colombia	111.0
27	Romania	96.0
28	Israel	89.1
29	Panama	87.7
30	Vietnam	77.8
31	Philippines	77.7
32	Peru	65.9
33	Pakistan	65.5
34	Iraq	60.0
35	Croatia	49.4
	Sudan	49.4
37	Egypt	46.6
38	Sri Lanka	43.9
39	Morocco	43.0
40	Bangladesh	38.6
41	Belarus	37.9
42	Bulgaria	37.5
43	Kuwait	35.4
44	Lebanon	35.1
45	Serbia	30.8
46	Nigeria	29.0
47	Cuba	28.9
48	Angola	28.0
49	Bahrain	27.7
50	Tunisia	27.4

Highest foreign debt burden[a]

Total foreign debt as % of GDP, 2015

1	Mongolia	183.5
2	Panama	171.5
3	Hong Kong	159.0
4	Singapore	156.8
5	Ukraine	135.5
6	Mauritius	125.3
7	Kyrgyzstan	112.1
8	Hungary	104.8
9	Papua New Guinea	102.7
10	Croatia	101.5
11	Jamaica	100.1
12	Georgia	95.3
13	Bahrain	88.9
14	Moldova	88.7
15	Laos	87.4
16	Qatar	87.1
17	Kazakhstan	86.0
18	Armenia	84.8
19	Serbia	82.9
20	Nicaragua	82.6
21	Estonia	81.5
22	Mauritania	79.1
23	Bosnia & Herz.	77.1
24	Bulgaria	74.7
25	Lebanon	72.9
26	Albania	72.5
27	Poland	69.5
28	Belarus	69.4
29	Macedonia	69.1
30	Jordan	68.6
31	Czech Republic	68.2
32	Mozambique	67.9
33	Chile	64.9
34	Malaysia	64.4
35	Tunisia	63.6
36	Zimbabwe	60.6
37	El Salvador	58.7
38	Paraguay	57.0
	Tajikistan	57.0

a Foreign debt is debt owed to non-residents and repayable in foreign currency; the figures shown include liabilities of government, public and private sectors. Longer-established developed countries have been excluded.

Highest foreign debt[a]

As % of exports of goods and services, 2015

1	Sudan	888.8	**15**	Uruguay	211.1
2	Mongolia	394.5	**16**	Jamaica	206.4
3	Venezuela	310.8	**17**	Papua New Guinea	205.4
4	Laos	309.4	**18**	Colombia	203.4
5	Central African Rep.	304.4	**19**	Mauritania	201.3
6	Panama	290.6	**20**	Chile	201.1
7	Kazakhstan	280.0	**21**	Sierra Leone	197.9
8	Ethiopia	262.9	**22**	Turkey	195.0
9	Brazil	227.7	**23**	Albania	191.2
10	Mozambique	226.3	**24**	Sri Lanka	182.8
11	Burundi	218.2	**25**	Kyrgyzstan	182.3
12	Argentina	217.2	**26**	Croatia	179.8
13	Niger	212.7	**27**	Georgia	175.2
14	Ukraine	211.3	**28**	Nicaragua	174.8

Highest debt service ratio[b]

Average, %, 2015

1	Syria	68.4	**15**	Mauritius	28.3
2	Kazakhstan	63.4	**16**	Armenia	28.1
3	Venezuela	60.3	**17**	Turkey	26.9
4	Jamaica	58.8	**18**	Hungary	25.9
5	Ukraine	56.9	**19**	Colombia	25.6
6	Brazil	37.6	**20**	Georgia	24.5
7	Croatia	35.5	**21**	Argentina	24.4
8	Chile	33.1	**22**	Dominican Rep.	23.3
9	Cuba	32.6	**23**	Russia	23.0
10	Mongolia	32.1	**24**	Bosnia & Herz.	22.9
11	Bulgaria	30.3	**25**	Serbia	22.5
	Indonesia	30.3	**26**	Ecuador	21.9
13	Romania	30.1	**27**	Albania	21.0
14	Sudan	28.4	**28**	Macedonia	20.5

Household debt[c]

As % of net disposable income, 2015

1	Denmark	292.0	**13**	Japan[d]	129.5
2	Netherlands	277.1	**14**	Spain	121.9
3	Norway	221.8	**15**	Greece	118.5
4	Australia	211.8	**16**	Belgium	114.3
5	Switzerland	211.2	**17**	United States	111.6
6	Sweden	179.1	**18**	France	108.3
7	Ireland	177.9	**19**	Austria	93.5
8	Canada	175.1	**20**	Germany	92.9
9	South Korea	169.9	**21**	Italy	89.2
10	United Kingdom	149.5	**22**	Estonia	81.9
11	Portugal	136.4	**23**	Czech Republic	68.7
12	Finland	129.7	**24**	Slovakia	68.0

b Debt service is the sum of interest and principal repayments (amortisation) due on outstanding foreign debt. The debt service ratio is debt service as a percentage of exports of goods, non-factor services, primary income and workers' remittances.
c OECD countries. d 2012

Aid

Largest recipients of bilateral and multilateral aid

$bn, 2015

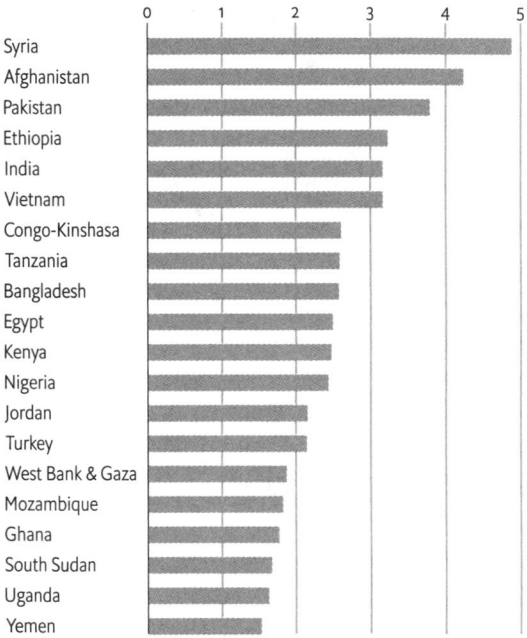

$ per person, 2015

1	West Bank & Gaza	423.6
2	Jordan	283.1
3	Syria	263.9
4	Kosovo	243.7
5	Liberia	243.0
6	Timor-Leste	170.5
7	Lebanon	166.7
8	Montenegro	160.6
9	Sierra Leone	146.7
10	South Sudan	135.7
11	Afghanistan	130.3
12	Kyrgyzstan	129.1
13	Georgia	121.7
14	Somalia	116.2
15	Albania	115.7
16	Armenia	115.2
17	Fiji	114.9
18	Macedonia	103.1
19	Central African Rep.	99.4
20	Haiti	97.3
21	Bosnia & Herz.	93.2
	Rwanda	93.2
23	Moldova	87.9
24	Mongolia	79.6
25	Mauritania	78.2
26	Papua New Guinea	77.4
27	Nicaragua	74.7
28	Bolivia	73.4
29	Swaziland	72.0
30	Laos	69.3
31	Mali	68.2
32	Honduras	66.5
33	Maldives	65.6
34	Mozambique	64.9
35	Ghana	64.5
36	Malawi	61.0
37	Mauritius	60.6
38	Senegal	58.1
39	Namibia	57.9
40	Gabon	57.2

Largest bilateral and multilateral donors[a]

$m, 2015			As % of GDP
1	United States	30,986	0.17
2	United Kingdom	18,545	0.70
3	Germany	17,940	0.52
4	Japan	9,203	0.21
5	France	9,039	0.37
6	Sweden	7,089	1.40
7	Saudi Arabia	6,758	1.05
8	Netherlands	5,726	0.75
9	United Arab Emirates	4,381	1.18
10	Norway	4,278	1.05
11	Canada	4,277	0.28
12	Italy	4,004	0.22
13	Turkey	3,919	0.50
14	Switzerland	3,562	0.52
15	Australia	3,494	0.29
16	Denmark	2,566	0.85
17	South Korea	1,915	0.14
18	Belgium	1,905	0.42
19	Spain	1,397	0.12
20	Austria	1,324	0.35
21	Finland	1,288	0.55
22	Russia	1,161	0.09
23	Ireland	718	0.32
24	New Zealand	442	0.27
25	Poland	441	0.10
26	Luxembourg	363	0.95
27	Portugal	308	0.16
28	Kuwait	304	0.26
29	Taiwan	255	0.05
30	Greece	239	0.12

Biggest changes to aid

2015 compared with 2011, $m

Increases			*Decreases*		
1	Syria	4,546.4	1	Congo-Kinshasa	-2,927.2
2	Egypt	2,063.4	2	Afghanistan	-2,627.9
3	South Sudan	1,239.0	3	Turkey	-1,143.5
4	Jordan	1,175.9	4	Serbia	-1,066.6
5	Bangladesh	1,078.7	5	Sudan	-842.5
6	Yemen	1,054.4	6	Ivory Coast	-782.9
7	Myanmar	788.6	7	Mexico	-664.3
8	Philippines	699.0	8	Haiti	-649.1
9	Ukraine	679.7	9	West Bank & Gaza	-561.6
10	Nigeria	663.9	10	Libya	-483.5
11	Sierra Leone	522.5	11	Vietnam	-461.8
12	Lebanon	499.7	12	Tunisia	-450.7
13	Cuba	465.7	13	Indonesia	-444.7
14	Guinea	336.3	14	Iraq	-429.7
15	Liberia	332.2	15	Togo	-342.8
16	Colombia	329.8	16	Bosnia & Herz.	-270.7
17	Nepal	329.1	17	Peru	-266.0
18	Pakistan	292.4	18	Ethiopia	-258.6
19	China	271.1	19	Mozambique	-250.4
20	Malawi	251.9	20	Benin	-242.4
21	Kyrgyzstan	245.7	21	Nicaragua	-237.4
22	Uzbekistan	243.7	22	Zambia	-236.3
23	Madagascar	229.9	23	Azerbaijan	-217.8
24	Niger	221.2	24	Burundi	-205.2
25	Central African Rep.	218.2	25	El Salvador	-189.6
26	Thailand	192.8	26	Sri Lanka	-186.1
27	Angola	187.2	27	Rwanda	-181.1
28	Brazil	177.6	28	Senegal	-175.4

a China also provides aid, but does not disclose amounts.

Industry and services

Largest industrial output

$bn, 2015

1	China	4,529
2	United States[a]	3,471
3	Japan[a]	1,224
4	Germany	923
5	India	563
6	Canada[b]	498
7	United Kingdom	495
8	South Korea	476
9	France	422
10	Russia	389
11	Italy	385
12	Mexico	349
13	Brazil	346
14	Indonesia	345
15	Australia	319
16	Saudi Arabia	297
17	Spain	256
18	Taiwan	185
19	United Arab Emirates	177
20	Turkey	168
21	Switzerland	166
	Venezuela[b]	166
23	Iran[a]	159
24	Poland	144
25	Thailand	141
26	Argentina	138
27	Netherlands	135
28	Egypt	122
29	Norway	119
30	Sweden	115
31	Ireland	109
32	Malaysia	108
33	Nicarugua	98
	Puerto Rico[b]	98
35	Qatar	96
36	Austria	95
37	Colombia	91
38	Belgium	90
	Philippines	90
40	South Africa	83
41	Iraq	76
42	Singapore	73
43	Chile	72

Highest growth in industrial output

Average annual % increase in real terms, 2007–15

1	Timor-Leste[c]	24.1
2	Liberia	16.9
3	Ethiopia	15.9
4	Myanmar	15.1
5	Laos	13.3
6	Panama	12.1
7	Uzbekistan	11.5
8	Ghana	10.3
9	Qatar	9.3
10	Chad	9.2
	China	9.2
12	Niger	9.1
13	Rwanda	9.0
14	Kosovo	8.5
15	Bangladesh	8.4
16	Tanzania	8.2
17	Cambodia	7.8
	Iraq	7.8
	Mongolia	7.8
20	Macedonia	7.5

Lowest growth in industrial output

Average annual % change in real terms, 2006–14

1	Cyprus	-7.8
2	Bermuda[d]	-7.5
3	Greece	-7.2
4	Ukraine	-6.3
5	Finland	-3.2
6	Croatia	-3.1
	Spain	-3.1
8	Italy	-2.6
9	Latvia	-2.5
10	Portugal	-2.4
11	Brunei	-2.2
	Jamaica	-2.2
13	Botswana	-1.7
14	Luxembourg	-1.6
15	Slovenia	-1.5
	Trinidad & Tobago	-1.5
17	Armenia	-1.3
	Central African Rep.	-1.3
19	Iran[c]	-1.1
20	France	-1.0
	Netherlands	-1.0
	Puerto Rico[e]	-1.0

a 2014 b 2013 c 2007–14 d 2007–12 e 2007–13

Largest manufacturing output

$bn, 2015

1	China[a]	2,857
2	United States	2,068
3	Japan[b]	851
4	Germany	690
5	South Korea	370
6	India	315
7	Italy	258
8	United Kingdom	249
9	France	243
10	Mexico	196
11	Canada[a]	183
12	Brazil	182
13	Indonesia	180
14	Russia	169
15	Taiwan	158
16	Spain	154
17	Switzerland	117
18	Turkey	112
19	Thailand	106
20	Ireland	97
21	Argentina	85
	Australia	85
23	Poland	83
24	Netherlands	79
	Saudi Arabia	79
26	Sweden	75
27	Malaysia	68
28	Austria	63
29	Philippines	59
30	Belgium	58
31	Egypt	56
32	Singapore	55
33	Iran[b]	49
34	Puerto Rico[a]	48
35	Nigeria	46
36	Czech Republic	45
37	Venezuela[a]	43
38	Romania[b]	42
39	Denmark	38a

Largest services output

$bn, 2015

1	United States[b]	13,084
2	China	5,558
3	Japan[b]	3,528
4	Germany	2,085
5	United Kingdom	2,039
6	France	1,703
7	Italy	1,214
8	Canada[a]	1,196
9	Brazil	1,126
10	India	1,007
11	Australia	899
12	Spain	799
13	Russia	748
	South Korea	748
15	Mexico	677
16	Netherlands	527
17	Switzerland	479
18	Turkey	412
19	Indonesia	400
20	Saudi Arabia	335
21	Taiwan	328
22	Argentina	323
23	Sweden	318
24	Belgium	314
25	Nigeria	283
26	Hong Kong	274
27	Poland	268
28	Austria	236
29	Norway	219
30	Iran[b]	218
	Thailand	218
32	Singapore	202
33	Denmark	198
34	South Africa	193
35	United Arab Emirates	191
36	Egypt	176
37	Philippines	172
38	Malaysia	163
39	Colombia	158
40	Venezuela[a]	155
41	Ireland	151
42	Pakistan	142
43	Finland	142
44	Chile	139
45	Greece	138
46	Portugal	131
47	New Zealand[c]	115
48	Kazakhstan	109
49	Bangladesh	105
50	Peru	102
51	Czech Republic	99
52	Iraq	96

a 2013 b 2014 c 2012

Agriculture and fisheries

Largest agricultural output

$bn, 2015

1	China	977
2	India	332
3	United States[a]	224
4	Indonesia	117
5	Nigeria	100
6	Brazil	77
7	Pakistan	65
8	Russia	55
9	Turkey	54
10	Japan[a]	53
11	Iran[a]	39
12	France	38
	Mexico	38
14	Egypt	37
	Italy	37
16	Thailand	36
17	Vietnam	33
18	Canada	32
19	Australia	31
	Sudan	31
21	Argentina	30
	Philippines	30
23	Bangladesh	29
	South Korea	29
25	Spain	28
26	Malaysia	25
27	Ethiopia	23
28	Algeria	19
	Germany	19
	Kenya	19

Most economically dependent on agriculture

% of GDP from agriculture, 2015

1	Sierra Leone	61.3
2	Chad	52.4
3	Guinea-Bissau[b]	43.7
4	Burundi	43.0
5	Central African Rep.	42.4
6	Ethiopia	41.0
	Mali	41.0
8	Togo	40.7
9	Niger	39.9
10	Sudan	39.3
11	Liberia	35.0
12	Rwanda	34.6
13	Burkina Faso	34.2
14	Nepal	33.0
15	Kenya	32.9
16	Tanzania	31.1
17	Malawi	29.5
18	Cambodia	28.2
19	Laos	27.4
20	Myanmar	26.7
21	Uganda	25.8
22	Madagascar	25.6
23	Benin	25.3
24	Mozambique	25.2
25	Pakistan	25.1
26	Tajikistan	25.0
27	Cameroon	22.8
28	Ivory Coast	22.7

Least economically dependent on agriculture

% of GDP from agriculture, 2015

1	Macau	0.0
	Singapore	0.0
3	Hong Kong	0.1
4	Luxembourg	0.2
	Qatar	0.2
6	Bahrain	0.3
7	Trinidad & Tobago	0.5
8	Andorra[b]	0.6
	Germany	0.6
	Kuwait	0.6
11	Belgium	0.7
	Switzerland	0.7
	United Kingdom	0.7
14	Bermuda[c]	0.8
	Puerto Rico[b]	0.8
16	Ireland	1.0
17	Brunei	1.1
	Japan[a]	1.1
19	Denmark	1.2
20	Austria	1.3
	Sweden	1.3
	United States[a]	1.3
23	Malta	1.4
24	Oman	1.6

a 2014 b 2013 c 2012

Fisheries and aquaculture production

Fish, crustaceans and molluscs, million tonnes, 2015

1	China	64.1	**16**	Malaysia	1.7
2	Indonesia	10.7	**17**	Mexico	1.6
3	India[a]	10.1	**18**	Egypt[a]	1.5
4	Vietnam	6.2	**19**	Morocco	1.4
5	United States	5.5	**20**	Brazil[a]	1.3
6	Peru	4.9		Iceland	1.3
7	Russia	4.6		Spain	1.3
8	Japan	4.1		Taiwan	1.3
9	Bangladesh	3.7	**24**	Ecuador	1.1
	Norway	3.7	**25**	Canada	1.0
11	Myanmar[a]	2.9		Iran	1.0
	Philippines	2.9		Nigeria	1.0
13	Chile	2.8	**28**	Denmark	0.9
14	Thailand	2.5		United Kingdom	0.9
15	South Korea[a]	2.1	**30**	Argentina	0.8

Biggest producers

'000 tonnes, 2014

Cereals

1	China	557,407	**6**	Indonesia	89,855
2	United States	442,849	**7**	France	73,331
3	India	295,360	**8**	Ukraine	63,378
4	Russia	103,136	**9**	Bangladesh	55,759
5	Brazil	101,402	**10**	Germany	52,010

Meat

1	China	84,798	**6**	India	6,601
2	United States	42,565	**7**	Mexico	6,224
3	Brazil	26,053	**8**	Spain	5,742
4	Russia	9,070	**9**	France	5,489
5	Germany	8,356	**10**	Argentina	5,193

Fruit

1	China	158,424	**6**	Spain	17,764
2	India	88,475	**7**	Indonesia	17,365
3	Brazil	37,410	**8**	Philippines	16,233
4	United States	25,952	**9**	Italy	15,645
5	Mexico	17,851	**10**	Turkey	14,291

Vegetables

1	China	596,110	**6**	Egypt	19,352
2	India	126,579	**7**	Vietnam	17,951
3	United States	36,599	**8**	Russia	16,894
4	Turkey	28,186	**9**	Mexico	14,286
5	Iran	21,456	**10**	Spain	14,173

Roots and tubers

1	China	173,355	**5**	Thailand	30,484
2	Nigeria	108,069	**6**	Brazil	27,716
3	India	55,622	**7**	Indonesia	27,599
4	Russia	31,501	**8**	Ghana	25,079

a Estimate.

Commodities

Wheat

Top 10 producers, 2015–16
'000 tonnes

1	EU28	159,600
2	China	130,200
3	India	86,500
4	Russia	61,000
5	United States	56,100
6	Canada	27,600
7	Ukraine	27,300
8	Pakistan	25,500
9	Australia	24,200
10	Turkey	22,600

Top 10 consumers, 2015–16
'000 tonnes

1	EU28	128,890
2	China	116,900
3	India	88,710
4	Russia	37,140
5	United States	32,060
6	Pakistan	24,330
7	Egypt	20,430
8	Turkey	20,370
9	Iran	18,180
10	Ukraine	11,800

Rice[a]

Top 10 producers, 2015–16
'000 tonnes

1	China	145,770
2	India	104,408
3	Indonesia	36,200
4	Bangladesh	34,500
5	Vietnam	27,584
6	Thailand	15,800
7	Myanmar	12,160
8	Philippines	11,000
9	Japan	7,670
10	Brazil	7,210

Top 10 consumers, 2015–16
'000 tonnes

1	China	144,000
2	India	93,568
3	Indonesia	37,800
4	Bangladesh	35,100
5	Vietnam	22,600
6	Philippines	13,000
7	Myanmar	10,750
8	Thailand	9,100
9	Japan	8,600
10	Brazil	7,850

Sugar[b]

Top 10 producers, 2015
'000 tonnes

1	Brazil	34,240
2	India	28,870
3	EU28	15,300
4	Thailand	11,000
5	China	10,260
6	United States	7,700
7	Pakistan	6,130
8	Mexico	5,880
9	Russia	5,100
10	Australia	4,820

Top 10 consumers, 2015
'000 tonnes

1	India	26,000
2	EU28	17,880
3	China	15,450
4	Brazil	11,010
5	United States	10,830
6	Indonesia	6,050
7	Russia	5,500
8	Pakistan	4,860
9	Mexico	4,370
10	Egypt	3,270

Coarse grains[c]

Top 5 producers, 2015–16
'000 tonnes

1	United States	367,399
2	China	233,325
3	EU28	152,157
4	Brazil	68,729
5	Argentina	48,334

Top 5 consumers, 2015–16
'000 tonnes

1	United States	313,248
2	China	240,059
3	EU28	149,378
4	Brazil	60,063
5	Mexico	45,718

a Milled. b Raw. c Includes: maize (corn), barley, sorghum, oats, rye, millet, triticale and other. d Tonnes at 65 degrees brix.

Tea

Top 10 producers, 2014
'000 tonnes

1	China	2,096
2	India	1,207
3	Kenya	445
4	Sri Lanka	338
5	Vietnam	228
6	Turkey	227
7	Indonesia	154
8	Iran	119
9	Myanmar	99
10	Argentina	85

Top 10 consumers, 2015
'000 tonnes

1	China	1,978
2	India	999
3	Turkey	306
4	Russia	165
5	Pakistan	152
6	United States	127
7	United Kingdom	115
8	Japan	110
9	Egypt	90
10	Bangladesh	78

Coffee

Top 10 producers, 2016
'000 tonnes

1	Brazil	3,300
2	Vietnam	1,530
3	Colombia	870
4	Indonesia	600
5	Ethiopia	396
6	Honduras	356
7	India	320
8	Peru	228
	Uganda	228
10	Guatemala	210

Top 10 consumers, 2015–16
'000 tonnes

1	EU28	2,573
2	United States	1,520
3	Brazil	1,230
4	Japan	467
5	Indonesia	270
6	Russia	258
7	Ethiopia	222
8	Canada	212
9	Vietnam	138
10	India	135

Cocoa

Top 10 producers, 2015–16
'000 tonnes

1	Ivory Coast	1,581
2	Ghana	778
3	Indonesia	320
4	Ecuador	232
5	Cameroon	211
6	Nigeria	200
7	Brazil	140
8	Peru	95
9	Dominican Rep.	72
10	Colombia	53

Top 10 consumers, 2015–16
'000 tonnes

1	Netherlands	535
2	Ivory Coast	492
3	Germany	430
4	United States	398
5	Indonesia	382
6	Brazil	335
7	Ghana	202
8	Malaysia	194
9	France	138
10	Spain	112

Orange juice[d]

Top 5 producers, 2015–16
'000 tonnes

1	Brazil	848
2	United States	383
3	Mexico	165
4	EU28	100
5	South Africa	45

Top 5 consumers, 2015–16
'000 tonnes

1	EU28	825
2	United States	634
3	Canada	94
4	China	83
5	Japan	78

Copper

Top 10 producers[a], 2015
'000 tonnes

1	Chile	5,764
2	Peru	1,705
3	China	1,667
4	United States	1,410
5	Congo-Kinshasa	1039
6	Australia	964
7	EU28	861
8	Zambia	758
9	Russia	740
10	Canada	697

Top 10 consumers[b], 2015
'000 tonnes

1	China	11,353
2	EU28	3,338
3	United States	1,796
4	Germany	1,219
5	Japan	997
6	South Korea	705
7	Italy	613
8	India	491
9	Taiwan	471
10	Turkey	455

Lead

Top 10 producers[a], 2014
'000 tonnes

1	China	2,335
2	Australia	653
3	United States	371
4	Peru	316
5	Mexico	254
6	EU28	208
7	Russia	196
8	India	139
9	Sweden	79
10	Turkey	76

Top 10 consumers[b], 2015
'000 tonnes

1	China	3,804
2	EU28	1,617
3	United States	1,590
4	South Korea	602
5	India	539
6	Germany	357
7	Japan	269
8	Brazil	240
9	Spain	238
10	Mexico	235

Zinc

Top 10 producers[a], 2015
'000 tonnes

1	China	4,750
2	Australia	1,583
3	Peru	1,422
4	India	826
5	United States	808
6	EU28	699
7	Mexico	677
8	Bolivia	442
9	Kazakhstan	384
10	Canada	277

Top 10 consumers[c], 2015
'000 tonnes

1	China	6,483
2	EU28	2,114
3	United States	931
4	India	612
5	South Korea	590
6	Germany	479
	Japan	479
8	Belgium	450
9	Italy	258
10	Turkey	230

Tin

Top 5 producers[a], 2015
'000 tonnes

1	China	146.6
2	Indonesia	68.4
3	Myanmar	28.6
4	Brazil	25.5
5	Bolivia	20.1

Top 5 consumers[b], 2015
'000 tonnes

1	China	175.8
2	EU28	51.5
3	United States	31.4
4	Japan	26.8
5	Germany	17.9

Nickel

Top 10 producers[a], 2015
'000 tonnes

1	Philippines	464.5
2	Russia	261.0
3	Canada	234.9
4	Australia	225.2
5	New Caledonia	186.1
6	Indonesia	128.6
7	China	100.8
8	Brazil	89.3
9	South Africa	56.7
10	Guatemala	56.5

Top 10 consumers[b], 2015
'000 tonnes

1	China	836.1
2	EU28	301.6
3	United States	152.0
4	Japan	150.6
5	South Korea	83.4
6	Italy	60.5
7	Germany	60.2
8	Taiwan	60.0
9	India	37.1
10	Belgium	35.0

Aluminium

Top 10 producers[d], 2015
'000 tonnes

1	China	31,410
2	Russia	3,529
3	Canada	2,880
4	United Arab Emirates	2,464
5	EU28	2,217
6	India	1,886
7	Australia	1,646
8	United States	1,587
9	Norway	1,241
10	Bahrain	961

Top 10 consumers[e], 2015
'000 tonnes

1	China	31,068
2	EU28	6,679
3	United States	5,325
4	Germany	2,163
5	Japan	1,779
6	India	1,476
7	South Korea	1,366
8	Turkey	952
9	United Arab Emirates	835
10	Brazil	801

Precious metals

Gold[a]
Top 10 producers, 2015
tonnes

1	China	450.1
2	Australia	277.8
3	Russia	255.8
4	United States	212.3
5	Canada	160.8
6	Peru	145.0
7	South Africa	144.5
8	Mexico	124.6
9	Uzbekistan	103.0
10	Indonesia	92.2

Silver[a]
Top 10 producers, 2015
tonnes

1	Mexico	5,592
2	Peru	4,102
3	China	3,393
4	EU28	2,024
5	Russia	1,571
6	Chile	1,504
7	Australia	1,430
8	Bolivia	1,306
9	Kazakhstan	1,305
10	Poland	1,230

Platinum
Top 3 producers, 2015
tonnes

1	South Africa	142.1
2	Russia	20.8
3	Zimbabwe	12.5

Palladium
Top 3 producers, 2015
tonnes

1	South Africa	76.1
2	Russia	69
3	United States/Canada	24.6

a Mine production. b Refined consumption. c Slab consumption.
d Primary refined production. e Primary refined consumption.

Rubber (natural and synthetic)

Top 10 producers, 2015
'000 tonnes

1	Thailand	4,724
2	China	3,645
3	Indonesia	3,145
4	United States	2,392
5	EU28	2,381
6	Japan	1,668
7	South Korea	1,502
8	Russia	1,390
9	Vietnam	1,017
10	India	767

Top 10 consumers, 2015
'000 tonnes

1	China	8,897
2	EU28	3,629
3	United States	2,905
4	Japan	1,587
5	India	1,536
6	Thailand	1,072
7	Brazil	929
8	Malaysia	898
9	Russia	520
10	Indonesia	509

Cotton

Top 10 producers, 2015–16
'000 tonnes

1	India	5,746
2	China	4,753
3	United States	2,806
4	Pakistan	1,537
5	Brazil	1,289
6	Uzbekistan	832
7	Turkey	640
8	Australia	626
9	Turkmenistan	315
10	Burkina Faso	244

Top 10 consumers, 2015–16
'000 tonnes

1	China	7,442
2	India	5,296
3	Pakistan	2,256
4	Turkey	1,500
5	Bangladesh	1,324
6	Vietnam	1,007
7	United States	751
8	Brazil	733
9	Indonesia	654
10	Mexico	418

Major oil seeds[a]

Top 5 producers, 2015–16
'000 tonnes

1	United States	115,879
2	Brazil	98,974
3	Argentina	60,777
4	China	54,454
5	India	29,043

Top 5 consumers, 2015–16
'000 tonnes

1	China	141,677
2	United States	63,104
3	EU28	51,515
4	Brazil	45,568
5	India	28,659

Major vegetable oils[b]

Top 5 producers, 2015–16
'000 tonnes

1	Indonesia	32,000
2	China	22,329
3	Malaysia	17,801
4	EU28	16,096
5	United States	10,883

Top 5 consumers, 2015–16
'000 tonnes

1	China	29,859
2	EU28	23,185
3	India	18,345
4	United States	13,028
5	Indonesia	9,463

a Soyabeans, rapeseed (canola), cottonseed, sunflowerseed and groundnuts (peanuts). b Palm, soyabean, rapeseed and sunflowerseed oil.
c Includes crude oil, shale oil, oil sands and natural gas liquids. d Opec member.
e Opec membership suspended 30 November 2016.

Oil[c]

Top 10 producers, 2016
'000 barrels per day

1	United States	12,354
2	Saudi Arabia[e]	12,349
3	Russia	11,227
4	Iran[d]	4,600
5	Iraq[d]	4,465
6	Canada	4,460
7	United Arab Emirates[d]	4,073
8	China	3,999
9	Kuwait[d]	3,151
10	Brazil	2,605

Top 10 consumers, 2016
'000 barrels per day

1	United States	19,631
2	China	12,381
3	India	4,489
4	Japan	4,037
5	Saudi Arabia[d]	3,906
6	Russia	3,203
7	Brazil	3,018
8	South Korea	2,763
9	Germany	2,394
10	Canada	2,343

Natural gas

Top 10 producers, 2016
Billion cubic metres

1	United States	749.2
2	Russia	579.4
3	Iran[d]	202.4
4	Qatar[d]	181.2
5	Canada	152.0
6	China	138.4
7	Norway	116.6
8	Saudi Arabia[d]	109.4
9	Algeria[d]	91.3
10	Australia	91.2

Top 10 consumers, 2016
Billion cubic metres

1	United States	778.6
2	Russia	390.9
3	China	210.3
4	Iran[e]	200.8
5	Japan	111.2
6	Saudi Arabia[d]	109.4
7	Canada	99.9
8	Mexico	89.5
9	Germany	80.5
10	United Arab Emirates[d]	76.6

Coal

Top 10 producers, 2016
Million tonnes oil equivalent

1	China	1,685.7
2	United States	364.8
3	Australia	299.3
4	India	288.5
5	Indonesia[e]	255.7
6	Russia	192.8
7	South Africa	142.4
8	Colombia	62.5
9	Poland	52.3
10	Kazakhstan	44.1

Top 10 consumers, 2016
Million tonnes oil equivalent

1	China	1,887.6
2	India	411.9
3	United States	358.4
4	Japan	119.9
5	Russia	87.3
6	South Africa	85.1
7	South Korea	81.6
8	Germany	75.3
9	Indonesia[e]	62.7
10	Poland	48.8

Oil reserves[c]

Top proved reserves, end 2016
% of world total

1	Venezuela[d]	17.6
2	Saudi Arabia[d]	15.6
3	Canada	10
4	Iran[d]	9.3
5	Iraq[d]	9.0
6	Russia	6.4
7	Kuwait[d]	5.9
8	United Arab Emirates[d]	5.7
9	Libya[d]	2.8
	United States	2.8

Energy

Largest producers

Million tonnes of oil equivalent, 2014

1	China	3,073
2	United States	2,451
3	Russia	772
4	India	623
5	Japan	477
6	Canada	364
7	Germany	322
8	Brazil	321
9	South Korea	281
10	Iran	265
11	Saudi Arabia	255
12	France	254
13	United Kingdom	201
14	Mexico	188
15	Indonesia	185
16	Italy	160
17	Australia	142
	South Africa	142
19	Spain	137
20	Turkey	131
21	Thailand	129
22	Taiwan	115
23	United Arab Emirates	107
24	Ukraine	106
25	Poland	98
26	Netherlands	96
27	Argentina	94
28	Egypt	90
29	Malaysia	87
30	Venezuela	83

Largest consumers

Million tonnes of oil equivalent, 2013

1	China	3,073
2	United States	2,451
3	Russia	772
4	India	623
5	Japan	477
6	Canada	364
7	Germany	322
8	Brazil	321
9	South Korea	281
10	Iran	265
11	Saudi Arabia	255
12	France	254
13	United Kingdom	201
14	Mexico	188
15	Indonesia	185
16	Italy	160
17	Australia	142
	South Africa	142
19	Spain	137
20	Turkey	131
21	Thailand	129
22	Taiwan	115
23	United Arab Emirates	107
24	Ukraine	106
25	Poland	98
26	Netherlands	96
27	Argentina	94
28	Egypt	90
29	Malaysia	87
30	Venezuela	83

Energy efficiency[a]

GDP per unit of energy use, 2014

Most efficient

1	South Sudan	32.8
2	Hong Kong	26.8
3	Sri Lanka	20.6
4	Cuba	19.6
5	Switzerland	18.5
6	Panama	18.4
7	Colombia	17.9
8	Ireland	17.7
9	Dominican Rep.	17.2
	Malta	17.2
11	Mauritius	16.4

Least efficient

1	Congo-Kinshasa	1.9
2	Trinidad & Tobago	2.2
3	Iceland	2.3
4	Mozambique	2.5
5	Ethiopia	2.9
	Togo	2.9
	Turkmenistan	2.9
8	Ukraine	3.4
9	Bahrain	4.1
10	Haiti	4.2
11	South Africa	4.6

a 2011 PPP $ per kg of oil equivalent.

Net energy importers

% of commercial energy use, 2014

Highest

1	Hong Kong	99.0
2	Lebanon	98.0
	Malta	98.0
	Singapore	98.0
5	Jordan	97.0
6	Luxembourg	96.0
7	Cyprus	94.0
	Japan	94.0
9	Morocco	91.0
10	Moldova	90.0
11	Belarus	87.0
	Dominican Rep.	87.0

Lowest

1	South Sudan	-1,058
2	Norway	-583
3	Angola	-541
4	Congo-Brazzaville	-497
5	Qatar	-399
6	Kuwait	-391
7	Brunei	-357
8	Azerbaijan	-310
9	Colombia	-274
10	Iraq	-229
11	Gabon	-213
12	Oman	-206

Largest consumption per person

Kg of oil equivalent, 2014

1	Qatar	20,292
2	Iceland	17,916
3	Trinidad & Tobago	14,447
4	Bahrain	10,395
5	Kuwait	9,027
6	Brunei	8,515
7	Canada	7,874
8	United Arab Emirates	7,756
9	United States	6,949
10	Saudi Arabia	6,913
11	Luxembourg	6,861
12	Finland	6,213
13	Oman	5,743
14	Norway	5,596
15	Australia	5,338
16	South Korea	5,323
17	Singapore	5,122
18	Turkmenistan	5,040
19	Sweden	4,966
20	Russia	4,943
21	Belgium	4,699
22	Estonia	4,593

Sources of electricity

% of total, 2014

Oil

1	South Sudan	99.6
2	Benin	99.5
	Eritrea	99.5
4	Lebanon	98.9
5	Malta	96.7

Gas

1	Bahrain	100.0
	Qatar	100.0
	Turkmenistan	100.0
4	Trinidad & Tobago	99.8
5	Brunei	99.0

Hydropower

1	Albania	100.0
	Paraguay	100.0
3	Congo-Kinshasa	99.9
4	Nepal	99.8
5	Namibia	99.1

Nuclear power

1	France	78.6
2	Slovakia	57.1
3	Belgium	53.3
4	Hungary	48.6
5	Sweden	47.2

Coal

1	Kosovo	96.9
2	Botswana	95.8
3	South Africa	93.0
4	Mongolia	92.3
5	Estonia	87.4

Renewables excl. hydropower

1	Denmark	55.8
2	Nicaragua	45.7
3	El Salvador	45.0
4	Iceland	33.8
5	Portugal	32.1

Labour markets

Labour-force participation

% of working-age population[a] working or looking for work, 2016 or latest

Highest

1	Madagascar	86.4
2	Uganda	85.0
3	Rwanda	84.9
4	Qatar	84.1
5	Eritrea	83.9
6	Burundi	83.7
7	Burkina Faso	83.4
8	Ethiopia	83.0
	Nepal	83.0
10	Zimbabwe	82.5
11	Guinea	82.3
12	Equatorial Guinea	82.0
13	Malawi	81.1
14	Cambodia	81.0
15	Togo	80.9
16	North Korea	79.5
	United Arab Emirates	79.5
18	Mozambique	79.1
19	Tanzania	78.5
20	Vietnam	78.4
21	Central African Rep.	78.1
22	Myanmar	77.8
23	Laos	77.6
24	Botswana	77.5
25	Ghana	77.1
26	Cameroon	76.1
27	Zambia	75.3
28	Peru	74.3

Lowest

1	Jordan	40.1
2	Timor-Leste	41.4
3	Syria	41.7
4	Moldova	42.3
5	Puerto Rico	42.5
6	Iraq	42.6
7	Algeria	43.8
8	Iran	44.7
9	Bosnia & Herz.	46.0
10	Lebanon	47.2
11	Mauritania	47.3
12	Tunisia	47.7
13	Sudan	48.2
14	Italy	48.3
15	Montenegro	48.8
16	Gabon	49.2
17	Morocco	49.3
18	Egypt	49.6
19	Yemen	49.8
20	Albania	50.3
	Turkey	50.3
22	Serbia	51.4
23	Sri Lanka	51.7
24	Greece	51.8
25	Croatia	52.2
	Swaziland	52.2

Most male workforce

Highest % men in workforce, 2016

1	United Arab Emirates	87.6
2	Oman	87.2
3	Syria	85.3
4	Saudi Arabia	84.8
5	Qatar	84.7
6	Jordan	82.5
7	Afghanistan	82.4
8	Iraq	82.2
9	Iran	81.9
10	Algeria	80.7
11	Bahrain	80.2
12	West Bank & Gaza	79.6
13	Pakistan	77.8
14	Egypt	76.9
15	India	75.7
16	Lebanon	75.1

Most female workforce

Highest % women in workforce, 2016

1	Mozambique	54.4
	Rwanda	54.4
3	Burundi	51.7
4	Togo	51.2
5	Laos	51.0
6	Nepal	50.8
7	Malawi	50.5
8	Congo-Kinshasa	50.1
9	Ghana	50.0
10	Barbados	49.9
	Lithuania	49.9
12	Myanmar	49.7
13	Latvia	49.6
14	Sierra Leone	49.5
15	Benin	49.4

a Aged 15 and over.

Highest rate of unemployment

% of labour force[a], 2016

1	Kosovo[b]	32.9
2	Réunion[b]	30.2
3	Gambia, The	29.7
4	Lesotho	27.4
5	Macedonia	26.7
6	Guadeloupe[b]	26.2
7	South Africa	25.9
	West Bank & Gaza[b]	25.9
9	Bosnia & Herz.	25.8
10	Namibia	25.6
11	Swaziland	25.3
12	Mozambique	24.4
13	Greece	23.9
14	French Guiana[b]	23.8
15	Martinique[b]	23.2
16	Spain	19.4
17	Libya	19.2
18	Gabon	18.5
19	Botswana	18.4
20	French Polynesia	17.9
21	Montenegro	17.5
	Oman	17.5
23	Yemen	17.1
24	Armenia	16.8
25	Serbia	16.5
26	Albania	16.3
27	Iraq	16.0
28	Bahamas	15.3
29	New Caledonia	14.9
30	Tunisia	14.8
31	Dominican Rep.	14.4
32	Syria	14.3
33	Croatia	13.5
34	Jamaica	13.3
	Sudan	13.3
36	Haiti	13.2
	Jordan	13.2
38	Puerto Rico	12.6
39	Egypt	12.0
40	Cyprus	11.7
	Mauritania	11.7
42	Georgia	11.6
43	Brazil	11.5
	Italy	11.5
45	Barbados	11.4
	Guyana	11.4

Highest rate of youth unemployment

% of labour force[a] aged 15–24, 2016 estimates

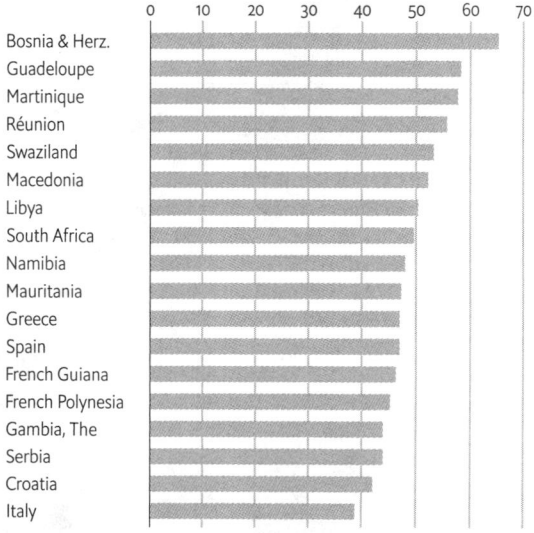

a ILO definition. b 2015

Minimum wage

As % of the median wage of full-time workers[a], 2015

1	Turkey	70.2
2	Chile	66.2
3	France	62.3
4	New Zealand	59.8
	Slovenia	59.8
6	Israel	58.1
7	Portugal	56.9
8	Luxembourg	54.8
9	Australia	53.5
10	Hungary	52.5
11	Latvia	51.8
12	Poland	51.3
13	Belgium	49.2
14	United Kingdom	48.7
15	South Korea	48.4
16	Germany	47.8
17	Greece	47.4
18	Slovakia	47.3
19	Netherlands	45.9
20	Canada	44.5
21	Ireland	44.4
22	Estonia	41.3
23	Japan	39.8
24	Czech Republic	38.8
25	Mexico	37.5
26	Spain	36.8
27	United States	35.8

Average hours worked

Per employed person per week, 2015

1	Nepal	53.6
2	Egypt	53.0
3	Myanmar	50.8
4	Qatar	50.0
5	Pakistan	47.4
6	Turkey	46.7
7	Macau	46.0
8	Malaysia	45.4
9	Mongolia	45.0
10	Peru	44.6
11	Singapore	44.2
12	Saudi Arabia	44.1
13	Hong Kong	44.0
14	South Korea	43.6
15	Vietnam	43.5
16	South Africa	43.4
17	Costa Rica	43.0
18	Mexico	42.7
19	Serbia	42.6
20	Colombia	42.2
21	Guatemala	42.0
22	Dominican Rep.	41.7
23	Macedonia	41.5
	Montenegro	41.5

Poverty pay

% of workers paid $2 or less per day, 2015

1	Madagascar	94.6
2	Liberia	93.0
3	Central African Rep.	90.7
4	Burundi	88.7
5	Afghanistan	87.5
6	Congo-Kinshasa	86.7
7	Malawi	81.6
8	Guinea-Bissau	79.9
9	Mali	79.0
10	Guinea	72.3
11	Zambia	71.6
12	Eritrea	71.1
13	Nigeria	68.9
14	Rwanda	68.6
15	Niger	67.6
16	Bangladesh	62.8
17	Benin	62.6
	Tanzania	62.6
19	Zimbabwe	62.5
20	Mozambique	61.3
21	Togo	60.7
22	Sierra Leone	57.8
23	Laos	56.9
24	Senegal	56.6
25	Burkina Faso	56.2
26	India	53.3
27	Uganda	53.1
28	Congo-Brazzaville	51.8
29	Chad	51.2
30	Lesotho	49.4

a OECD countries.

Business costs and foreign direct investment

Office rents

Rent, taxes and operating expenses, Q1 2016, $ per sq. ft.

Foreign direct investment[a]

Inflows, $m, 2015

1	United States	379,894
2	Hong Kong	174,892
3	China	135,610
4	Ireland	100,542
5	Netherlands	72,649
6	Switzerland	68,838
7	Singapore	65,262
8	Brazil	64,648
9	Canada	48,643
10	India	44,208
11	France	42,883
12	United Kingdom	39,533
13	Germany	31,719
14	Belgium	31,029
15	Mexico	30,285
16	Luxembourg	24,596
17	Australia	22,264

Outflows, $m, 2015

1	United States	299,969
2	Japan	128,654
3	China	127,560
4	Netherlands	113,429
5	Ireland	101,616
6	Germany	94,313
7	Switzerland	70,277
8	Canada	67,182
9	Hong Kong	55,143
10	Luxembourg	39,371
11	Belgium	38,547
12	Singapore	35,485
13	France	35,069
14	Spain	34,586
15	South Korea	27,640
16	Italy	27,607
17	Russia	26,558

Note: CBD is Central Business District.
a Investment in companies in a foreign country.

Business creativity and research

Entrepreneurial activity

Percentage of population aged 18–64 who are either a nascent entrepreneur[a] or owner-manager of a new business, average 2011–16

Highest			*Lowest*		
1	Zambia	40.7	**1**	Suriname	3.6
2	Senegal	38.6	**2**	Bulgaria	4.2
3	Nigeria	36.6		Japan	4.2
4	Uganda	32.2	**4**	Italy	4.3
5	Ecuador	32.1	**5**	Morocco	5.0
6	Malawi	31.8	**6**	Germany	5.1
7	Ghana	31.2		Russia	5.1
8	Cameroon	30.1	**8**	Denmark	5.2
9	Botswana	28.6		France	5.2
10	Burkina Faso	28.3	**10**	Malaysia	5.3
11	Bolivia	27.4	**11**	Belgium	5.5
12	Lebanon	25.7		Spain	5.5
	Namibia	25.7	**13**	United Arab Emirates	5.9
14	Angola	25.4	**14**	Slovenia	6.0
15	Chile	24.6	**15**	Finland	6.1
16	Peru	23.8	**16**	Norway	6.3
17	Colombia	22.3	**17**	Macedonia	6.6
18	Thailand	18.4	**18**	Greece	6.7
19	Brazil	18.1	**19**	Sweden	7.0
20	Guatemala	18.0	**20**	Switzerland	7.2
	Philippines	18.0	**21**	Croatia	7.4
22	Indonesia	17.9	**22**	Czech Republic	7.5
	Trinidad & Tobago	17.9		South Korea	7.5
24	Argentina	17.0		Tunisia	7.5
25	El Salvador	16.3	**25**	Algeria	7.6
26	Barbados	16.1			

Brain drains[b]

Highest, 2016			*Lowest, 2016*		
1	Serbia	1.7	**1**	Switzerland	6.1
	Venezuela	1.7	**2**	United Arab Emirates	5.6
3	Bosnia & Herz.	1.9		United States	5.6
	Moldova	1.9	**4**	Norway	5.5
	Yemen	1.9		Qatar	5.5
6	Romania	2.1		Singapore	5.5
7	Burundi	2.2	**7**	United Kingdom	5.4
	Croatia	2.2	**8**	Malaysia	5.3
9	Hungary	2.4	**9**	Finland	5.2
	Zimbabwe	2.4		Hong Kong	5.2
11	Kyrgyzstan	2.5		Netherlands	5.2
	Mongolia	2.5	**12**	Luxembourg	5.1
	Ukraine	2.5	**13**	Sweden	5.0
			14	Chile	4.9
				Iceland	4.9
			16	Canada	4.8
				Germany	4.8

a An individual who has started a new firm which has not paid wages for over three months.
b Scores: 1 = talented people leave for other countries; 7 = they stay and pursue opportunities in the country.

Total expenditure on R&D

	$bn, 2015			*% of GDP, 2015*	
1	United States	502.9	**1**	Israel	4.30
2	China	227.6	**2**	South Korea	4.23
3	Japan	144.0	**3**	Japan	3.49
4	Germany	96.7	**4**	Sweden	3.28
5	South Korea	58.3	**5**	Austria	3.10
6	France	53.9	**6**	Taiwan	3.06
7	United Kingdom	48.7	**7**	Denmark	3.02
8	Brazil[b]	39.7	**8**	Switzerland[c]	2.97
9	Australia[b]	32.3	**9**	Finland	2.93
10	Canada[a]	28.8	**10**	Germany	2.88
11	Italy	24.3	**11**	United States	2.80
12	Switzerland[c]	19.7	**12**	Belgium	2.46
13	India[a]	18.3	**13**	France	2.23
14	Sweden	16.2	**14**	Slovenia	2.21
15	Taiwan	16.0	**15**	Iceland	2.20
	Netherlands	15.1		Singapore[a]	2.20
17	Russia	15.0	**17**	Australia[b]	2.15
18	Spain	14.6	**18**	China	2.09
19	Israel	12.7	**19**	Netherlands	2.01
20	Austria	11.6	**20**	Czech Republic	1.98

Innovation index[d]

2016, 100=maximum score

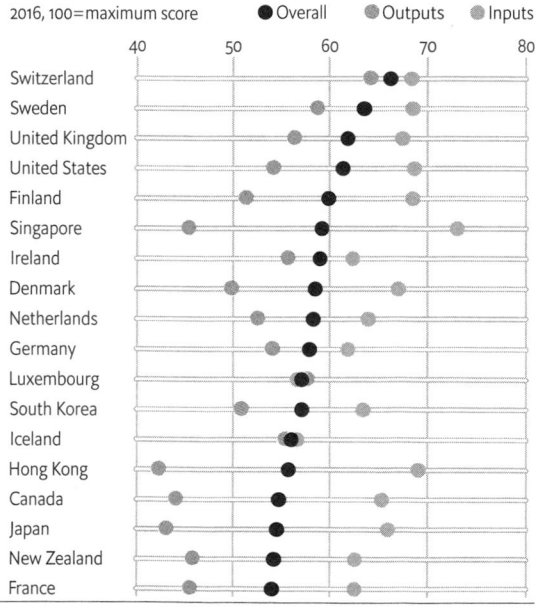

a 2014 b 2013 c 2012

d The innovation index averages countries' capacity for innovation (inputs) and success in innovation (outputs), based on 79 indicators.

Businesses and banks

Largest non-financial companies

By market capitalisation, $bn, end December 2016

By net profit, $bn, 2016

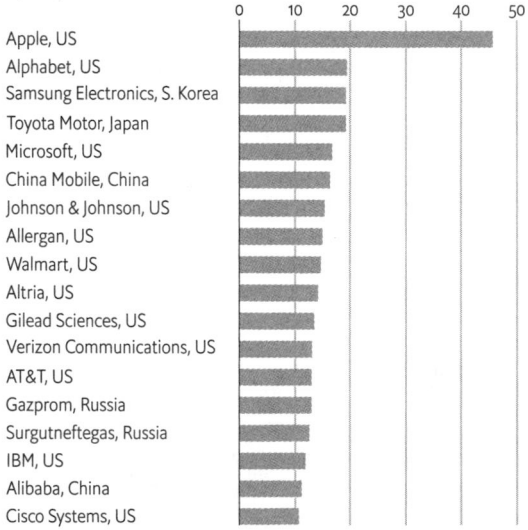

Largest banks

By market capitalisation, $bn, end December 2016

1	JPMorgan Chase	United States	308.8
2	Wells Fargo	United States	276.8
3	Industrial & Commercial Bank of China	China	223.4
4	Bank of America	United States	223.3
5	China Construction Bank	China	192.6
6	Citigroup	United States	169.4
7	HSBC	United Kingdom	161.1
8	Agricultural Bank of China	China	144.0
9	Bank of China	China	141.6
10	Commonwealth Bank of Australia	Australia	102.5
11	Royal Bank of Canada	Canada	100.4
12	TD Bank Group	Canada	91.5
13	Mitsubishi UFJ	Japan	87.5
14	BNP Paribas	France	79.6
15	Westpac	Australia	79.0

By assets, $bn, end December 2016

1	Industrial & Commercial Bank of China	China	3,478
2	China Construction Bank	China	3,021
3	Agricultural Bank of China	China	2,820
4	Bank of China	China	2,615
5	Mitsubishi UFJ	Japan	2,590
6	JPMorgan Chase	United States	2,546
7	HSBC	United Kingdom	2,375
8	Bank of America	United States	2,248
9	BNP Paribas	France	2,191
10	Wells Fargo	United States	1,952
11	Citigroup	United States	1,822
12	Japan Post	Japan	1,802
13	Mizuho	Japan	1,752
14	Deutsche Bank	Germany	1,674
15	Crédit Agricole	France	1,608

Largest sovereign-wealth funds

By assets, $bn, April 2017

1	Government Pension Fund, Norway	922
2	Abu Dhabi Investment Authority, UAE	828
3	China Investment Corporation	814
4	Kuwait Investment Authority	592
5	SAMA Foreign Holdings, Saudi Arabia	514
6	Hong Kong Monetary Authority Investment Portfolio	457
7	SAFE Investment Company, China[a]	441
8	Government of Singapore Investment Corporation	350
9	Qatar Investment Authority	335
10	China National Social Security Fund	295

Note: Countries listed refer to the company's domicile.
a Estimate.

Stockmarkets

Largest market capitalisation

$bn, end 2016

1	NYSE	19,573
2	Nasdaq – US	7,779
3	Japan Exchange Group	5,062
4	Shanghai SE	4,104
5	London SE Group	3,496
6	Euronext	3,493
7	Shenzhen SE	3,217
8	Hong Kong Exchanges	3,193
9	TMX Group	2,042
10	Deutsche Börse	1,732
11	BSE India	1,561
12	National Stock Exchange of India	1,534
13	SIX Swiss Exchange	1,415
14	Australian Securities Exchange[a]	1,317
15	Korea Exchange[b]	1,282
16	Nasdaq OMX Nordic Exchanges[c]	1,260
17	Johannesburg SE	959
18	Taiwan SE	862
19	BM&FBOVESPA	774
20	BME Spanish Exchanges	711
21	Singapore Exchange	649
22	Moscow Exchange	622
23	Saudi SE Tadawul	449
24	Stock Exchange of Thailand	437
25	Indonesia Stock Exchange	434
26	Bursa Malaysia	363
27	Bolsa Mexicana de Valores	334
28	Philippine Stock Exchange	240
29	Oslo Bors	234
30	Tel-Aviv Stock Exchange	215
31	Bolsa de Comercio de Santiago	212
32	Borsa Istanbul	158
33	Qatar Stock Exchange	155
34	Warsaw Stock Exchange	141
35	Abu Dhabi Securities Exchange	121
	Irish Stock Exchange	121
37	Bolsa de Valores de Colombia	103
38	Tehran Stock Exchange	101
	Wiener Borse	101

Stockmarket gains and losses

$ terms, % change December 31st 2015 to December 30th 2016

Largest gains

1	Russia (RTS)	82.1
2	Brazil (BVSP)	68.9
3	Pakistan (KSE)	46.2
4	Hungary (BUX)	32.9
5	Colombia (IGBC)	25.0
6	Canada (S&P TSX)	21.7
7	Norway (OSEAX)	21.2
8	Chile (IGPA)	20.9
9	Thailand (SET)	20.4
10	Argentina (MERV)	18.5
11	Indonesia (JSX)	18.0
12	US (DJIA)	13.4
13	South Africa (FTSE JSE)	13.2
14	Taiwan (TWI)	13.1
15	US (S&P 500)	9.5
16	US (NAScomp)	7.5
17	Netherlands (AEX)	6.2
18	Australia (ASX)	6.1
	Austria (ATX)	6.1
20	Poland (WIG)	5.4

Largest losses

1	Venezuela (IBC)	-95.6
2	China (SSEB)	-25.1
3	Egypt (Case 30)	-23.9
4	China (SSEA)	-18.0
5	Denmark (OMXCB)	-14.2
6	Italy (FTSE MIB)	-12.8
7	Mexico IPC	-11.0
8	Turkey (BIST)	-9.6
9	Switzerland (SMI)	-8.2
10	Malaysia (KLSE)	-7.2
11	Czech Republic (PX)	-6.4
12	Belgium (Bel 20)	-5.4
13	Spain (Madrid SE)	-5.1
14	UK (FTSE 100)	-4.1
15	Europe (FTSEurofirst 300)	-3.5
16	Sweden (OMXS30)	-2.7
17	Euro area (EURO STOXX 50)	-2.2
18	Singapore (STI)	-1.9
19	Israel (TA 125)	-1.8
20	Euro area (FTSE Euro 100)	-1.3

a Includes investment funds. b Includes Kosdaq. c Copenhagen, Helsinki, Iceland, Stockholm, Tallinn, Riga and Vilnius stock exchanges.

Value traded[a]

$bn, 2016

1	Nasdaq – US	31,944
2	NYSE	19,737
3	BATS Global Markets – US	13,683
4	Shenzhen SE	11,673
5	Shanghai SE	7,535
6	Japan Exchange Group Inc.	6,354
7	BATS Chi-x Europe	3,215
8	London SE Group	3,121
9	Euronext	1,802
10	Korea Exchange[b]	1,688
11	Hong Kong Exchanges	1,350
12	Deutsche Börse	1,324
13	TMX Group	1,176
14	Australian Securities Exchange[c]	911
15	SIX Swiss Exchange	870
16	Nasdaq OMX Nordic Exchange[d]	779
17	BME Spanish Exchanges	714
18	National Stock Exchange of India	691
19	BM&FBOVESPA	535
20	Taiwan SE	522
21	Johannesburg SE	404
22	Stock Exchange of Thailand	340
23	Borsa Istanbul	331
24	Saudi SE – Tadawul	309
25	Singapore Exchange	197
26	Taipei Exchange	157
27	Moscow Exchange	139
	Indonesia SE	139
29	Mexican Exchange	123
30	Oslo Bors	119
31	Bursa Malaysia	116
32	BSE India	110
33	Tel-Aviv SE	59
34	Warsaw SE	53

Number of listed companies[e]

End 2016

1	BSE India Limited	5,821
2	Japan Exchange Group Inc.	3,541
3	BME Spanish Exchanges	3,506
4	TMX Group	3,419
5	Nasdaq – US	2,897
6	LSE Group	2,588
7	NYSE	2,307
8	Australian Securities Exchange[c]	2,095
9	Korea Exchange[b]	2,059
10	Hong Kong Exchanges	1,973
11	Shenzhen Stock Exchange	1,870
12	National Stock Exchange of India	1,840
13	Shanghai Stock Exchange	1,182
14	Euronext	1,051
15	Nasdaq Nordic Exchanges[d]	938
16	Taiwan Stock Exchange	911
17	Bursa Malaysia	903
18	Warsaw Stock Exchange	893
19	Singapore Exchange	757
20	Taipei Exchange	732
21	Stock Exchange of Thailand	656
22	Deutsche Börse	592
23	Indonesia Stock Exchange	537
24	Tel-Aviv Stock Exchange	451
25	Borsa Istanbul	381
26	Hanoi Stock Exchange	376
	Johannesburg Stock Exchange	376
28	BM&F BOVESPA	349
29	Tehran Stock Exchange	325
30	Hochiminh Stock Exchange	320
31	Bolsa de Comercio de Santiago	298
32	Colombo Stock Exchange	295
33	Dhaka Stock Exchange	294
34	Philippine Stock Exchange	265
35	Bolsa de Valores de Lima	264
	SIX Swiss Exchange	264

Note: Figures are not entirely comparable due to different reporting rules and calculations.
a Includes electronic and negotiated deals. b Includes Kosdaq. c Includes investment funds. d Copenhagen, Helsinki, Iceland, Stockholm, Tallinn, Riga and Vilnius stock exchanges. e Domestic and foreign.

Public finance

Government debt

As % of GDP, 2016

1	Japan	233.7
2	Greece	185.7
3	Italy	159.3
4	Portugal	151.0
5	Belgium	127.0
6	France	122.7
7	Spain	118.4
8	United States	115.6
9	United Kingdom	112.5
10	Euro area (15)	109.1
11	Austria	106.0
12	Canada	100.4
13	Slovenia	99.4
14	Hungary	97.5
15	Ireland	91.0
16	Finland	78.0
17	Netherlands	76.1
18	Germany	74.7
19	Poland	67.5
20	Iceland	64.4
21	Israel	62.7
22	Slovakia	59.2
23	Denmark	53.7
24	Sweden	52.9
25	Czech Republic	52.3
26	Latvia	46.2
27	Australia	45.4
28	South Korea	44.2
29	Switzerland	43.1
30	Norway	41.7

Government spending

As % of GDP, 2016

1	Finland	57.5
2	France	56.5
3	Denmark	55.4
4	Belgium	53.2
5	Greece	52.3
6	Austria	51.1
7	Norway	51.0
8	Sweden	50.3
9	Hungary	49.9
10	Italy	49.5
11	Euro area (15)	48.1
12	Portugal	46.2
13	Slovenia	45.5
14	Netherlands	44.7
15	Germany	44.3
16	Slovakia	43.6
17	Spain	42.8
18	Luxembourg	42.4
19	Poland	41.7
20	Iceland	41.4
21	United Kingdom	41.3
22	Canada	41.1
23	Japan	41.0
	New Zealand	41.0
25	Czech Republic	40.4
26	Estonia	40.0
27	Israel	39.3
28	United States	38.0
29	Latvia	37.1
30	Australia	36.4

Tax revenue

As % of GDP, 2015

1	Denmark	46.6
2	France	45.5
3	Belgium	44.8
4	Finland	44.0
5	Austria	43.5
6	Italy	43.3
	Sweden	43.3
8	Hungary	39.4
9	Norway	38.1
10	Netherlands	37.8
11	Iceland	37.1
12	Luxembourg	37.0
13	Germany	36.9
14	Greece	36.8
15	Slovenia	36.6
16	Portugal	34.5
17	Spain	33.8
18	Estonia	33.6
19	Czech Republic	33.5
20	New Zealand	32.8
21	United Kingdom	32.5
22	Slovakia	32.3
23	Poland	32.1
24	Japan	32.0
25	Canada	31.9
26	Israel	31.4

Note: Includes only OECD countries.

Democracy

Democracy index

Most democratic = 100, 2016

Most

1	Norway	87.1
2	Switzerland	86.7
3	Sweden	86.2
4	Finland	86.0
5	Denmark	85.1
6	Netherlands	83.3
7	New Zealand	81.4
8	Germany	81.3
9	Ireland	80.9
10	Australia	80.5
11	Belgium	80.3
12	Austria	79.9
	Canada	79.9
14	United Kingdom	79.6
15	France	78.2
16	United States	76.5
17	Slovenia	75.9
18	Japan	75.5
19	Spain	75.3
20	Portugal	74.8

Least

1	Yemen	22.5
2	Libya	29.5
3	Pakistan	34.9
4	Egypt	35.7
5	Ivory Coast	38.1
6	China	38.3
7	Bahrain	38.6
8	Haiti	39.0
9	Nigeria	39.3
10	Guinea	39.4
	Togo	39.4
12	Mali	39.5
13	Venezuela	42.2
14	Morocco	42.5
	Mozambique	42.5
16	Lebanon	42.9
17	Kyrgyzstan	43.0
	Russia	43.0
19	Niger	43.2
20	Burkina Faso	45.3

Parliamentary seats

Lower or single house, seats per 100,000 population, April 2017

Most

1	Liechtenstein	62.5
2	Monaco	60.0
3	Andorra	28.0
4	Maldives	21.3
5	Iceland	21.0
6	Malta	16.3
7	Montenegro	13.5
8	Equatorial Guinea	12.5
9	Brunei	11.3
10	Suriname	10.2

Fewest

1	India	0.04
2	United States	0.14
3	Pakistan	0.18
4	Nigeria	0.20
5	Bangladesh	0.22
	China	0.22
	Indonesia	0.22
8	Brazil	0.25
9	Philippines	0.29
10	Russia	0.31

Women in parliament

Lower or single house, women as % of total seats, April 2017

1	Rwanda	61.3
2	Bolivia	53.1
3	Cuba	48.9
4	Iceland	47.6
5	Nicaragua	45.7
6	Sweden	43.6
7	Senegal	42.7
8	Mexico	42.6
9	South Africa	42.1
10	Finland	42.0
11	Namibia	41.3
12	Mozambique	39.6
	Norway	39.6
14	Spain	39.1
15	Argentina	38.9
16	Ethiopia	38.8
17	Timor-Leste	38.5
18	Angola	38.2
19	Belgium	38.0
	Ecuador	38.0
21	Denmark	37.4
22	Germany	37.0

Education

Primary enrolment

Number enrolled as % of relevant age group

Highest

1	Madagascar	149
2	Malawi	146
3	Timor-Leste	137
4	Nepal	136
5	Rwanda	134
6	Benin	129
7	Sierra Leone	128
8	Burundi	124
9	Suriname	123
10	Togo	122
11	Sweden	121
12	Bangladesh	120
13	Cambodia	117
	Cameroon	117
	Georgia	117
	Philippines	117

Lowest

1	Eritrea	50
2	South Sudan	64
3	Sudan	70
4	Niger	73
5	Mali	76
6	Congo-Brazzaville	77
7	Equatorial Guinea	79
8	Syria	80
9	Senegal	82
	Tanzania	82
11	Guyana	85
12	Burkina Faso	88
13	Puerto Rico	89
	Turkmenistan	89

Highest secondary enrolment

Number enrolled as % of relevant age group

1	Belgium	165
2	Finland	149
3	Australia	138
4	Sweden	133
5	Netherlands	132
6	Denmark	130
	Spain	130
8	Thailand	129
9	United Kingdom	128
10	Ireland	127
11	Costa Rica	123
12	Iceland	119
13	New Zealand	117
14	Liechtenstein	116
	Portugal	116
16	Estonia	115
	Latvia	115
18	Norway	113
19	Kazakhstan	112
20	France	111
	Slovenia	111
22	Canada	110

Highest tertiary enrolment[a]

Number enrolled as % of relevant age group

1	Greece	114
2	South Korea	95
3	Australia	90
	Spain	90
5	Chile	89
6	Belarus	88
7	Finland	87
8	Turkey	86
	United States	86
10	Puerto Rico	84
11	Argentina	83
	Slovenia	83
13	Austria	82
	Denmark	82
	Ukraine	82
16	Iceland	81
	New Zealand	81
18	Netherlands	79
	Russia	79
20	Ireland	78

Notes: Latest available year 2012–16. The gross enrolment ratios shown are the actual number enrolled as a percentage of the number of children in the official primary age group. They may exceed 100 when, eg, children outside the primary age group are receiving primary education.

a Tertiary education includes all levels of post-secondary education including courses leading to awards not equivalent to a university degree, courses leading to a first university degree and postgraduate courses.

Least literate

% adult population

1	Niger	19.1
2	Guinea	30.5
3	South Sudan	32.0
4	Mali	33.1
5	Central African Rep.	36.8
6	Burkina Faso	37.7
7	Afghanistan	38.2
8	Benin	38.4
9	Chad	40.0
10	Ivory Coast	43.3
11	Liberia	47.6
12	Sierra Leone	48.4
13	Ethiopia	49.0
14	Mauritania	52.1
15	Gambia, The	55.6
	Senegal	55.6
17	Pakistan	56.4
18	Sudan	58.6
19	Mozambique	58.8
20	Nigeria	59.6
21	Guinea-Bissau	59.8
22	Haiti	60.7
23	Bangladesh	61.5
24	Papua New Guinea	63.4
25	Timor-Leste	64.1
26	Madagascar	64.7
	Nepal	64.7
28	Malawi	66.0
29	Togo	66.5
30	Yemen	70.0
31	Angola	71.2
	Rwanda	71.2
33	Morocco	71.7
34	India	72.2
35	Eritrea	73.8
	Uganda	73.8

Education spending

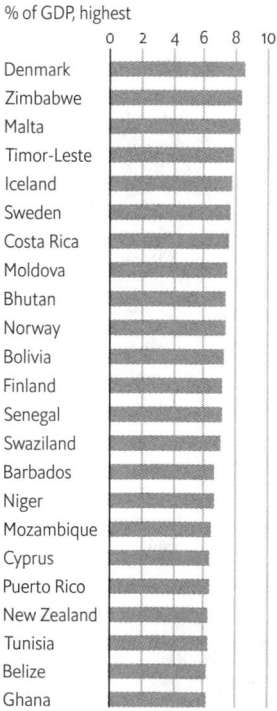

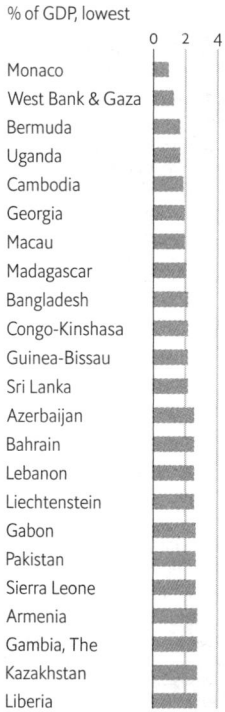

Marriage and divorce

Highest marriage rates

Number of marriages per 1,000 population, 2015 or latest available year

1	Tajikistan	11.6
2	Lebanon	11.2
3	Egypt	11.0
4	Kazakhstan	9.9
5	China	9.6
	Uzbekistan	9.6
	West Bank & Gaza	9.6
8	Iran	9.3
9	Jordan	9.2
10	Azerbaijan	8.9
	Belarus	8.9
12	Kyrgyzstan	8.7
13	Russia	8.5
14	Guam	8.3
15	Albania	8.2
	Bermuda	8.2
17	Hong Kong	7.8
	Turkey	7.8
19	Mauritius	7.7
20	Lithuania	7.6
21	Singapore	7.3
22	Moldova	7.2
23	Georgia	7.0
24	Ukraine	6.9
25	Jamaica	6.8
	United States	6.8
27	Barbados	6.7
	Macedonia	6.7
	Malta	6.7
30	Israel	6.5
31	Cyprus	6.4
32	Guyana	6.3
	Latvia	6.3
34	Armenia	6.0
35	Romania	5.9
	South Korea	5.9
	Trinidad & Tobago	5.9
38	Bahamas	5.8
	Macau	5.8
	Mongolia	5.8
41	Montenegro	5.7

Lowest marriage rates

Number of marriages per 1,000 population, 2015 or latest available year

1	Qatar	1.8
2	Martinique	2.5
3	Argentina	2.8
4	Guadeloupe	3.0
	Luxembourg	3.0
	Portugal	3.0
	Uruguay	3.0
	Venezuela	3.0
9	Italy	3.1
	Peru	3.1
11	Slovenia	3.2
12	Panama	3.3
	Réunion	3.3
14	Bulgaria	3.4
	Spain	3.4
16	Chile	3.5
17	Belgium	3.6
18	Andorra	3.7
	France	3.7
20	Suriname	3.8
21	Hungary	3.9
	Netherlands	3.9
	New Caledonia	3.9
24	Kuwait	4.0
25	Austria	4.3
	Czech Republic	4.3
27	Finland	4.5
	New Zealand	4.5
	United Kingdom	4.5
30	Croatia	4.6
	Iceland	4.6
	Norway	4.6
33	Estonia	4.7
34	Bosnia & Herz.	4.8
	Dominican Rep.	4.8
	Germany	4.8
	Ireland	4.8
	Mexico	4.8
39	Greece	4.9
	Puerto Rico	4.9
	Slovakia	4.9
42	Denmark	5.0
	Liechtenstein	5.0
	Poland	5.0

Note: The data are based on latest available figures (no earlier than 2010) and hence will be affected by the population age structure at the time. Marriage rates refer to registered marriages only and, therefore, reflect the customs surrounding registry and efficiency of administration.

Highest divorce rates

Number of divorces per 1,000 population, 2015 or latest available year[a]

1	Russia	4.5
2	Belarus	3.7
3	Guam	3.6
4	Denmark	3.4
	Puerto Rico	3.4
6	Lithuania	3.3
7	Latvia	3.1
8	Cuba	3.0
	Kazakhstan	3.0
	Moldova	3.0
	Ukraine	3.0
12	United States	2.8
13	Sweden	2.7
14	Luxembourg	2.6
15	Belgium	2.5
	Czech Republic	2.5
	Finland	2.5
18	Estonia	2.4
	Jordan	2.4
	Liechtenstein	2.4
21	Cyprus	2.2
	Portugal	2.2
	Spain	2.2

Lowest divorce rates

Number of divorces per 1,000 population, 2015 or latest available year[a]

1	Chile	0.1
2	Guatemala	0.3
3	Bosnia & Herz.	0.4
	Peru	0.4
5	Ireland	0.6
	Jamaica	0.6
7	Qatar	0.7
8	Malta	0.8
9	Italy	0.9
	Mexico	0.9
	Montenegro	0.9
	Uzbekistan	0.9
13	Armenia	1.0
14	Macedonia	1.1
	Martinique	1.1
	Panama	1.1
	Serbia	1.1
	Tajikistan	1.1
19	Bahamas	1.2
	New Caledonia	1.2
	Slovenia	1.2
22	Albania	1.3
	Azerbaijan	1.3
	Mongolia	1.3
25	Kyrgyzstan	1.4
	Romania	1.4
	Suriname	1.4
28	Bulgaria	1.5
	Greece	1.5

Mean age of women at first marriage

Years, 2012 or latest available year

Youngest[a]			*Oldest[b]*		
1	Niger	15.7	**1**	Sweden	32.9
2	Bangladesh	16.0	**2**	Denmark	32.1
	Chad	16.0		Iceland	32.1
4	Guinea	16.5	**4**	Ireland	31.2
5	Mali	16.7	**5**	Norway	31.0
6	Sierra Leone	17.1		Spain	31.0
7	Ethiopia	17.4	**7**	Netherlands	30.4
8	Mozambique	17.5	**8**	Finland	30.3
9	India	17.8		Germany	30.3
10	Burkina Faso	17.9	**10**	Italy	30.1
	Malawi	17.9	**11**	France	30.0
	Nepal	17.9	**12**	Luxembourg	29.9
13	Afghanistan	18.0		United Kingdom	29.9
14	Nicaragua	18.1	**14**	Switzerland	29.4

a No earlier than 2010. b No earlier than 2000.

Households, living costs and giving

Number of households

Biggest, m, 2015

1	China	452.8
2	India	268.6
3	United States	124.5
4	Indonesia	65.3
5	Brazil	62.1
6	Russia	56.5
7	Japan	53.0
8	Germany	41.6
9	Nigeria	38.3
10	Bangladesh	37.1
11	Mexico	32.8
12	France	29.3
13	Pakistan	28.1
14	Italy	27.3
15	United Kingdom	27.2
16	Vietnam	27.1
17	Iran	24.3
18	Egypt	23.4
19	Philippines	22.9
20	Thailand	22.5
21	Ethiopia	21.9
22	Turkey	21.2
23	Spain	18.8
24	South Korea	18.7
25	Ukraine	17.7
26	South Africa	15.3
27	Poland	14.1
28	Canada	14.0
29	Argentina	13.5
30	Colombia	13.3
31	Congo-Kinshasa	11.5
32	Tanzania	11.2
33	Myanmar	11.1
34	Kenya	10.8
35	North Korea	9.6
36	Australia	8.8
37	Uganda	8.2
38	Venezuela	7.9
39	Peru	7.8
	Taiwan	7.8

Average household size, people

Biggest, 2015

1	Guinea	8.6
2	Angola	8.5
3	Senegal	8.2
4	Chad	7.9
	Equatorial Guinea	7.9
	Gambia, The	7.9
7	Gabon	7.8
	Guinea-Bissau	7.8
9	Oman	6.9
10	Congo-Kinshasa	6.7
	Mauritania	6.7
	Pakistan	6.7
	Yemen	6.7
14	Maldives	6.5
15	Iraq	6.3
	Papua New Guinea	6.3
	Tajikistan	6.3
	Turkmenistan	6.3
19	Libya	6.1
	Mali	6.1
21	Niger	6.0
22	Kosovo	5.9

Smallest, 2015

1	Germany	1.9
	Sweden	1.9
3	Luxembourg	2.0
4	Finland	2.1
5	France	2.2
	Italy	2.2
	Lithuania	2.2
	Netherlands	2.2
9	Austria	2.3
	Czech Republic	2.3
	Estonia	2.3
12	Bulgaria	2.4
	Denmark	2.4
	Hungary	2.4
	Japan	2.4
	Latvia	2.4
	Slovenia	2.4
	United Kingdom	2.4
19	Portugal	2.5
	Russia	2.5
	Spain	2.5
	Ukraine	2.5

a The cost of living index shown is compiled by the Economist Intelligence Unit for use by companies in determining expatriate compensation: it is a comparison of the cost of maintaining a typical international lifestyle in the country rather than a comparison of the purchasing power of a citizen of the country. The index is based on typical urban prices an international executive and family will face abroad. The prices

Cost of living[a]

December 2016, US = 100

Highest

1	Singapore	120
2	Hong Kong	114
3	Japan	110
4	South Korea	108
5	France	107
	Switzerland	107
7	Denmark	100
	United States	100
9	Israel	99
	Norway	99
11	Australia	98
12	Finland	92
	Iceland	92
	New Zealand	92
15	Austria	91
16	United Kingdom	89
17	Ireland	88
18	Jordan	85
19	Italy	82
20	Belgium	81
	Canada	81
	New Caledonia	81
23	Spain	80
	Sweden	80
25	China	79

Lowest

1	Kazakhstan	38
2	Nigeria	39
3	Pakistan	44
4	Algeria	45
5	India	47
	Romania	47
	Ukraine	47
8	Zambia	49
9	Iran	50
	Syria	50
	Venezuela	50
12	Nepal	51
13	Paraguay	51
	South Africa	51
15	Bulgaria	54
	Panama	54
	Saudi Arabia	54
18	Serbia	55
19	Hungary	56
	Senegal	56
	Sri Lanka	56
22	Morocco	57
23	Oman	58
	Poland	58

World Giving Index[b]

Top givers, % of population, 2015

1	Myanmar	70
2	United States	61
3	Australia	60
4	New Zealand	59
5	Sri Lanka	57
6	Canada	56
	Indonesia	56
8	Ireland	54
	United Kingdom	54
10	United Arab Emirates	53
11	Kenya	52
	Netherlands	52
	Uzbekistan	52
14	Norway	50
	Turkmenistan	50
16	Iceland	49
	Malta	49
18	Kuwait	48
19	Denmark	47
	Germany	47
21	Finland	46
	Malaysia	46
	Switzerland	46
24	Sweden	45
25	Mongolia	44
	Singapore	44
	Uganda	44

are for products of international comparable quality found in a supermarket or department store. Prices found in local markets and bazaars are not used unless the available merchandise is of the specified quality and the shopping area itself is safe for executive and family members. New York City prices are used as the base, so United States = 100.

b Three criteria are used to assess giving: in the previous month those surveyed either gave money to charity, gave time to those in need or helped a stranger.

Transport: roads and cars

Longest road networks

Km of road per km² land area, 2015 or latest

1	Monaco	38.5
2	Macau	13.6
3	Malta	9.7
4	Bermuda	8.9
5	Bahrain	5.3
6	Belgium	5.1
7	Singapore	4.9
8	Netherlands	4.1
9	Barbados	3.7
10	Japan	3.4
11	Puerto Rico	3.0
12	Liechtenstein	2.5
13	Hungary	2.3
14	Bangladesh	2.0
	France	2.0
	Hong Kong	2.0
	Jamaica	2.0
	Luxembourg	2.0
19	Guam	1.9
	India	1.9
	Slovenia	1.9
22	Denmark	1.8
	Germany	1.8
	Switzerland	1.8
25	Czech Republic	1.7
	Italy	1.7
	United Kingdom	1.7
28	Austria	1.5
	Sri Lanka	1.5
30	Cyprus	1.4
	Estonia	1.4
	Ireland	1.4
	Poland	1.4
34	Lithuania	1.3
	Spain	1.3
36	Taiwan	1.2
37	Latvia	1.1
	Mauritius	1.1
	South Korea	1.1
	Sweden	1.1
41	Romania	1.0
42	Greece	0.9
	Israel	0.9
	Portugal	0.9
	Slovakia	0.9
46	Costa Rica	0.8
	Qatar	0.8

Densest road networks

Km of road per km² land area, 2015 or latest

1	Monaco	38.5
2	Macau	13.6
3	Malta	9.7
4	Bermuda	8.9
5	Bahrain	5.3
6	Belgium	5.1
7	Singapore	4.9
8	Netherlands	4.1
9	Barbados	3.7
10	Japan	3.4
11	Puerto Rico	3
12	Liechtenstein	2.5
13	Hungary	2.3
14	Bangladesh	2
	France	2
	Hong Kong	2
	Jamaica	2
	Luxembourg	2
19	Guam	1.9
	India	1.9
	Slovenia	1.9
22	Denmark	1.8
	Germany	1.8
	Switzerland	1.8
25	Czech Republic	1.7
	Italy	1.7
	United Kingdom	1.7
28	Austria	1.5
	Sri Lanka	1.5
30	Cyprus	1.4
	Estonia	1.4
	Ireland	1.4
	Poland	1.4
34	Lithuania	1.3
	Spain	1.3
36	Taiwan	1.2
37	Latvia	1.1
	Mauritius	1.1
	South Korea	1.1
	Sweden	1.1
41	Romania	1
42	Greece	0.9
	Israel	0.9
	Portugal	0.9
	Slovakia	0.9

Most crowded road networks

Number of vehicles per km of road network, 2014 or latest

1	Japan	628.4
2	United Arab Emirates	479.0
3	Monaco	427.3
4	Hong Kong	310.6
5	Kuwait	263.7
6	Bahrain	252.3
7	Singapore	239.5
8	Macau	238.0
9	South Korea	190.4
10	Taiwan	176.2
11	Israel	150.3
12	Jordan	148.3
13	Puerto Rico	122.5
14	Mauritius	111.8
15	Guam	108.8
16	Guatemala	108.0
17	Malta	101.8
18	Qatar	97.7
19	Mexico	93.8
20	Syria	91.9
21	United Kingdom	88.1
22	Bulgaria	85.6
23	Italy	85.0
24	Thailand	79.8
25	Luxembourg	79.5
26	Liechtenstein	77.3
27	Germany	74.1
28	Armenia	73.3
29	Tunisia	71.5
30	Dominican Rep.	68.1
31	Brunei	67.9
32	Barbados	67.5
	Switzerland	67.5
34	Portugal	67.1
35	Netherlands	66.5
36	Croatia	61.5
37	Malaysia	58.1
38	Argentina	58.0
39	Bermuda	57.9
40	Morocco	57.6
41	Poland	56.8
42	Ukraine	56.2
43	Chile	55.4
44	Greece	55.2
45	Moldova	53.9
46	Slovakia	52.4
47	Kazakhstan	50.0
48	Ecuador	49.5
49	Bahamas	48.2
50	Finland	48.1

Most road deaths

Fatalities per 100,000 population, 2015

1	Zimbabwe	45.4
2	Venezuela	41.7
3	Liberia	35.1
4	Malawi	34.2
5	Congo-Kinshasa	33.5
6	Tanzania	33.4
7	Mozambique	33.1
8	Rwanda	32.9
9	Burundi	32.7
10	Togo	31.9
11	Central African Rep.	31.8
12	Thailand	31.7
13	Madagascar	31.4
14	Burkina Faso	30.7
15	Kenya	30.5
16	Gambia, The	30.4
17	South Sudan	29.3
18	Sierra Leone	28.5
19	Niger	28.4
20	Cameroon	28.1
	Guinea	28.1
22	Iran	28.0
	Senegal	28.0
24	Dominican Rep.	27.8
25	Benin	27.7
26	Saudi Arabia	27.5
27	Ethiopia	27.3
	Uganda	27.3
29	Somalia	26.9
30	Guinea-Bissau	26.8
31	Congo-Brazzaville	26.7
32	Ghana	26.1
	Lesotho	26.1
34	Libya	25.3
	Mali	25.3
36	Oman	25.0
37	Eritrea	24.9
	Swaziland	24.9
39	Zambia	24.7
40	Sudan	24.6
41	Angola	24.4
42	Chad	24.3
43	Mauritania	24.2
44	Ivory Coast	24.0
	Vietnam	24.0
46	Algeria	23.7

Fastest-growing car ownership

Change in number of cars per 1,000 population, 1995–2014[a]

1	Bahrain	458.5	**26**	Canada	101.6
2	Brunei	257.5	**27**	Norway	100.1
3	Kuwait	208.6	**28**	Australia	96.9
	Puerto Rico	208.6	**29**	Iceland	96.7
5	Poland	200.0	**30**	Bosnia & Herz.	96.0
6	Qatar	175.7	**31**	Uruguay	95.3
7	New Zealand	173.7	**32**	Syria	95.0
8	Kazakhstan	166.9	**33**	South Korea	93.4
9	Libya	152.4	**34**	Czech Republic	91.4
10	Malta	149.9	**35**	Mexico	90.8
11	Malaysia	148.2	**36**	Georgia	81.4
12	Suriname	146.0	**37**	Chile	78.6
13	Finland	144.6	**38**	Greece	72.8
14	Lithuania	138.2	**39**	Romania	71.4
15	Luxembourg	131.7	**40**	Brazil	71.0
16	Russia	125.0	**41**	Mauritius	70.8
17	Estonia	122.5	**42**	Iran	69.8
18	Belarus	120.2	**43**	Botswana	68.5
19	Slovakia	117.8	**44**	Jordan	68.3
20	Argentina	117.5	**45**	China	67.8
21	United Arab Emirates	110.0	**46**	Bulgaria	66.9
22	Oman	109.0	**47**	Costa Rica	66.7
23	Kyrgyzstan	108.8	**48**	Saudi Arabia	66.3
24	Israel	104.9	**49**	Thailand	66.0
25	Cyprus	102.9	**50**	Guam	65.5

Slowest-growing car ownership

Change in number of cars per 1,000 population, 1995–2014[a]

1	Latvia	-42.3	**22**	Madagascar	4.9
2	Germany	-20.4	**23**	El Salvador	5.1
3	Zambia	-3.6	**24**	Philippines	5.2
4	Ethiopia	0.2	**25**	Mali	5.4
5	Sudan	0.3	**26**	Benin	5.5
6	Burundi	0.6	**27**	Pakistan	5.6
	Haiti	0.6	**28**	Mozambique	5.8
8	Bangladesh	0.9	**29**	Ivory Coast	6.7
9	Bermuda	1.1	**30**	Tunisia	7.9
10	Malawi	1.5	**31**	Yemen	8.5
11	Honduras	1.7	**32**	Jamaica	8.6
12	Liberia	1.8	**33**	Kenya	9.5
13	Mauritania	2.0	**34**	Nigeria	9.7
14	Uganda	2.1	**35**	Sri Lanka	10.2
15	Congo-Kinshasa	2.2	**36**	Bolivia	10.5
16	Cuba	2.9	**37**	Senegal	10.8
17	Nicaragua	3.1	**38**	India	11.3
18	Cameroon	3.2	**39**	Zimbabwe	13.7
19	Burkina Faso	3.7	**40**	Vietnam	14.9
20	Tanzania	3.9	**41**	Ghana	15.9
21	Togo	4.1	**42**	Egypt	16.2

a Based on 2014 population.

Car production

Number of cars produced, m, 2015

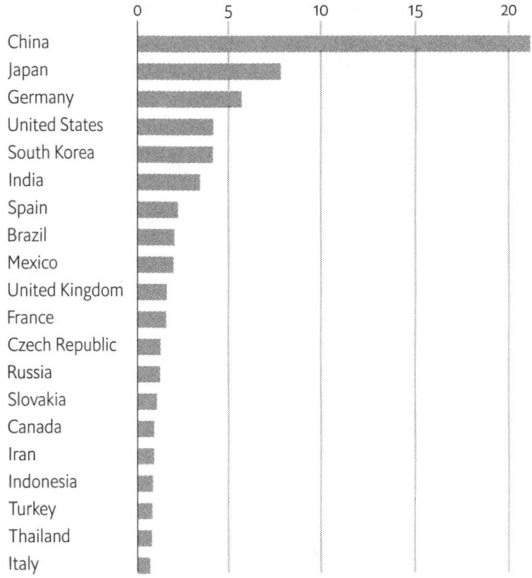

Cars sold

New car registrations, '000, 2015

1	China	21,210
2	United States	7,517
3	Japan	4,216
4	Germany	3,206
5	India	2,772
6	United Kingdom	2,634
7	Brazil	2,123
8	France	1,917
9	Italy	1,576
10	South Korea	1,534
11	Russia	1,283
12	Spain	1,094
13	Iran	1,055
14	Australia	924
15	Indonesia	756
16	Turkey	726
17	Saudi Arabia	672
18	Malaysia	591
19	Belgium	501
20	Argentina	481
21	Netherlands	449
22	Thailand	356
23	Poland	355
24	Sweden	345
25	Switzerland	324
26	Austria	309
27	Israel	247
28	Colombia	237
29	Czech Republic	231
30	United Arab Emirates	214
31	Chile	212
	Taiwan	212
33	Denmark	208
34	Pakistan	182
35	Portugal	179
36	Norway	151
37	Peru	137
38	Ireland	125
39	Kuwait	124
40	Oman	121
41	Vietnam	117
42	Philippines	116
43	Finland	109
44	Romania	98

Transport: planes and trains

Most air travel

Passengers carried, m, 2015

1	United States	798.2
2	China	436.2
3	United Kingdom	131.4
4	Germany	115.5
5	Japan	113.8
6	Ireland	113.1
7	Brazil	102.0
8	India	98.9
9	Turkey	96.6
10	Indonesia	88.7
11	United Arab Emirates	84.7
12	Canada	80.2
13	Australia	69.3
14	France	65.0
15	Spain	60.8
16	Thailand	54.3
17	Malaysia	50.3
18	Mexico	45.6
19	Netherlands	34.9
20	Singapore	33.3
21	Saudi Arabia	32.8
22	Philippines	32.2
23	Colombia	30.7
24	Vietnam	29.9
25	Switzerland	26.8
26	Italy	26.0
27	Qatar	25.3
28	Hungary	20.0
29	South Africa	17.2
30	New Zealand	15.3

Busiest airports

Total passengers, m, 2016

1	Atlanta, Hartsfield	104.2
2	Beijing, Capital	94.4
3	Dubai Intl.	83.6
4	Los Angeles, Intl.	80.9
5	Tokyo, Haneda	79.7
6	Chicago, O'Hare	78.3
7	London, Heathrow	75.7
8	Hong Kong, Intl.	70.3
9	Shanghai, Pudong Intl.	66.0
10	Paris, Charles de Gaulle	65.9
11	Dallas, Ft Worth	65.7
12	Amsterdam, Schiphol	63.6
13	Frankfurt, Main	60.8
14	Istanbul, Ataturk	60.2
15	Guangzhou Baiyun, Intl	59.7

Total cargo, m tonnes, 2016

1	Hong Kong, Intl.	4.62
2	Memphis, Intl.	4.32
3	Shanghai, Pudong Intl.	3.44
4	Dubai, Intl.	2.95
5	Seoul, Incheon	2.71
6	Anchorage, Intl.	2.54
7	Louisville, Standiford Field	2.44
8	Tokyo, Narita	2.17
9	Paris, Charles de Gaulle	2.14
10	Frankfurt, Main	2.11
11	Taiwan, Taoyuan Intl.	2.10
12	Miami, Intl.	2.01
	Singapore, Changi	2.01
14	Los Angeles, Intl.	1.99
15	Beijing, Capital	1.93

Average daily aircraft movements, take-offs and landings, 2016

1	Atlanta, Hartsfield	2,461
2	Chicago, O'Hare	2,377
3	Los Angeles, Intl.	1,910
4	Dallas, Ft Worth	1,843
5	Beijing, Capital	1,661
6	Denver, Intl.	1,569
7	Charlotte/Douglas, Intl.	1,495
8	Las Vegas, McCarran Intl.	1,483
9	Shanghai, Pudong Intl.	1,315
10	Amsterdam, Schiphol	1,312
11	London, Heathrow	1,301
12	Paris, Charles de Gaulle	1,296
13	Houston, George Bush Intercontinental	1,290
14	Istanbul, Ataturk	1,275
15	Frankfurt, Main	1,268
16	Toronto, Pearson Intl.	1,251
17	Dubai, Intl.	1,244
18	New York, JFK	1,239
19	San Francisco	1,234
20	Mexico City, Intl.	1,228
21	Tokyo, Haneda	1,221
22	Phoenix, Skyharbor Intl.	1,207
23	Guangzhou Baiyun, Intl	1,192
24	Newark	1,182
25	Miami	1,135

Longest railway networks

'000 km, 2015 or latest

1	United States	228.2
2	Russia	85.3
3	China	67.2
4	India	66.0
5	Canada	52.1
6	Germany	33.3
7	Australia	32.8
8	France	30.0
9	Brazil	29.8
10	Mexico	26.7
11	Argentina	25.0
12	Ukraine	21.0
13	South Africa	20.5
14	Japan	19.2
15	Poland	18.5
16	Italy	16.7
17	United Kingdom	16.1
18	Spain	15.7
19	Kazakhstan	14.8
20	Romania	10.8
21	Turkey	10.1
22	Sweden	9.7
23	Czech Republic	9.5
24	Pakistan	9.3
25	Iran	8.6
26	Hungary	7.9
27	Finland	5.9
28	Belarus	5.5
	Chile	5.5
30	Thailand	5.3
31	Egypt	5.2
32	Austria	4.9
33	Indonesia	4.7
34	Sudan	4.3
35	Norway	4.2
	Uzbekistan	4.2
37	Bulgaria	4.0
	Switzerland	4.0
39	South Korea	3.9

Most rail passengers

Km per person per year, 2015 or latest

1	Switzerland	2,311
2	Japan	1,633
3	Russia	1,439
4	Austria	1,359
5	France	1,315
6	Denmark	1,054
7	Netherlands	1,051
8	Germany	982
9	Kazakhstan	971
10	United Kingdom	963
11	Belgium	914
12	India	875
13	Taiwan	844
14	Ukraine	839
15	Belarus	749
16	Finland	748
17	Czech Republic	683
18	Italy	657
19	Sweden	642
20	Luxembourg	622
21	Norway	594
22	Hungary	571
	Slovakia	571
24	Spain	557

Most rail freight

Million tonne-km per year, 2015 or latest

1	United States	2,547,253
2	Russia	2,304,759
3	China	1,980,061
4	India	681,696
5	Canada	352,535
6	Brazil	267,700
7	Ukraine	195,054
8	Kazakhstan	189,759
9	South Africa	134,600
10	Mexico	78,770
11	Germany	72,913
12	Australia	59,649
13	Belarus	40,785
14	France	33,116
15	Poland	28,720
16	Iran	25,014
17	Uzbekistan	22,686
18	Austria	20,804
19	Japan	20,255
20	Lithuania	14,036
21	Latvia	13,023
22	Argentina	12,111
23	Turkmenistan	11,992
24	Mongolia	11,463

Transport: shipping

Merchant fleets

Number of vessels, by country of domicile, January 2016

1	China	4,960	**11**	Turkey	1,540
2	Greece	4,136	**12**	United Kingdom	1,329
3	Japan	3,969	**13**	Netherlands	1,229
4	Germany	3,361	**14**	Denmark	960
5	Singapore	2,553	**15**	India	947
6	United States	1,995	**16**	Taiwan	898
7	Norway	1,854	**17**	Vietnam	896
8	Indonesia	1,712	**18**	United Arab Emirates	815
9	Russia	1,680	**19**	Italy	802
10	South Korea	1,634	**20**	Malaysia	621

Ships' flags

Largest registered fleets, 2016

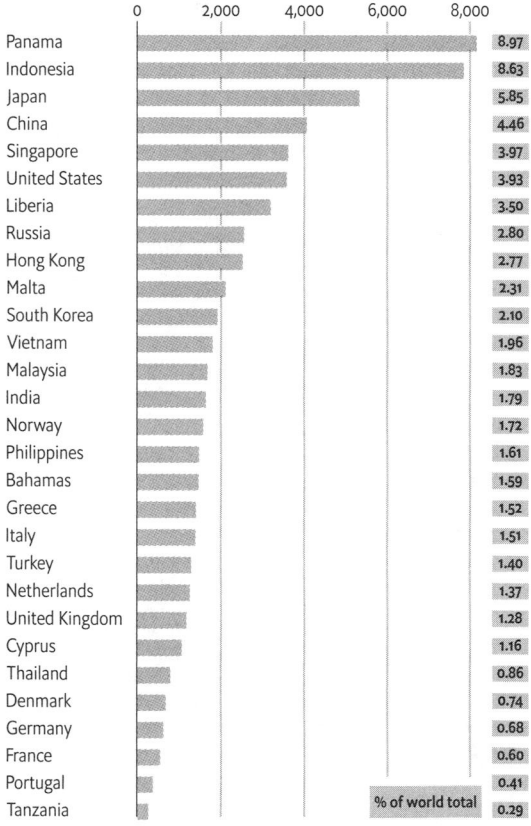

Crime and punishment

Murders

Homicides per 100,000 pop., 2014 or latest

1	Honduras	74.6
2	El Salvador	64.2
3	Venezuela	62.0
4	Virgin Islands (US)	52.6
5	Lesotho	38.0
6	Jamaica	36.1
7	Belize	34.4
8	South Africa	33.0
9	Guatemala	31.2
10	Bahamas	29.8
11	Colombia	27.9
12	Trinidad & Tobago	25.9
13	Brazil	24.6
14	Guyana	20.4
15	Puerto Rico	18.5
16	Dominican Rep.	17.4
	Panama	17.4
	Swaziland	17.4
19	Namibia	16.9
20	Mexico	15.7

Robberies

Per 100,000 pop., 2014 or latest

1	Belgium	1,529
2	Costa Rica	1,096
3	Argentina	958
4	Chile	599
5	Mexico	589
6	Ecuador	571
7	Uruguay	543
8	Brazil	496
	Nicaragua	496
	Panama	496
11	Paraguay	307
12	Peru	251
13	Honduras	238
14	Maldives	208
15	Guyana	201
16	Colombia	198
17	Trinidad & Tobago	197
18	France	178
19	Spain	153
20	Portugal	150

Prisoners

Total prison pop., 2017 or latest

1	United States	2,145,100
2	China	1,649,804
3	Brazil	650,956
4	Russia	627,702
5	India	419,623
6	Thailand	286,861
7	Mexico	233,469
8	Iran	225,624
9	Indonesia	210,682
10	Turkey	201,177
11	South Africa	161,984
12	Philippines	142,168
13	Vietnam	130,679
14	Colombia	119,269
15	Ethiopia	111,050
16	Egypt	106,000
17	United Kingdom	85,442
18	Peru	82,200
19	Pakistan	80,169
20	Morocco	79,368
21	Argentina	72,693
22	Poland	72,677
23	Myanmar	70,000
24	Bangladesh	69,719
25	France	68,432
26	Nigeria	68,259
27	Germany	62,865

Per 100,000 pop., 2017 or latest

1	United States	666
2	Turkmenistan	583
3	El Salvador	579
4	Virgin Islands (US)	542
5	Cuba	510
6	Guam	438
7	Russia	434
	Rwanda	434
9	Panama	426
10	Thailand	424
11	Bahamas	363
12	Bermuda	354
13	Costa Rica	352
14	Puerto Rico	349
15	Barbados	322
16	Brazil	316
17	Belarus	314
18	Bahrain	301
19	South Africa	291
	Uruguay	291
21	Iran	287
22	Swaziland	282
23	Trinidad & Tobago	272
24	Taiwan	266
25	Israel	265
26	Mongolia	262
27	Peru	259

War and terrorism

Defence spending

As % of GDP, 2016

1	Oman	15.3
2	Afghanistan	14.0
3	Iraq	11.6
4	Saudi Arabia	8.9
5	Congo-Brazzaville	6.4
6	Algeria	6.3
7	Israel	6.1
8	Bahrain	4.8
9	Botswana	4.4
	Jordan	4.4
11	Namibia	4.1
12	Armenia	4.0
	Azerbaijan	4.0
14	Iran	3.9
	Mali	3.9
16	Brunei	3.8
17	Russia[a]	3.7
18	Lebanon	3.5
	Singapore	3.5
20	Colombia	3.4
21	Myanmar	3.3
	United States	3.3
23	Cambodia	3.2
	Morocco	3.2

Defence spending

$bn, 2016

1	United States	604.5
2	China	145
3	Saudi Arabia	56.9
4	United Kingdom	52.5
5	India	51.1
6	Japan	47.3
7	France	47.2
8	Russia[a]	46.6
9	Germany	38.3
10	South Korea	33.8
11	Australia	24.2
12	Italy	22.3
13	Iraq	17.9
14	Iran	15.9
	Israel	15.9

Per person, $, 2016

1	Oman	2,714
2	Israel	2,322
3	Saudi Arabia	2,021
4	Qatar	1,950
5	United States	1,866
6	Singapore	1,773
7	Norway	1,134
8	Bahrain	1,110
9	Australia	1,052
10	Brunei	920
11	United Kingdom	815
12	France	706
13	South Korea	663
14	Denmark	634
15	Finland	597

Armed forces

'000, 2017[b]

		Regulars	Reserves
1	China	2,183	510
2	India	1,395	1,155
3	United States	1,347	865
4	Russia[a]	831	2,000
5	Pakistan	654	0
6	South Korea	630	4,500
7	Iran	523	350
8	Vietnam	482	5,000
9	Egypt	439	479
10	Myanmar	406	0
11	Indonesia	396	400
12	Thailand	361	200
13	Turkey	355	379
14	Brazil	335	1,340
15	Colombia	293	35
16	Mexico	277	82
17	Saudi Arabia	227	0
18	Taiwan	215	1,657
19	Ukraine	204	900
20	France	203	28
21	Sri Lanka	203	6
22	Morocco	196	150
23	South Sudan	185	0
24	Israel	177	465
25	Georgia	177	28
26	Italy	175	18
27	Afghanistan	171	0
28	United Kingdom	152	81
29	Greece	143	221
30	Congo-Kinshasa	134	0

a National defence budget only. b Estimates.

Arms exporters

$m, 2016

1	United States	9,894
2	Russia	6,432
3	Germany	2,813
4	France	2,226
5	China	2,123
6	United Kingdom	1,393
7	Israel	1,260
8	Italy	802
9	South Korea	534
10	Ukraine	528
11	Spain	483
12	Netherlands	466
13	Turkey	277
14	Sweden	249
15	Switzerland	186
16	Portugal	169
17	Norway	150
18	Czech Republic	129
19	Australia	127
	Canada	127

Arms importers

$m, 2016

1	Saudi Arabia	2,979
2	Algeria	2,882
3	India	2,547
4	Iraq	1,734
5	Egypt	1,483
6	South Korea	1,333
7	United Arab Emirates	1,278
8	Vietnam	1,196
9	Australia	1,060
10	China	993
11	Qatar	901
12	Italy	868
13	Pakistan	759
14	Israel	607
15	United States	512
16	Bangladesh	438
17	Turkey	437
18	Oman	393
19	Turkmenistan	392
20	Mexico	388

Terrorist attacks

Number of incidences, 2015

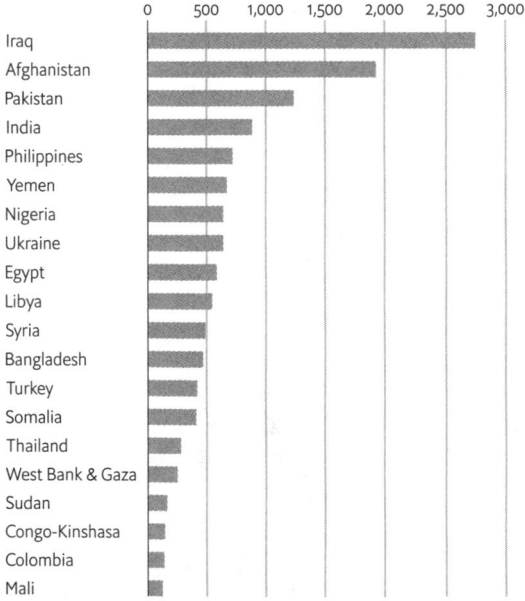

Space and peace

Manned space missions

Firsts and selected events

1957	Man-made satellite
	Dog in space, Laika
1961	Human in space, Yuri Gagarin
1963	Woman in space, Valentina Tereshkova
1964	Space crew, one pilot and two passengers
1965	Spacewalk, Alexei Leonov
	Eight days in space achieved (needed to travel to moon and back)
1968	Live television broadcast from space
1968	Moon orbit
1969	Moon landing
1971	Space station, Salyut
	Drive on Moon
1973	Space laboratory, Skylab
1978	Non-Amercian, non-Soviet, Vladimir Remek (Czechoslovakia)
1982	Space shuttle, *Columbia* (first craft to carry four crew members)
1986	Space shuttle explosion, *Challenger*
	Mir space station activated
1990	Hubble telescope deployed
2001	Dennis Tito, paying space tourist
2003	China manned space flight, Yang Liwei
2004	*SpaceShipOne*, successful private manned suborbital space flight
2010	SpaceX's privately funded spacecraft made an orbital flight
2014	Rosetta probe landed on comet *67P* after 12-year mission

Orbital launches

2016	*Commercial*	*Non-commercial*[a]	*Total*	*2005–16*
1 United States	11	11	22	218
2 China	0	22	22	163
3 Russia	2	15	17	330
4 Europe	8	3	11	92
5 India	0	7	7	37
6 Japan	0	4	4	36
7 Israel	0	1	1	4
North Korea	0	1	1	4

Global Peace Index[b]

Most peaceful, 2017

1	Iceland	1.111
2	New Zealand	1.241
3	Portugal	1.258
4	Austria	1.265
5	Denmark	1.337
6	Czech Republic	1.360
7	Slovenia	1.364
8	Canada	1.371
9	Switzerland	1.373
10	Ireland	1.408

Least peaceful, 2017

1	Syria	3.814
2	South Sudan	3.524
3	Iraq	3.556
4	Afghanistan	3.567
5	Somalia	3.387
6	Yemen	3.412
7	Ukraine	3.184
8	Sudan	3.213
9	Libya	3.328
10	Pakistan	3.058

a Government and non-profit launches.
b Ranks 163 countries using 23 indicators which gauge the level of safety and security in society, the extent of domestic or international conflict and the degree of militarisation.

Environment

Biggest emitters of carbon dioxide

Million tonnes, 2013

1	China	10,249.5
2	United States	5,186.2
3	India	2,034.8
4	Russia	1,789.1
5	Japan	1,243.4
6	Germany	757.3
7	Iran	617.0
8	South Korea	592.5
9	Saudi Arabia	541.4
10	Brazil	503.7
11	Mexico	488.6
12	Indonesia	479.4
13	Canada	475.7
14	South Africa	471.2
15	United Kingdom	457.5
16	Australia	377.9
17	Italy	344.8
18	France	333.2
19	Turkey	323.5
20	Thailand	303.1
21	Poland	302.3
22	Taiwan	295.0
23	Ukraine	271.1
24	Kazakhstan	262.9
25	Spain	237.0
26	Malaysia	236.5
27	Egypt	213.0
28	Argentina	189.8
29	Venezuela	185.5
30	Netherlands	170.0
31	United Arab Emirates	169.1
32	Iraq	167.8
33	Pakistan	153.4
34	Vietnam	152.6
35	Algeria	134.2
36	Uzbekistan	103.2
37	Czech Republic	98.7
38	Philippines	98.2
39	Kuwait	98.0
40	Nigeria	95.7
41	Belgium	93.6
42	Colombia	89.6
43	Qatar	85.0
44	Chile	83.2
45	Israel	71.1
46	Romania	70.7
47	Greece	69.2
48	Bangladesh	69.0
49	Turkmenistan	66.9
50	Belarus	63.8
51	Austria	62.4
52	Oman	61.2
53	Norway	59.6
54	Morocco	58.6
55	Peru	57.2
56	Libya	51.0
57	Singapore	50.6
58	North Korea	50.1
59	Trinidad & Tobago	46.5

Largest amount of carbon dioxide emitted per person

Tonnes, 2013

1	Qatar	40.5
2	Trinidad & Tobago	34.5
3	Kuwait	27.3
4	Bahrain	23.7
5	Brunei	18.9
6	Luxembourg	18.7
	United Arab Emirates	18.7
8	Saudi Arabia	17.9
9	United States	16.4
10	Australia	16.3
11	Oman	15.7
12	Kazakhstan	15.4
13	Estonia	15.1
14	New Caledonia	14.7
15	Mongolia	14.5
16	Canada	13.5
17	Turkmenistan	12.8
18	Taiwan	12.6
19	Russia	12.5
20	South Korea	11.8
21	Norway	11.7
22	Netherlands	10.1
23	Japan	9.8
24	Guam	9.7
25	Czech Republic	9.4
	Singapore	9.4
27	Germany	9.2
28	South Africa	8.9
29	Israel	8.8
30	Finland	8.5
31	Belgium	8.4
32	Bahamas	8.2
33	Libya	8.1

Most polluted capital cities

Annual mean particulate matter concentration[a], micrograms per cubic metre 2014 or latest

1	Riyadh, Saudi Arabia	368.0	**13**	Beijing, China	108.0
2	Kabul, Afghanistan	260.0	**14**	Tunis, Tunisia	90.0
3	Delhi, India	229.1	**15**	Kathmandu, Nepal	88.3
4	Islamabad, Pakistan	216.9	**16**	Lima, Peru	87.8
5	Baghdad, Iraq	208.0	**17**	Muscat, Oman	82.1
6	Cairo, Egypt	179.0	**18**	San Salvador, El Salvador	77.2
7	Kampala, Uganda	170.4	**19**	Ankara, Turkey	77.0
8	Doha, Qatar	167.6	**20**	Tehran, Iran	76.9
9	Ulaanbaatar, Mongolia	165.1	**21**	Skopje, Macedonia	73.8
10	Dhaka, Bangladesh	158.1	**22**	Amman, Jordan	68.0
11	Dakar, Senegal	141.3	**23**	Yaoundé, Cameroon	65.0
12	Abu Dhabi, UAE	132.0	**24**	Santiago, Chile	64.4

Lowest access to an improved water source

% of population, 2014

1	South Sudan	6.7	**15**	Benin	19.6
2	Niger	10.8	**16**	Guinea	20.0
3	Togo	11.6	**17**	Mozambique	20.4
4	Madagascar	11.9	**18**	Guinea-Bissau	20.7
5	Chad	12.0	**19**	Central African Rep.	21.7
6	Sierra Leone	13.1	**20**	Ivory Coast	22.3
7	Ghana	14.8	**21**	Sudan	23.6
8	Congo-Brazzaville	14.9	**22**	Mali	24.2
9	Tanzania	15.0	**23**	Ethiopia	26.8
10	Eritrea	15.6	**24**	Haiti	27.4
11	Liberia	16.6	**25**	Congo-Kinshasa	28.3
12	Papua New Guinea	18.9	**26**	Nigeria	29.3
13	Uganda	19.0	**27**	Kenya	30.1
14	Burkina Faso	19.4	**28**	Lesotho	30.2

Lowest access to electricity

% of population, 2013

1	South Sudan	4.0	**17**	Papua New Guinea	19.7
2	Burundi	6.5	**18**	Mozambique	20.2
3	Chad	7.6	**19**	Zambia	23.6
4	Malawi	9.0	**20**	Ethiopia	25.2
5	Liberia	9.8	**21**	Lesotho	25.3
6	Central African Rep.	11.8	**22**	Mali	26.1
7	Madagascar	12.9	**23**	Guinea	26.8
8	Sierra Leone	13.5	**24**	Kenya	28.2
9	Niger	13.8	**25**	North Korea	31.2
10	Guinea-Bissau	13.9	**26**	Angola	33.3
	Uganda	13.9	**27**	Mauritania	36.2
12	Congo-Kinshasa	14.8	**28**	Zimbabwe	36.5
13	Rwanda	15.2	**29**	Benin	37.3
14	Tanzania	16.4	**30**	Haiti	37.5
15	Burkina Faso	16.9	**31**	Sudan	38.5
16	Somalia	18.1	**32**	Congo-Brazzaville	42.1

a Particulates less than 10 microns in diameter.

Largest forests

Sq km, 2014

1	Russia	8,149,715
2	Brazil	4,945,220
3	Canada	3,471,156
4	United States	3,098,200
5	China	2,067,791
6	Congo-Kinshasa	1,528,894
7	Australia	1,244,430
8	Indonesia	916,944
9	Peru	741,406
10	India	705,036
11	Mexico	661,316
12	Colombia	585,285
13	Angola	579,808
14	Bolivia	550,530
15	Zambia	488,016
16	Venezuela	468,474
17	Tanzania	464,320
18	Mozambique	381,464
19	Papua New Guinea	335,618
20	Myanmar	295,874
21	Sweden	280,730
22	Argentina	274,088
23	Japan	249,596
24	Gabon	228,000
25	Congo-Brazzaville	223,494
26	Finland	222,180
27	Central African Rep.	221,856
28	Malaysia	221,808
29	Sudan	193,844
30	Cameroon	190,360

Most forested

% of land area, 2014

1	Suriname	98.3
2	Gabon	88.5
3	Guyana	84.0
4	Laos	80.5
5	Papua New Guinea	74.1
6	Finland	73.1
7	Brunei	72.1
8	Guinea-Bissau	70.5
9	Sweden	68.9
10	Japan	68.5
11	Malaysia	67.5
12	Congo-Kinshasa	67.4
13	Zambia	65.6
14	Congo-Brazzaville	65.4
15	South Korea	63.5
16	Panama	62.3
17	Slovenia	62.0
18	Montenegro	61.5
19	Brazil	59.2
20	Peru	57.9
21	Equatorial Guinea	56.3
22	Puerto Rico	55.5
23	Fiji	55.4
24	Cambodia	54.3
25	Latvia	54.0
26	Costa Rica	53.4
27	Venezuela	53.1
28	Colombia	52.8
29	Estonia	52.7
30	Tanzania	52.4

Deforestation

Biggest % change in forested land, 1990–2014

Decrease

1	Togo	-69.7
2	Nigeria	-57.0
3	Uganda	-53.4
4	Mauritania	-45.1
5	Honduras	-42.1
6	Niger	-40.6
7	Pakistan	-40.0
8	North Korea	-37.1
9	Sudan	-36.9
10	Zimbabwe	-35.1
11	Nicaragua	-31.0
12	El Salvador	-28.5
13	Mali	-28.3
14	Timor-Leste	-27.8
15	Cambodia	-26.0
	Paraguay	-26.0
17	Ethiopia	-25.6

Increase

1	Iceland	197.5
2	French Polynesia	181.8
3	Bahrain	168.2
4	Uruguay	128.4
5	Kuwait	81.2
6	Dominican Rep.	76.5
7	Puerto Rico	71.7
8	Egypt	64.5
9	Ireland	60.9
10	Tunisia	60.3
11	Vietnam	56.4
12	Cuba	52.9
13	Rwanda	48.8
14	Spain	33.1
15	Montenegro	32.1
16	Syria	32.0
17	China	31.6

Dams and reservoirs

Most dams[a]

1	China	23,842
2	United States	9,261
3	India	5,102
4	Japan	3,112
5	Brazil	1,411
6	Canada	1,170
7	South Africa	1,114
8	Spain	1,063
9	Turkey	972
10	Iran	802
11	France	712
12	United Kingdom	596
13	Mexico	571
14	Australia	570
15	Italy	542
16	Germany	371
17	Norway	335
18	Albania	307
19	Zimbabwe	254
20	Romania	246
21	Thailand	218
22	Portugal	217
23	Sweden	190
24	Bulgaria	181
25	Austria	171
26	Switzerland	167
27	Greece	164
28	Pakistan	163
29	Algeria	154
30	Morocco	150

Dams

Largest reservoir capacity[a], cubic kms

Slums

% of urban population living in slums, 2014

1	South Sudan	95.6
2	Central African Rep.	93.3
3	Sudan	91.6
4	Chad	88.2
5	Guinea-Bissau	82.3
6	Mozambique	80.3
7	Mauritania	79.9
8	Madagascar	77.2
9	Sierra Leone	75.6
10	Congo-Kinshasa	74.8
11	Haiti	74.4
12	Ethiopia	73.9
13	Somalia	73.6
14	Niger	70.1

a As of April 2017. b Under construction spring 2017.

Environmental Performance Index

Scores on biodiversity[a], 2016, 0=lowest, 100=highest

Best			*Worst*		
1	Belgium	100.0	**1**	Somalia	20.9
	Czech Republic	100.0	**2**	Afghanistan	21.3
	Estonia	100.0	**3**	Turkey	22.5
	Germany	100.0	**4**	Haiti	24.4
	Hungary	100.0	**5**	Libya	24.7
	Luxembourg	100.0	**6**	Lesotho	26.2
	Slovakia	100.0	**7**	Barbados	26.5
	Slovenia	100.0	**8**	Syria	31.2
9	Poland	99.8	**9**	Iraq	34.6
10	France	99.5	**10**	Maldives	35.9
11	Croatia	99.0	**11**	Bosnia & Herz.	36.6
	Italy	99.0	**12**	Eritrea	41.1
	United Kingdom	99.0	**13**	Sudan	42.8
14	Lithuania	98.6	**14**	Jordan	42.9
15	Latvia	97.8		Mauritania	42.9
16	Denmark	97.6	**16**	Gambia, The	43.6
17	Zambia	97.1	**17**	Lebanon	43.9
18	Finland	96.9	**18**	Papua New Guinea	46.5
19	Spain	96.7	**19**	Yemen	48.0
20	Portugal	95.8	**20**	Oman	48.7
	Romania	95.8	**21**	Liberia	49.7
22	Namibia	95.7	**22**	Turkmenistan	49.9
	Venezuela	95.7	**23**	Guyana	51.3
24	Greece	94.8	**24**	Swaziland	52.9

Worst natural catastrophes

2015

	Country/region	*Type of disaster*	*Deaths*
1	Nepal	Earthquake	8,960
2	India	Heatwave	2,248
3	Pakistan	Heatwave	1,270
4	Europe	Heatwave	1,200
5	Malawi/Mozambique/Zimbabwe	Floods	451
6	China	Ship hit by strong wind	442
7	Afghanistan	Earthquake	399
8	Guatemala	Landslide	350
9	Afghanistan	Avalanches	291
10	India (Chennai)	Flash floods	289
11	India	Monsoon floods	206
12	Pakistan	Monsoon floods	166
13	Myanmar	Monsoon floods	125
14	Egypt	Heatwave	110
15	India (Purnia)	Thunderstorms/hail	100
16	Colombia	Flash floods	93
17	Kenya	Floods	89
18	Philippines/Japan/North Korea	Flooding/landslides	82
19	India (Andhra Pradesh)	Monsoon floods	81
	India (Gujarat)	Monsoon rains	81

a Based on protection of species, land and marine area.

Life expectancy

Highest life expectancy

Years, 2015–20

1	Monaco[a]	89.5
2	Hong Kong	84.5
3	Japan	84.1
4	Italy	83.8
5	Singapore	83.7
6	Switzerland	83.6
7	Spain	83.2
8	Iceland	83.1
9	Australia	83.0
	Israel	83.0
11	France	82.9
12	Andorra[a]	82.8
	South Korea	82.8
	Sweden	82.8
15	Chile	82.7
16	Canada	82.6
	Martinique	82.6
18	New Zealand	82.4
19	Luxembourg	82.3
20	Austria	82.1
	Netherlands	82.1
	Norway	82.1
23	Guadeloupe	82.0
24	Liechtenstein[a]	81.9
25	Portugal	81.7
26	Greece	81.6
27	Finland	81.5
	Germany	81.5
	Ireland	81.5
30	Belgium	81.4
	Macao	81.4
32	Bermuda[a]	81.3
	United Kingdom	81.3
34	Channel Islands	81.2
	Malta	81.2
	Virgin Islands (US)	81.2
37	Slovenia	81.0
38	Cyprus	80.8
	Réunion	80.8
40	Denmark	80.7
41	French Guiana	80.3
	Lebanon	80.3
43	Puerto Rico	80.2
44	Costa Rica	80.1
	Taiwan[a]	80.1
46	Cuba	80.0
	Guam	80.0
48	United States	79.6

Highest male life expectancy

Years, 2015–20

1	Monaco[a]	85.6
2	Hong Kong	81.7
	Iceland	81.7
4	Switzerland	81.6
5	Israel	81.3
	Italy	81.3
7	Australia	81.1
	Sweden	81.1
9	Canada	80.8
	Japan	80.8
	New Zealand	80.8
12	Andorra[a]	80.6
	Singapore	80.6
14	Spain	80.5
15	Netherlands	80.3
16	Luxembourg	80.2
	Norway	80.2
18	France	80.0

Highest female life expectancy

Years, 2015–20

1	Monaco[a]	93.5
2	Hong Kong	87.4
3	Japan	87.3
4	Singapore	86.7
5	Italy	86.0
6	Spain	85.8
7	South Korea	85.7
8	France	85.6
9	Martinique	85.5
	Switzerland	85.5
11	Chile	85.3
12	Andorra[a]	85.1
13	Australia	85.0
	Guadeloupe	85.0
15	Israel	84.6
	Liechtenstein[a]	84.6
17	Bermuda[a]	84.5
	Iceland	84.5

a 2016 estimate.

Lowest life expectancy

Years, 2015–20

1	Swaziland	48.7
2	Lesotho	50.4
3	Sierra Leone	52.1
4	Chad	52.5
5	Ivory Coast	52.8
6	Central African Rep.	53.3
7	Angola	53.7
8	Nigeria	53.8
9	Guinea-Bissau	56.2
10	Mozambique	56.2
11	Somalia	56.5
12	Cameroon	57.0
13	South Sudan	57.1
14	South Africa	57.7
15	Burundi	58.1
16	Equatorial Guinea	58.6
17	Mali	59.7
18	Burkina Faso	59.8
19	Congo-Kinshasa	59.9
20	Guinea	60.2
21	Benin	60.3
22	Uganda	61.0
23	Gambia, The	61.1
	Togo	61.1
25	Afghanistan	61.5
26	Ghana	62.0
	Liberia	62.0
28	Zambia	62.3
29	Zimbabwe	62.4
30	Niger	62.8
31	Papua New Guinea	63.2
32	Kenya	63.3
33	Mauritania	63.6
34	Congo-Brazzaville	63.9
	Haiti	63.9
36	Sudan	64.2
37	Yemen	64.5
38	Botswana	64.6
39	Eritrea	65.1
40	Namibia	65.3
41	Ethiopia	65.8
	Malawi	65.8
43	Gabon	66.0
	Rwanda	66.0
45	Turkmenistan	66.1
46	Madagascar	66.4
	Tanzania	66.4
48	Myanmar	66.5
49	Guyana	66.8
	Pakistan	66.8

Lowest male life expectancy

Years, 2015–20

1	Swaziland	49.5
2	Lesotho	50.3
3	Central African Rep.	51.1
4	Chad	51.4
5	Sierra Leone	51.5
6	Ivory Coast	52.0
7	Angola	52.2
8	Nigeria	53.3
9	Guinea-Bissau	54.4
10	Somalia	54.9
11	Mozambique	55.0
12	South Africa	55.7
13	Cameroon	55.9
14	Burundi	56.0
15	South Sudan	56.1
16	Equatorial Guinea	57.3
17	Congo-Kinshasa	58.4
18	Burkina Faso	58.5
19	Benin	58.8
20	Uganda	58.9

Lowest female life expectancy

Years, 2015–20

1	Swaziland	47.7
2	Lesotho	50.2
3	Sierra Leone	52.7
4	Chad	53.6
5	Ivory Coast	53.8
6	Nigeria	54.1
7	Angola	55.2
8	Central African Rep.	55.5
9	Mozambique	57.3
10	Guinea-Bissau	58.0
11	South Sudan	58.1
12	Cameroon	58.2
	Somalia	58.2
14	South Africa	59.3
15	Mali	59.6
16	Equatorial Guinea	60.0
17	Burundi	60.2
18	Guinea	60.7

Death rates and infant mortality

Highest death rates

Number of deaths per 1,000 population, 2015–20

1	Lithuania	16.2
2	Ukraine	15.7
3	Bulgaria	15.6
4	Latvia	15.4
5	Swaziland	14.9
6	Lesotho	14.7
7	Belarus	14.6
8	Russia	14.3
9	Romania	13.7
10	Hungary	13.5
11	Chad	13.3
12	Central African Rep.	13.1
	Serbia	13.1
14	Croatia	12.8
	Ivory Coast	12.8
	Sierra Leone	12.8
17	Angola	12.7
	Estonia	12.7
19	South Africa	12.6
20	Nigeria	12.2
21	Moldova	11.7
22	Georgia	11.5
23	Guinea-Bissau	11.4
24	Germany	11.3
	Greece	11.3
	Somalia	11.3
27	Bosnia & Herz.	11.1
28	Barbados	10.9
	Japan	10.9
	South Sudan	10.9
31	Mozambique	10.8
32	Portugal	10.7
33	Cameroon	10.6
	Czech Republic	10.6
35	Burundi	10.5
36	Poland	10.4
37	Equatorial Guinea	10.3
	Montenegro	10.3
39	Italy	10.2
	Slovakia	10.2
41	Slovenia	10.0
42	Finland	9.9
43	Trinidad and Tobago	9.8
44	Belgium	9.7
	Macedonia	9.7
46	Armenia	9.6
	Congo-Kinshasa	9.6
	Denmark	9.6
	Monaco[a]	9.6
50	Austria	9.5
51	North Korea	9.4
	Uruguay	9.4
53	Mali	9.3
	Malta	9.3
55	Guinea	9.2
56	Channel Islands	9.1
	France	9.1
	Spain	9.1
	United Kingdom	9.1
60	Benin	9.0
	Kazakhstan	9.0
	Martinique	9.0
	Sweden	9.0
64	Burkina Faso	8.9
65	Netherlands	8.8
66	Ghana	8.5
	Guyana	8.5
	Haiti	8.5
	Uganda	8.5
70	Bermuda[a]	8.4
	Myanmar	8.4
	Thailand	8.4
	United States	8.4
74	Niger	8.3
75	Cuba	8.2
	Gambia, The	8.2
	Togo	8.2
78	Liberia	8.1
	Virgin Islands (US)	8.1
80	Mauritius	8.0
	Puerto Rico	8.0
	Switzerland	8.0
	Zambia	8.0
84	Gabon	7.9
	Norway	7.9
86	Congo-Brazzaville	7.8
	Turkmenistan	7.8
	Zimbabwe	7.8
89	Albania	7.7
	Botswana	7.7
	Mauritania	7.7
92	Afghanistan	7.6
	Azerbaijan	7.6
	Kenya	7.6
	Papua New Guinea	7.6
	Suriname	7.6

Note: Both death and, in particular, infant mortality rates can be underestimated in certain countries where not all deaths are officially recorded. a 2016 estimate.

Highest infant mortality

Number of deaths per 1,000 live births, 2015–20

1	Angola	88
2	Chad	87
3	Central African Rep.	84
4	Guinea-Bissau	82
5	Sierra Leone	81
6	Burundi	71
7	Mali	70
	Somalia	70
9	Nigeria	68
	South Sudan	68
11	Congo-Kinshasa	66
12	Cameroon	65
13	Afghanistan	64
14	Benin	63
	Ivory Coast	63
	Mauritania	63
	Pakistan	63
18	Equatorial Guinea	62
19	Burkina Faso	58
	Swaziland	58
21	Mozambique	57
22	Uganda	56
23	Liberia	52
	Malawi	52
25	Guinea	50
	Lesotho	50
	Niger	50
28	Yemen	49
29	Kenya	48
	Sudan	48
31	Ghana	47
	Zambia	47
33	Papua New Guinea	45
34	Congo-Brazzaville	44
35	Ethiopia	43
	Gambia, The	43
	Myanmar	43
	Rwanda	43
	Turkmenistan	43
40	Haiti	42
	Togo	42
42	Uzbekistan	41
43	Zimbabwe	39

Lowest death rates

No. deaths per 1,000 pop., 2015–20

1	Qatar	1.5
2	United Arab Emirates	1.8
3	Bahrain	2.5
4	Kuwait	2.6
5	Oman	2.7
6	French Guiana	3.0
7	Brunei	3.2
8	Saudi Arabia	3.5
	West Bank & Gaza	3.5
10	Maldives	3.7
11	Jordan	3.8
12	Lebanon	4.5
13	Iran	4.6
14	Nicaragua	4.8
15	Guam	4.9
	Macau	4.9
	Mexico	4.9
18	Costa Rica	5.0
	Honduras	5.0
	Iraq	5.0
21	Algeria	5.1
	Ecuador	5.1
	Panama	5.1
	Singapore	5.1

Lowest infant mortality

No. deaths per 1,000 live births, 2015–20

1	Luxembourg	1
	Singapore	1
3	Czech Republic	2
	Finland	2
	Greece	2
	Hong Kong	2
	Iceland	2
	Ireland	2
	Italy	2
	Japan	2
	Monaco[a]	2
	Norway	2
	South Korea	2
	Sweden	2

Death and disease

Diabetes

Prevalence in pop. aged 20–79, %
2015 age-standardised estimate[a]

1	Mauritius	22.3
2	Kuwait	20.0
	Qatar	20.0
	Saudi Arabia	20.0
5	Bahrain	19.6
6	New Caledonia	19.6
7	French Polynesia	19.4
8	United Arab Emirates	19.3
9	Guam	18.7
10	Malaysia	17.9
11	Egypt	16.7
12	Mexico	15.8
	Réunion	15.8
14	Papua New Guinea	15.3
15	Oman	14.8
16	Fiji	13.8

Cardiovascular disease

No. of deaths per 100,000 pop.,
2012 age standardised estimate[a]

1	Turkmenistan	712.1
2	Kazakhstan	635.5
3	Mongolia	586.7
4	Uzbekistan	577.7
5	Kyrgyzstan	549.4
6	Guyana	544.8
7	Ukraine	536.1
8	Russia	531.0
9	Afghanistan	511.5
10	Tajikistan	510.3
11	Moldova	507.7
12	Armenia	473.9
13	Belarus	464.2
14	Egypt	445.1
15	Azerbaijan	442.2
16	Albania	436.2

Chronic respiratory diseases

Deaths per 100,000 population,
2012 age-standardised estimate[a]

1	India	154.8
2	Nepal	152.3
3	North Korea	133.6
4	Liberia	125.5
5	Myanmar	114.1
6	Bangladesh	106.7
7	Papua New Guinea	106.4
8	Mali	102.5
9	Lesotho	91.9
10	Pakistan	91.4
11	Swaziland	89.5
12	Laos	80.2
13	Central African Rep.	79.5
14	China	77.1
15	Equatorial Guinea	76.3
16	Angola	74.4
17	Afghanistan	65.5
18	Timor-Leste	63.2
19	Namibia	63.1
20	Congo-Kinshasa	61.4
21	Sierra Leone	61.1
22	Philippines	60.7
23	Maldives	60.2

Tuberculosis

Incidence per 100,000 pop., 2015

1	South Africa	834
2	Lesotho	788
3	Swaziland	565
4	North Korea	561
5	Mozambique	551
6	Timor-Leste	498
7	Namibia	489
8	Gabon	465
9	Papua New Guinea	432
10	Mongolia	428
11	Indonesia	395
12	Central African Rep.	391
	Zambia	391
14	Cambodia	380
15	Congo-Brazzaville	379
16	Guinea-Bissau	373
17	Angola	370
18	Myanmar	365
19	Botswana	356
20	Nigeria	322
	Philippines	322
22	Liberia	308
23	Sierra Leone	307
24	Tanzania	306
25	Somalia	274

a Assumes that every country and region has the same age profile (the age profile of the world population has been used).

Note: Statistics are not available for all countries. The number of cases diagnosed and reported depends on the quality of medical practice and administration and can be under-reported in a number of countries.

Measles immunisation

Lowest % of children aged 12–23 months, 2015

1	South Sudan	20
2	Equatorial Guinea	27
3	Somalia	46
4	Central African Rep.	49
5	Guinea	52
6	Haiti	53
	Syria	53
8	Nigeria	54
9	Angola	55
10	Ukraine	56
11	Iraq	57
12	Madagascar	58
13	Papua New Guinea	60
14	Pakistan	61
15	Chad	62
16	Liberia	64
	Montenegro	64
18	Yemen	67

DPT[a] immunisation

Lowest % of children aged 12–23 months, 2015

1	Equatorial Guinea	16
2	Ukraine	23
3	South Sudan	31
4	Syria	41
5	Somalia	42
6	Central African Rep.	47
7	Guinea	51
8	Liberia	52
9	Chad	55
10	Nigeria	56
11	Iraq	58
12	Haiti	60
	Philippines	60
14	Papua New Guinea	62
15	Angola	64
16	Niger	65
17	Mali	68

HIV/AIDS

Prevalence in adults aged 15–49, %, 2015

1	Swaziland	28.8
2	Lesotho	22.7
3	Botswana	22.2
4	South Africa	19.2
5	Zimbabwe	14.7
6	Namibia	13.3
7	Zambia	12.9
8	Mozambique	10.5
9	Malawi	9.1
10	Uganda	7.1
11	Kenya	5.9
12	Equatorial Guinea	4.9
13	Tanzania	4.7
14	Cameroon	4.5
15	Gabon	3.8
16	Central African Rep.	3.7
17	Bahamas	3.2
	Ivory Coast	3.2
19	Rwanda	2.9
20	South Sudan	2.5
21	Togo	2.4
22	Angola	2.2
23	Chad	2.0
24	Gambia, The	1.8
25	Haiti	1.7

AIDS

Deaths per 100,000 population, 2015

1	Lesotho	464
2	South Africa	330
3	Swaziland	295
4	Zimbabwe	186
5	Central African Rep.	159
6	Malawi	157
7	Botswana	141
	Cameroon	141
9	Mozambique	139
10	Equatorial Guinea	130
11	Bahamas	129
12	Namibia	126
13	Zambia	123
14	Ivory Coast	110
15	South Sudan	97
16	Kenya	78
17	Gabon	75
	Haiti	75
19	Uganda	72
20	Togo	70
21	Tanzania	67
22	Chad	61
23	Gambia, The	50
24	Angola	48
25	Ghana	47

a Diphtheria, pertussis and tetanus.

Health

Highest health spending

As % of GDP, 2014

1	United States	17.1
2	Haiti	13.2
3	Sweden	11.9
4	Switzerland	11.7
5	France	11.5
6	Germany	11.3
7	Austria	11.2
8	Cuba	11.1
	Sierra Leone	11.1
10	New Zealand	11.0
11	Netherlands	10.9
12	Denmark	10.8
13	Belgium	10.6
	Lesotho	10.6
15	Canada	10.4
	Serbia	10.4
17	Moldova	10.3
18	Japan	10.2
19	Liberia	10.0
20	Paraguay	9.8
21	Finland	9.7
	Malta	9.7
	Norway	9.7
24	Bosnia & Herz.	9.6
	Malawi	9.6

Lowest health spending

As % of GDP, 2014

1	Timor-Leste	1.5
2	Laos	1.9
3	Turkmenistan	2.1
4	Qatar	2.2
5	Myanmar	2.3
6	Brunei	2.6
	Congo-Kinshasa	2.6
	Pakistan	2.6
9	South Sudan	2.7
10	Bangladesh	2.8
	Indonesia	2.8
12	Kuwait	3.0
	Madagascar	3.0
14	Angola	3.3
	Eritrea	3.3
	Syria	3.3
17	Gabon	3.4
18	Sri Lanka	3.5
19	Bhutan	3.6
	Chad	3.6
	Ghana	3.6
	Oman	3.6
	United Arab Emirates	3.6
24	Nigeria	3.7
25	Equatorial Guinea	3.8
	Mauritania	3.8

Highest pop. per doctor

2014 or latest[a]

1	Liberia	71,429
2	Malawi	52,632
	Niger	52,632
4	Ethiopia	45,455
	Sierra Leone	45,455
6	Tanzania	32,258
7	Somalia	28,571
8	Gambia, The	26,316
9	Mozambique	25,000
10	Guinea-Bissau	22,222
11	Burkina Faso	21,277
12	Togo	18,868
13	Rwanda	17,857
14	Papua New Guinea	17,241
15	Benin	16,949
	Senegal	16,949
17	Mauritania	14,627
18	Timor-Leste	13,699
19	Mali	12,048
	Zimbabwe	12,048

Lowest pop. per doctor

2014 or latest[a]

1	Qatar	129
2	Monaco	140
3	Cuba	149
4	Greece	162
5	Spain	202
6	Belgium	205
7	Austria	207
8	Russia	232
9	Georgia	234
	Norway	234
11	Lithuania	243
12	Portugal	244
13	Switzerland	247
14	Andorra	250
15	Belarus	255
	Sweden	255
17	Germany	257
18	Argentina	259
	Bulgaria	259
20	Italy	266

a 2010–14

Obesity[a]

Adult population 18 years or over, % point increase 1975–2014

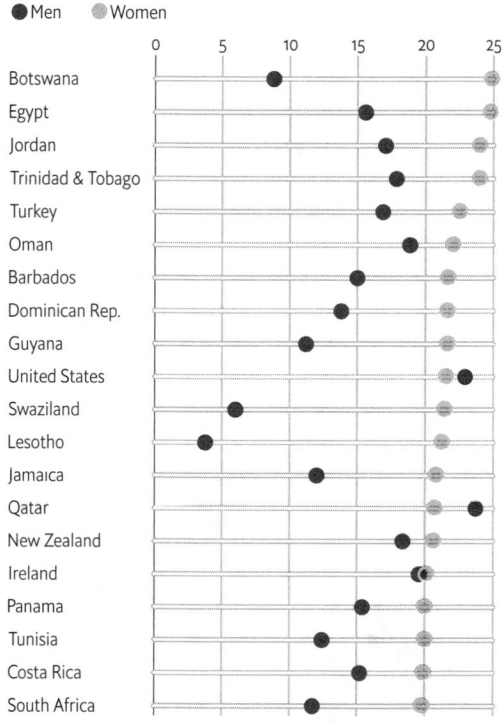

Food deficit

Average kilocalories needed[b] per person per day, 2016 or latest

Highest deficit			*Lowest deficit*		
1	Haiti	546	**1**	Turkey	1
2	Zambia	405	**2**	Argentina	2
3	Central African Rep.	380	**3**	Tunisia	3
4	North Korea	343	**4**	South Korea	4
5	Namibia	325	**5**	Cuba	7
6	Chad	261	**6**	Saudi Arabia	9
7	Zimbabwe	259		Venezuela	9
8	Liberia	256	**8**	Brazil	10
9	Tajikistan	250	**9**	Azerbaijan	12
10	Tanzania	238		Brunei	12
11	Ethiopia	236		Egypt	12
12	Rwanda	232	**12**	Jordan	13
				South Africa	13

a Defined as body mass index of 30 or more – see page 248.
b To lift the undernourished from their status.

Telephones and the internet

Mobile telephones

Subscribers per 100 population, 2015

1	Macau	324.4
2	Kuwait	231.8
3	Hong Kong	228.7
4	Maldives	206.7
5	United Arab Emirates	187.3
6	Bahrain	185.3
7	Jordan	179.4
8	Saudi Arabia	176.6
9	Panama	174.2
10	Botswana	169.0
11	South Africa	164.5
12	Montenegro	162.2
13	Gabon	161.1
14	Uruguay	160.2
15	Russia	160.0
16	Oman	159.9
17	Qatar	159.1
18	Trinidad & Tobago	157.7
19	Austria	157.4
20	Libya	157.0
21	Kazakhstan	156.9
22	Thailand	152.7
23	Costa Rica	150.7
24	Estonia	148.7
25	Luxembourg	148.5
26	Argentina	146.7
27	Singapore	146.5
28	Turkmenistan	145.9
29	El Salvador	145.3
30	Ukraine	144.0
31	Malaysia	143.9
32	Poland	142.7
33	Italy	142.1
34	Mauritius	140.6
35	Mali	139.6
36	Lithuania	139.5
37	Gambia, The	137.8
38	Suriname	136.8
39	Switzerland	136.5
40	Finland	135.4
41	Israel	133.5
42	Cambodia	133.0
43	Australia	132.8
	Kyrgyzstan	132.8
45	Indonesia	132.3
46	Vietnam	130.6
47	Sweden	130.4
48	Tunisia	129.9
49	Ghana	129.7
50	Chile	129.5

Landline telephones

Per 100 population, 2015

1	Monaco	128.1
2	Virgin Islands (US)	71.1
3	France	59.9
4	Taiwan	59.7
5	Hong Kong	59.2
6	South Korea	58.1
7	Germany	54.9
8	Barbados	54.6
9	Malta	53.4
10	United Kingdom	52.0
11	Luxembourg	51.0
12	Switzerland	50.3
13	Japan	50.2
14	Iceland	49.9
15	Belarus	49.0
16	Andorra	48.0
17	Greece	47.3
18	Liechtenstein	46.3
19	Portugal	44.1
20	Canada	43.5
21	Israel	43.1
22	Austria	42.2
23	Spain	41.5
24	Netherlands	41.3
25	Ireland	40.9
26	New Zealand	40.2
27	Belgium	40.1
28	Guam	40.0
29	United States	38.4
30	Iran	38.3

Internet users

Per 100 population, 2015

1	Bermuda	98.3
2	Iceland	98.2
3	Luxembourg	97.3
4	Andorra	96.9
5	Norway	96.8
6	Liechtenstein	96.6
7	Denmark	96.3
8	Bahrain	93.5
9	Monaco	93.4
10	Netherlands	93.1
11	Qatar	92.9
12	Finland	92.7
13	United Kingdom	92.0
14	United Arab Emirates	91.2
15	Japan	91.1
16	Sweden	90.6
17	South Korea	89.6
18	Canada	88.5
19	Estonia	88.4
20	New Zealand	88.2
21	Germany	87.6
22	Switzerland	87.5
23	Belgium	85.1
24	Hong Kong	84.9
25	France	84.7
26	Australia	84.6
27	Austria	83.9
28	Kuwait	82.1
	Singapore	82.1
30	Czech Republic	81.3
31	Ireland	80.1
32	Puerto Rico	79.5
33	Latvia	79.2
34	Spain	78.7
35	Bahamas	78.0
	Taiwan	78.0
37	Macau	77.6
	Slovakia	77.6
39	Israel	77.4
40	Azerbaijan	77.0
41	Malta	76.2
42	Barbados	76.1
43	United States	74.5
44	Oman	74.2
45	Lebanon	74.0
	New Caledonia	74.0
47	Guam	73.1
	Slovenia	73.1
49	Hungary	72.8
50	Cyprus	71.7

Broadband

Fixed-broadband subscriptions per 100 population, 2015

1	Monaco	47.9
2	Bermuda	45.7
3	Switzerland	45.1
4	Denmark	42.5
5	Liechtenstein	41.9
6	Netherlands	41.7
7	France	41.3
8	South Korea	40.2
9	Norway	39.7
10	United Kingdom	38.6
11	Andorra	37.9
12	Malta	37.8
13	Germany	37.2
14	Iceland	37.0
15	Belgium	36.8
16	Canada	36.3
17	Sweden	36.1
18	Luxembourg	35.9
19	Hong Kong	32.1
20	Finland	31.7
21	New Zealand	31.6
22	Belarus	31.4
23	United States	31.0
24	Greece	30.9
25	Japan	30.7
26	Estonia	30.0
27	Portugal	29.6
28	Macau	29.1
29	Austria	28.7
	Spain	28.7
31	Australia	28.5
32	Lithuania	27.8
33	Ireland	27.7
34	Slovenia	27.6
35	Hungary	27.4
	Israel	27.4
37	Czech Republic	27.3
38	Barbados	27.2
39	Singapore	26.4
40	Uruguay	26.3
41	Lebanon	25.4
42	Latvia	24.8
43	Italy	24.4
44	Taiwan	24.3

Arts and entertainment

Music sales

Total including downloads, $bn, 2016

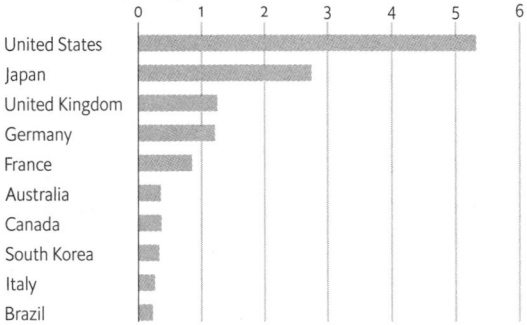

$ per person, 2016

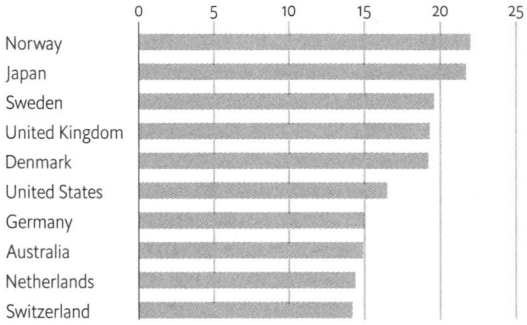

Book publishing

New titles per million population, 2015

1	United Kingdom	2,710	**15**	United States	1,043
2	Iceland	2,628	**16**	Georgia[b]	969
3	Denmark	2,326	**17**	Hungary[a]	920
4	Slovenia[a]	1,831	**18**	South Korea	909
	Taiwan[a]	1,831	**19**	Austria[a]	757
6	France	1,643	**20**	Bosnia & Herz.	731
7	Spain	1,552	**21**	Russia[a]	699
8	Czech Republic[a]	1,509	**22**	Sweden	695
9	Netherlands	1,482	**23**	Argentina	687
	Switzerland	1,482	**24**	Turkey[a]	670
11	Norway	1,268	**25**	Finland[b]	640
12	Australia[a]	1,176	**26**	Japan	603
13	Germany	1,084	**27**	Poland	547
14	Italy	1,078	**28**	Belgium	459

a 2013 b 2014

Cinema attendances

Total visits, m, 2015

1	India	2,191.9
2	United States	1,286.8
3	China	1,050.6
4	Mexico	276.0
5	South Korea	219.4
6	France	213.0
7	Russia	171.7
8	Japan	161.1
9	United Kingdom	157.8
10	Brazil	156.0
11	Germany	119.1
12	Italy	112.5
13	Spain	85.9
14	Australia	78.2
15	Malaysia	72.1
16	Turkey	65.4
17	Argentina	49.7
18	Colombia	49.1
19	Philippines	41.9
20	Poland	40.9
21	Peru	40.1
22	Netherlands	31.1
23	Thailand	28.9
24	Hong Kong	28.6
25	Venezuela	27.7
26	Chile	22.4
27	Singapore	22.2
28	South Africa	20.6
29	Belgium	20.4
30	United Arab Emirates	17.6

Visits per person, 2015

1	Iceland	4.3
	South Korea	4.3
3	Singapore	4.0
	United States	4.0
5	Hong Kong	3.9
6	Australia	3.3
	France	3.3
	New Zealand	3.3
9	Bahrain	3.1
	Ireland	3.1
11	United Kingdom	2.4
12	Malaysia	2.3
13	Luxembourg	2.2
	Mexico	2.2
	Norway	2.2
16	Denmark	2.1
	Estonia	2.1
18	Israel	2.0
	United Arab Emirates	2.0
20	Spain	1.9
21	Belgium	1.8
	Italy	1.8
	Netherlands	1.8
24	India	1.7
	Malta	1.7
	Sweden	1.7
	Switzerland	1.7
28	Austria	1.6
29	Germany	1.5
30	Finland	1.4

Oscar nominations by ethnicity

2001–17

Best actor

White	68
Black	11
Latino	5
Other	1

Best actress

White	76
Black	4
Latino	3
Other	2

Supporting actor

White	71
Black	7
Latino	4
Other	3

Supporting actress

White	68
Black	12
Latino	2
Other	3

The press

Daily newspapers

Highest daily circulation, m, 2015

1	India	285.1
2	China	142.1
3	Japan	44.2
4	United States	42.4
5	Germany	16.0
6	United Kingdom	11.3
7	Indonesia	10.9
8	South Korea	10.3
9	France	8.9
10	Brazil	8.4
11	Russia	8.3
12	Thailand	7.9
13	Mexico	7.0
14	Canada	5.2
15	Turkey	5.0
16	Egypt	4.7
17	Vietnam	4.0
18	Philippines	3.9
19	Hong Kong	3.8
20	Italy	3.7
21	Taiwan	3.5
22	Netherlands	3.4
23	Sweden	3.0
24	Austria	2.8
25	Malaysia	2.7
	Switzerland	2.7
27	Saudi Arabia	2.3
	Ukraine	2.3
29	Spain	2.1

Press freedom[a]

Scores, 1 = best, 100 = worst, 2015

Most free

1	Finland	8.6
2	Netherlands	8.8
	Norway	8.8
4	Denmark	8.9
5	New Zealand	10.0
6	Costa Rica	11.1
7	Switzerland	11.8
8	Sweden	12.3
9	Ireland	12.4
10	Jamaica	12.5
11	Austria	13.2
12	Slovakia	13.3
13	Belgium	14.2
14	Estonia	14.3
15	Luxembourg	14.4
16	Germany	14.8
17	Namibia	15.2
18	Canada	15.3
	Iceland	15.3
20	Uruguay	15.9
21	Czech Republic	16.7
22	Portugal	17.3
23	Latvia	17.4
24	Australia	17.8
25	Ghana	18.0
26	Cyprus	18.3
27	Liechtenstein	18.4
28	Chile	19.2

Least free

1	Eritrea	83.9
2	North Korea	83.8
3	Turkmenistan	83.4
4	Syria	81.4
5	China	81.0
6	Vietnam	74.3
7	Sudan	72.5
8	Laos	71.6
9	Cuba	70.2
10	Yemen	67.1
11	Equatorial Guinea	66.5
	Iran	66.5
13	Somalia	65.4
14	Uzbekistan	61.2
15	Saudi Arabia	59.7
16	Azerbaijan	57.9
	Libya	57.9
18	Bahrain	54.9
19	Kazakhstan	54.6
	Rwanda	54.6
21	Egypt	54.5
22	Iraq	54.4
23	Belarus	54.3
24	Burundi	54.1
25	Brunei	53.9
26	Singapore	53.0
27	Swaziland	52.4
28	Congo-Kinshasa	51.0
29	Turkey	50.8

a Based on data for deaths and violence against journalists, and attacks on organisations, plus 87 questions on media topics.

Nobel prize winners: 1901–2016

Nobel prize winners

By country of residence, 1901–2016

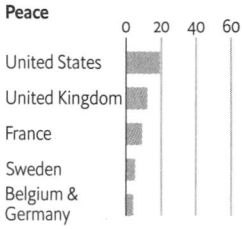

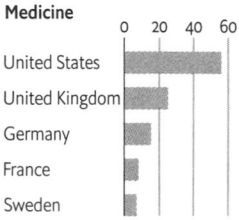

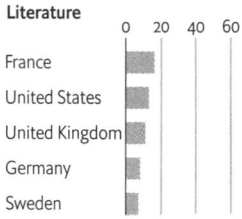

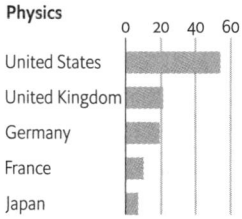

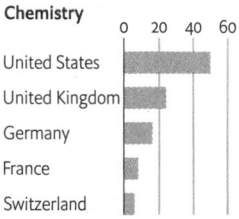

Nobel prize winners: 1901–2016

By country of birth

1	United States	259
2	United Kingdom	99
3	Germany	80
4	France	54
5	Sweden	29
6	Poland	26
	Russia	26
8	Japan	24
9	Italy	19
10	Canada	18
	Netherlands	18
12	Austria	16
	Switzerland	16
14	China	12
	Denmark	12
	Norway	12
17	Australia	10
18	Belgium	9
	Hungary	9
	South Africa	9
21	India	8
22	Spain	7
23	Czech Republic	6
	Egypt	6
	Israel	6

Notes: Prizes by country of residence at time awarded. When prizes have been shared in the same field, one credit given to each country. a Since 1969.

Sports champions and cheats

World Cup winners and finalists

Men's football (since 1930)		*Winner*	*Runner-up*
1	Brazil	5	2
2	Germany[a]	4	4
3	Italy	4	2
4	Argentina	2	3
5	Uruguay	2	0
6	France	1	1
7	England	1	0
	Spain	1	0
9	Netherlands	0	3
10	Czechoslovakia[b]	0	2
	Hungary	0	2
12	Sweden	0	1

Women's football (since 1991)		*Winner*	*Runner-up*
1	United States	3	1
2	Germany	2	1
	Japan	1	1
	Norway	1	1
5	Brazil	0	1
	China	0	1
	Sweden	0	1

Men's cricket (since 1975)		*Winner*	*Runner-up*
1	Australia	5	2
2	India	2	1
	West Indies	2	1
4	Sri Lanka	1	2
5	Pakistan	1	1
6	England	0	3
7	New Zealand	0	1

Women's cricket (since 1973)		*Winner*	*Runner-up*
1	Australia	6	2
2	England	3	3
3	New Zealand	1	3
4	India	0	1
	West Indies	0	1

Davis Cup, tennis (since 1900)[c]		*Winner*	*Runner-up*
1	United States	32	29
2	Australia	28	19
3	Great Britain	10	8
4	France	9	8
5	Sweden	7	5
6	Spain	5	4
7	Czech Republic[d]	3	2
	Germany[a]	3	2
9	Russia	2	3
10	Italy	1	6

Note: Data as of May 2016. a Including West Germany. b Until 1993.
c Excludes finalists who have never won. d Including Czechoslovakia.

Summer Olympics

Athletes sent per gold medal won, 1896–2016

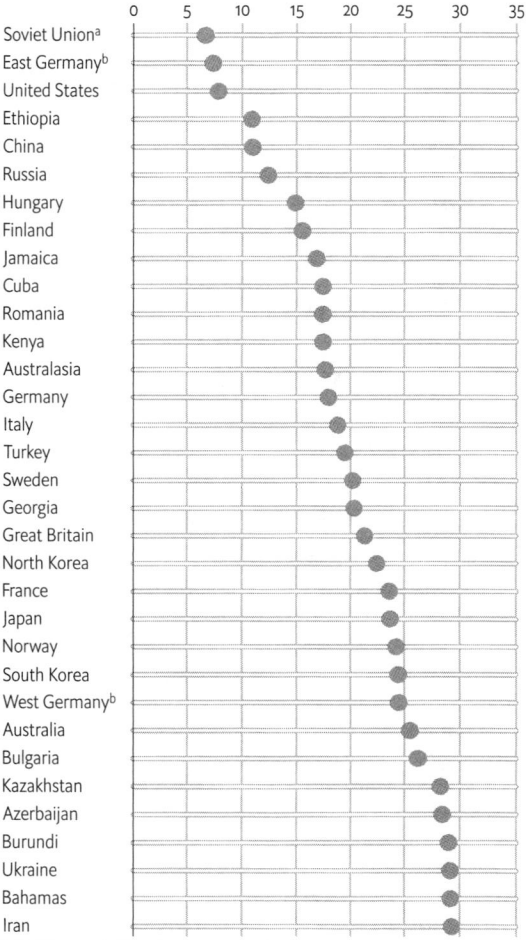

Doping

Anti-doping rule violations, 2015

1	Russia	176	**6**	South Africa	59
2	Italy	129		Turkey	59
3	India	117	**8**	South Korea	51
4	France	84	**9**	United States	50
5	Belgium	67	**10**	Iran	48

a Unified team 1952–92. b 1968–88

Vices

Beer drinkers

Consumption, litres per person, 2015

1	Czech Republic	142.4
2	Austria	104.7
	Germany	104.7
4	Namibia	102.7
5	Poland	99.0
6	Ireland	97.5
7	Lithuania	97.1
8	Romania	92.1
9	Estonia	91.5
10	Gabon	87.0
11	Spain	82.8
12	Slovenia	81.2
13	Panama	80.1
14	Slovakia	77.9
15	Finland	77.4
16	Latvia	77.3
17	Croatia	76.6
18	United States	75.4

Smokers

Av. ann. consumption of cigarettes per person per day, 2015

1	Moldova	7.1
2	Belarus	6.8
3	Lebanon	6.6
4	Russia	5.4
	Serbia	5.4
6	China	5.2
7	Macedonia	5.0
	Slovenia	5.0
9	Czech Republic	4.8
10	Bulgaria	4.6
11	Georgia	4.5
12	Taiwan	4.2
13	Austria	4.1
	Ukraine	4.1
15	Bosnia & Herz.	4.0
16	Azerbaijan	3.9
	Greece	3.9

Gambling losses[a]

Total, $bn, 2016

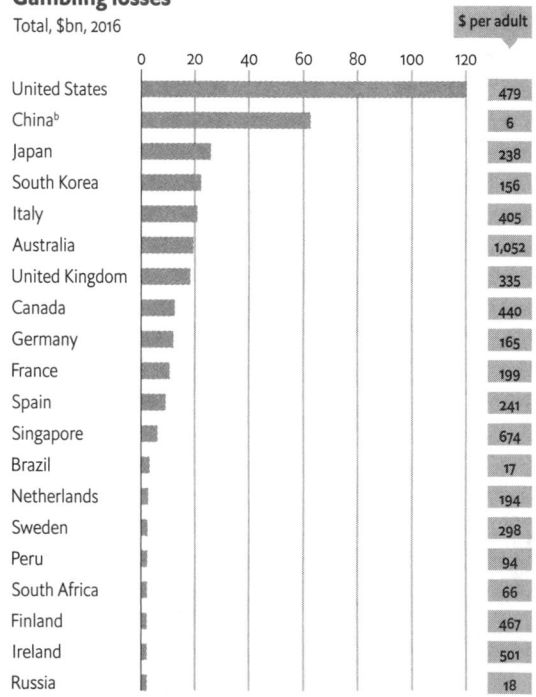

a Data according to H2 Gambling Capital – May 2017.
b Includes Macau and Hong Kong.

Tourism

Most tourist arrivals

Number of arrivals, '000, 2015

1	France	84,452
2	United States	77,510
3	Spain	68,215
4	China	56,886
5	Italy	50,732
6	Turkey	39,478
7	Germany	34,970
8	United Kingdom	34,436
9	Russia	33,729
10	Mexico	32,093
11	Thailand	29,923
12	Austria	26,719
13	Hong Kong	26,686
14	Malaysia	25,721
15	Greece	23,599
16	Japan	19,737
17	Saudi Arabia	17,994
18	Canada	17,971
19	Poland	16,722
20	Netherlands	15,007
21	Macau	14,308
22	India	13,284
23	South Korea	13,232
24	Croatia	12,683
25	Ukraine	12,428
26	Singapore	12,051
27	Bahrain	11,621
28	Taiwan	10,440
29	Denmark	10,424
30	Indonesia	10,407
31	Morocco	10,177
32	Portugal	9,957
33	Ireland	9,528
34	Romania	9,331
35	Switzerland	9,305
36	Egypt	9,139
37	South Africa	8,904
38	Czech Republic	8,707
39	Belgium	8,355
40	Vietnam	7,944

Biggest tourist spenders

$bn, 2015

1	China	292.2
2	United States	148.4
3	Germany	88.8
4	United Kingdom	79.6
5	France	46.8
6	Russia	38.4
7	Canada	29.5
8	Australia	28.3
9	South Korea	27.6
10	Italy	24.4
11	Japan	23.2
12	Hong Kong	23.1
13	Singapore	22.1
14	Saudi Arabia	21.7
15	Belgium	21.1
	Netherlands	21.1
17	Brazil	20.4
18	Switzerland	18.5
19	India	17.7
20	Spain	17.3
21	Norway	17.1
22	Sweden	14.4
23	Kuwait	13.1
24	Mexico	12.7

Largest tourist receipts

$bn, 2015

1	United States	246.2
2	China	114.1
3	United Kingdom	60.7
4	Spain	56.4
5	France	54.0
6	Thailand	48.5
7	Germany	47.4
8	Hong Kong	42.6
9	Italy	39.4
10	Turkey	35.4
11	Macau	32.0
12	Australia	31.3
13	Japan	27.3
14	India	21.5
15	Switzerland	19.6
16	Netherlands	19.3
17	South Korea	19.1
18	Mexico	18.7
19	Austria	18.3
20	Malaysia	17.6
21	Greece	17.3
22	Singapore	16.7
23	Canada	16.2
24	United Arab Emirates	16.0

Country profiles

110 Algeria
112 Argentina
114 Australia
116 Austria
118 Bangladesh
120 Belgium
122 Brazil
124 Bulgaria
126 Cameroon
128 Canada
130 Chile
132 China
134 Colombia
136 Czech Republic
138 Denmark
140 Egypt
142 Finland
144 France
146 Germany
148 Greece
150 Hong Kong
152 Hungary
154 India
156 Indonesia
158 Iran
160 Ireland
162 Israel
164 Italy
166 Ivory Coast
168 Japan
170 Kenya
172 Malaysia
174 Mexico
176 Morocco
178 Netherlands
180 New Zealand
182 Nigeria
184 Norway
186 Pakistan
188 Peru
190 Philippines
192 Poland
194 Portugal
196 Romania
198 Russia
200 Saudi Arabia
202 Singapore
204 Slovakia
206 Slovenia
208 South Africa
210 South Korea
212 Spain
214 Sweden
216 Switzerland
218 Taiwan
220 Thailand
222 Turkey
224 Ukraine
226 United Arab Emirates
228 United Kingdom
230 United States
232 Venezuela
234 Vietnam
236 Zimbabwe
238 Euro area
240 World

ALGERIA

Area, sq km	2,381,741	Capital	Algiers
Arable as % of total land	3.1	Currency	Algerian dinar (AD)

People

Population, m	39.7	Life expectancy: men	73.4 yrs
Pop. per sq km	16.7	women	78.0 yrs
Average annual growth in pop. 2015–20, %	1.6	Adult literacy	79.6
Pop. aged 0–24, %	45.2	Fertility rate (per woman)	2.8
Pop. aged 70 and over, %	3.9	Urban population, 2020, %	73.4
No. of men per 100 women	101.3		*per 1,000 pop.*
Human Development Index	74.5	Crude birth rate	21.5
		Crude death rate	5.1

The economy

GDP	$165bn	GDP per head	$4,151
GDP	AD16,592bn	GDP per head in purchasing power parity (USA=100)	26.1
Av. ann. growth in real GDP 2010–15	3.3%	Economic freedom index	46.5

Origins of GDP	*% of total*	**Components of GDP**	*% of total*
Agriculture	13	Private consumption	41
Industry, of which:	39	Public consumption	21
manufacturing	...	Investment	51
Services	48	Exports	24
		Imports	-37

Structure of employment

	% of total		*% of labour force*
Agriculture	8.8	Unemployed 2015	11.0
Industry	30.4	Av. ann. rate 2005–15	11.4
Services	60.5		

Energy

	m TOE		
Total output	164.0	Net energy imports as % of energy use	-177
Total consumption	59.0		
Consumption per head kg oil equivalent	1,327		

Inflation and finance

			av. ann. increase 2011–16
Consumer price inflation 2016	5.9%	Narrow money (M1)	6.0%
Av. ann. inflation 2011–16	6.3%	Broad money	7.0%
Treasury bill rate, Dec. 2016	1.55%		

Exchange rates

	end 2016		*December 2016*
AD per $	110.5	Effective rates	2010 = 100
AD per sdr	148.6	– nominal	86.7
AD per €	116.3	– real	104.2

Trade

Principal exports	$bn fob
Hydrocarbons	32.7
Semi-finished goods	1.7
Raw materials	0.1
Total incl. others	**34.7**

Principal imports	$bn cif
Capital goods	17.7
Intermediate goods	16.0
Food	9.3
Consumer goods	8.7
Total	**51.7**

Main export destinations	% of total
Spain	17.4
Italy	16.3
France	13.0
United Kingdom	7.6

Main origins of imports	% of total
China	16.0
France	10.5
Italy	9.4
Spain	7.6

Balance of payments, reserves and debt, $bn

Visible exports fob	34.3
Visible imports fob	-52.2
Trade balance	-17.8
Invisibles inflows	5.6
Invisibles outflows	-17.6
Net transfers	2.5
Current account balance	-27.2
– as % of GDP	-16.5
Capital balance	0.2
Overall balance	-27.4
Change in reserves	-35.8
Level of reserves end Dec.	150.6
No. months of import cover	25.9
Official gold holdings, m oz	5.6
Foreign debt	4.7
– as % of GDP	2.8
– as % of total exports	11.5
Debt service ratio	1.7

Health and education

Health spending, % of GDP	7.2
Doctors per 1,000 pop.	1.2
Hospital beds per 1,000 pop.	...
Improved-water source access, % of pop.	83.6
Education spending, % of GDP	...
Enrolment, %: primary	116
secondary	100
tertiary	37

Society

No. of households, m	7.3
Av. no. per household	5.4
Marriages per 1,000 pop.	...
Divorces per 1,000 pop.	...
Religion, % of pop.	
Muslim	97.9
Non-religious	1.8
Christian	0.2
Hindu	<0.1
Jewish	<0.1
Other	<0.1
Cost of living, Dec. 2016 New York = 100	45
Cars per 1,000 pop.	87
Colour TV households, % with:	
cable	...
satellite	93.1
Telephone lines per 100 pop.	8.0
Mobile telephone subscribers per 100 pop.	106.4
Broadband subs per 100 pop.	5.6
Internet users, % of pop.	38.1

ARGENTINA

Area, sq km	2,780,400	Capital	Buenos Aires
Arable as % of total land	14.3	Currency	Peso (P)

People

Population, m	43.4	Life expectancy: men	73.2 yrs
Pop. per sq km	15.6	women	80.6 yrs
Average annual growth in pop. 2015–20, %	0.9	Adult literacy	98.1
Pop. aged 0–24, %	41.1	Fertility rate (per woman)	2.2
Pop. aged 70 and over, %	7.4	Urban population, 2020, %	92.4
No. of men per 100 women	95.8		*per 1,000 pop.*
Human Development Index	82.7	Crude birth rate	16.9
		Crude death rate	7.5

The economy

GDP	$632bn	GDP per head	$14,553
GDP	P5,854bn	GDP per head in purchasing power parity (USA=100)	36.3
Av. ann. growth in real GDP 2010–15	1.4%	Economic freedom index	50.4

Origins of GDP	*% of total*	**Components of GDP**	*% of total*
Agriculture	6	Private consumption	65
Industry, of which:	28	Public consumption	18
manufacturing	17	Investment	17
Services	66	Exports	11
		Imports	-12

Structure of employment

	% of total		*% of labour force*
Agriculture	2.0	Unemployed 2015	6.6
Industry	24.6	Av. ann. rate 2005–15	8.1
Services	72.8		

Energy

	m TOE		
Total output	67.1	Net energy imports as % of energy use	13
Total consumption	94.0		
Consumption per head kg oil equivalent	2,179		

Inflation and finance

			av. ann. increase 2011–16
Consumer price inflation 2016	10.6%	Narrow money (M1)	29.1%
Av. ann. inflation 2011–16	10.8%	Broad money	32.0%
Money market rate, Dec. 2016	24.66%		

Exchange rates

	end 2016		*December 2016*
P per $	15.9	Effective rates	2010 = 100
P per sdr	21.4	– nominal	...
P per €	16.7	– real	...

Trade

Principal exports

	$bn fob
Processed agricultural products	23.3
Manufactures	18.0
Primary products	13.3
Fuels & energy	2.3
Total	**56.8**

Principal imports

	$bn cif
Intermediate goods	18.1
Capital goods	11.8
Consumer goods	6.8
Fuels	6.8
Total incl. others	**59.8**

Main export destinations

	% of total
Brazil	17.8
China	9.0
United States	6.0
Chile	4.2

Main origins of imports

	% of total
Brazil	21.9
China	19.7
United States	12.9
Germany	5.2

Balance of payments, reserves and debt, $bn

Visible exports fob	56.8
Visible imports fob	-57.2
Trade balance	-0.4
Invisibles inflows	16.3
Invisibles outflows	-32.3
Net transfers	-0.4
Current account balance	-16.8
– as % of GDP	-2.7
Capital balance	9.6
Overall balance	-8.4
Change in reserves	-5.9
Level of reserves end Dec.	25.5
No. months of import cover	3.4
Official gold holdings, m oz	2.0
Foreign debt	159.7
– as % of GDP	25.2
– as % of total exports	217.2
Debt service ratio	24.4

Health and education

Health spending, % of GDP	4.8
Doctors per 1,000 pop.	3.9
Hospital beds per 1,000 pop.	4.7
Improved-water source access, % of pop.	99.1
Education spending, % of GDP	5.5
Enrolment, %: primary	110
secondary	107
tertiary	83

Society

No. of households, m	13.5
Av. no. per household	3.2
Marriages per 1,000 pop.	2.8
Divorces per 1,000 pop.	...
Religion, % of pop.	
Christian	85.2
Non-religious	12.2
Other	1.1
Muslim	1.0
Jewish	0.5
Hindu	<0.1
Cost of living, Dec. 2016 New York = 100	66
Cars per 1,000 pop.	243
Colour TV households, % with:	
cable	64.8
satellite	14.4
Telephone lines per 100 pop.	23.9
Mobile telephone subscribers per 100 pop.	147.0
Broadband subs per 100 pop.	16.3
Internet users, % of pop.	69.4

AUSTRALIA

Area, sq km	7,741,000	Capital	Canberra
Arable as % of total land	6.1	Currency	Australian dollar (A$)

People

Population, m	24.0	Life expectancy: men	81.1 yrs
Pop. per sq km	3.1	women	85.0 yrs
Average annual growth in pop. 2015–20, %	1.3	Adult literacy	...
Pop. aged 0–24, %	31.9	Fertility rate (per woman)	1.8
Pop. aged 70 and over, %	10.1	Urban population, 2020, %	90.1
No. of men per 100 women	99.9		*per 1,000 pop.*
Human Development Index	93.9	Crude birth rate	13.0
		Crude death rate	6.7

The economy

GDP	$1,230bn	GDP per head	$51,238
GDP	A$ 1,634bn	GDP per head in purchasing power parity (USA=100)	85.0
Av. ann. growth in real GDP 2010–15	2.7%	Economic freedom index	81.0

Origins of GDP	*% of total*	**Components of GDP**	*% of total*
Agriculture	3	Private consumption	57
Industry, of which:	26	Public consumption	18
manufacturing	17	Investment	27
Services	72	Exports	20
		Imports	-21

Structure of employment

	% of total		*% of labour force*
Agriculture	2.7	Unemployed 2015	6.1
Industry	19.5	Av. ann. rate 2005–15	5.2
Services	78.0		

Energy

	m TOE		
Total output	360.1	Net energy imports as % of energy use	-192
Total consumption	141.6		
Consumption per head kg oil equivalent	5,338		

Inflation and finance

			av. ann. increase 2011–16
Consumer price inflation 2016	1.3%	Narrow money (M1)	5.4%
Av. ann. inflation 2011–16	4.0%	Broad money	6.8%
Money Market Rate, Dec. 2016	1.50%		

Exchange rates

	end 2016		*December 2016*
A$ per $	1.38	Effective rates	2010 = 100
A$ per sdr	1.86	– nominal	93.7
A$ per €	1.45	– real	95.1

Trade

Principal exports

	$bn fob
Crude materials	61.3
Fuels	46.8
Food	26.8
Machinery & transport equipment	12.1
Total incl. others	**187.7**

Principal imports

	$bn cif
Machinery & transport equipment	79.8
Miscellaneous manufactured articles	30.4
Manufactured goods	24.5
Mineral fuels	21.7
Total incl. others	**200.5**

Main export destinations

	% of total
China	32.4
Japan	16.0
South Korea	7.1
United States	5.5

Main origins of imports

	% of total
China	24.5
United States	11.9
Japan	7.8
South Korea	5.8

Balance of payments, reserves and aid, $bn

Visible exports fob	188.3
Visible imports fob	-207.2
Trade balance	-18.8
Invisibles inflows	87.7
Invisibles outflows	-125.4
Net transfers	-1.4
Current account balance	-58.0
– as % of GDP	-4.7
Capital balance	50.6
Overall balance	-2.3
Change in reserves	-4.6
Level of reserves end Dec.	49.3
No. months of import cover	1.8
Official gold holdings, m oz	2.6
Aid given	3.5
– as % of GDP	0.3

Health and education

Health spending, % of GDP	9.4
Doctors per 1,000 pop.	3.3
Hospital beds per 1,000 pop.	3.9
Improved-water source access, % of pop.	100
Education spending, % of GDP	5.3
Enrolment, %: primary	106
secondary	138
tertiary	90

Society

No. of households, m	8.8
Av. no. per household	2.7
Marriages per 1,000 pop.	5.2
Divorces per 1,000 pop.	2.0
Religion, % of pop.	
Christian	67.3
Non-religious	24.2
Other	4.2
Muslim	2.4
Hindu	1.4
Jewish	0.5
Cost of living, Dec. 2016 New York = 100	90
Cars per 1,000 pop.	563
Colour TV households, % with:	
cable	24.9
satellite	33.7
Telephone lines per 100 pop.	38.0
Mobile telephone subscribers per 100 pop.	132.8
Broadband subs per 100 pop.	28.5
Internet users, % of pop.	84.6

AUSTRIA

Area, sq km	82,523	Capital	Vienna
Arable as % of total land	16.5	Currency	Euro (€)

People

Population, m	8.6	Life expectancy: men	79.7 yrs
Pop. per sq km	104.2	women	84.4 yrs
Average annual growth in pop. 2015–20, %	0.3	Adult literacy	...
Pop. aged 0–24, %	25.9	Fertility rate (per woman)	1.5
Pop. aged 70 and over, %	13.7	Urban population, 2020, %	66.4
No. of men per 100 women	96.5		*per 1,000 pop.*
Human Development Index	89.3	Crude birth rate	9.7
		Crude death rate	9.5

The economy

GDP	$377bn	GDP per head	$43,855
GDP	€340bn	GDP per head in purchasing power parity (USA=100)	84.2
Av. ann. growth in real GDP 2010–15	1.0%	Economic freedom index	72.3

Origins of GDP	*% of total*	**Components of GDP**	*% of total*
Agriculture	1	Private consumption	53
Industry, of which:	28	Public consumption	20
manufacturing	19	Investment	24
Services	70	Exports	53
		Imports	-49

Structure of employment

	% of total		*% of labour force*
Agriculture	4.5	Unemployed 2015	5.7
Industry	25.8	Av. ann. rate 2005–15	5.1
Services	69.7		

Energy

	m TOE		
Total output	2.2	Net energy imports as % of energy use	62
Total consumption	35.4		
Consumption per head kg oil equivalent	3,765		

Inflation and finance

			av. ann. increase 2011–16
Consumer price inflation 2016	0.9%	Narrow money (M1)	8.1%
Av. ann. inflation 2011–16	3.7%	Broad money	3.6%
Deposit rate, Dec. 2016	0.30%		

Exchange rates

	end 2016		*December 2016*
€ per $	0.95	Effective rates	2010 = 100
€ per sdr	1.28	– nominal	98.5
		– real	100.4

Trade

Principal exports

	$bn fob
Machinery & transport equip.	61.9
Chemicals & related products	20.4
Food, drink & tobacco	11.1
Raw materials	4.7
Total incl. others	**152.9**

Principal imports

	$bn cif
Machinery & transport equip.	55.3
Chemicals & related products	20.9
Mineral fuels & lubricants	11.7
Food, drink & tobacco	11.6
Total incl. others	**156.1**

Main export destinations

	% of total
Germany	29.4
Italy	6.1
United States	6.3
Switzerland	5.7
EU28	70.1

Main origins of imports

	% of total
Germany	41.5
Italy	6.2
Switzerland	5.9
Czech Republic	4.2
EU28	76.8

Balance of payments, reserves and aid, $bn

Visible exports fob	142.1	Overall balance	-0.4
Visible imports fob	-140.4	Change in reserves	-2.8
Trade balance	1.7	Level of reserves end Dec.	22.2
Invisibles inflows	89.8	No. months of import cover	1.2
Invisibles outflows	-80.5	Official gold holdings, m oz	9.0
Net transfers	-3.8	Aid given	1.3
Current account balance	7.2	– as % of GDP	0.4
– as % of GDP	1.9		
Capital balance	-7.8		

Health and education

Health spending, % of GDP	11.2	Education spending, % of GDP	5.6
Doctors per 1,000 pop.	4.8	Enrolment, %: primary	103
Hospital beds per 1,000 pop.	7.6	secondary	100
Improved-water source access, % of pop.	100	tertiary	82

Society

No. of households, m	3.8	Cost of living, Dec. 2016 New York = 100	91
Av. no. per household	2.3	Cars per 1,000 pop.	552
Marriages per 1,000 pop.	4.3	Colour TV households, % with: cable	38.6
Divorces per 1,000 pop.	1.9	satellite	54.3
Religion, % of pop.		Telephone lines per 100 pop.	42.2
Christian	80.4	Mobile telephone subscribers per 100 pop.	157.4
Non-religious	13.5	Broadband subs per 100 pop.	28.7
Muslim	5.4	Internet users, % of pop.	83.9
Other	0.5		
Jewish	0.2		
Hindu	<0.1		

BANGLADESH

Area, sq km	130,170	Capital	Dhaka
Arable as % of total land	58.9	Currency	Taka (Tk)

People

Population, m	161.0	Life expectancy: men	71.6 yrs
Pop. per sq km	1,236.8	women	74.3 yrs
Average annual growth in pop. 2015–20, %	1.1	Adult literacy	61.5
Pop. aged 0–24, %	48.9	Fertility rate (per woman)	2.4
Pop. aged 70 and over, %	3.2	Urban population, 2020, %	38.0
No. of men per 100 women	102.0		*per 1,000 pop.*
Human Development Index	57.9	Crude birth rate	18.6
		Crude death rate	5.3

The economy

GDP	$207bn	GDP per head	$1,284
GDP	Tk16,227bn	GDP per head in purchasing power parity (USA=100)	6.4
Av. ann. growth in real GDP 2010–15	6.4%	Economic freedom index	55.0

Origins of GDP	*% of total*	**Components of GDP**	% of total
Agriculture	16	Private consumption	73
Industry, of which:	28	Public consumption	5
manufacturing	18	Investment	29
Services	56	Exports	17
		Imports	-25

Structure of employment

	% of total		*% of labour force*
Agriculture	47.5	Unemployed 2015	4.1
Industry	17.7	Av. ann. rate 2005–15	4.3
Services	35.3		

Energy

	m TOE		
Total output	22.6	Net energy imports as % of energy use	17
Total consumption	28.4		
Consumption per head kg oil equivalent	223		

Inflation and finance

			av. ann. increase 2011–16
Consumer price inflation 2016	6.7%	Narrow money (M1)	13.6%
Av. ann. inflation 2011–16	7.8%	Broad money	15.8%
Treasury bill rate, Dec. 2016	3.00%		

Exchange rates

	end 2016		*December 2016*
Tk per $	78.7	Effective rates	2010 = 100
Tk per sdr	105.8	– nominal	...
Tk per €	82.8	– real	...

Trade

Principal exports	$bn fob	Principal imports	$bn cif
Clothing	20.7	Textiles & yarns	3.9
Jute goods	0.7	Fuels	3.3
Fish & fish products	0.4	Iron & steel	2.9
Leather	0.3	Capital machinery	2.7
Total incl. others	**29.9**	Total incl. others	**39.5**

Main export destinations	% of total	Main origins of imports	% of total
United States	13.9	China	22.4
Germany	12.9	India	14.1
United Kingdom	8.9	Singapore	5.2
France	5.0	Japan	3.9

Balance of payments, reserves and debt, $bn

Visible exports fob	31.7	Change in reserves	5.2
Visible imports fob	-37.6	Level of reserves end Dec.	27.5
Trade balance	-5.9	No. months of import cover	6.9
Invisibles inflows	3.2	Official gold holdings, m oz	0.4
Invisibles outflows	-10.5	Foreign debt	38.6
Net transfers	15.9	– as % of GDP	19.8
Current account balance	2.7	– as % of total exports	76.8
– as % of GDP	1.3	Debt service ratio	2.9
Capital balance	3.6		
Overall balance	5.4		

Health and education

Health spending, % of GDP	2.8	Education spending, % of GDP	2.2
Doctors per 1,000 pop.	0.4	Enrolment, %: primary	120
Hospital beds per 1,000 pop.	0.6	secondary	64
Improved-water source access, % of pop.	86.9	tertiary	13

Society

No. of households, m	37.1	Cost of living, Dec. 2016 New York = 100	72
Av. no. per household	4.3	Cars per 1,000 pop.	3.0
Marriages per 1,000 pop.	...	Colour TV households, % with:	
Divorces per 1,000 pop.	...	cable	...
Religion, % of pop. of pop.		satellite	...
Muslim	89.8	Telephone lines per 100 pop.	0.5
Hindu	9.1	Mobile telephone subscribers per 100 pop.	81.9
Other	0.9	Broadband subs per 100 pop.	3.1
Christian	0.2	Internet users, % of pop.	14.4
Jewish	<0.1		
Non-religious	<0.1		

BELGIUM

Area, sq km	30,280	Capital	Brussels
Arable as % of total land	27.0	Currency	Euro (€)

People

Population, m	11.3	Life expectancy: men	79.1 yrs
Pop. per sq km	373.2	women	83.7 yrs
Average annual growth in pop. 2015–20, %	0.6	Adult literacy	...
Pop. aged 0–24, %	28.6	Fertility rate (per woman)	1.8
Pop. aged 70 and over, %	12.8	Urban population, 2020, %	98.0
No. of men per 100 women	96.8		*per 1,000 pop.*
Human Development Index	89.6	Crude birth rate	11.4
		Crude death rate	9.7

The economy

GDP	$455bn	GDP per head	$40,295
GDP	€410bn	GDP per head in purchasing power parity (USA=100)	78.4
Av. ann. growth in real GDP 2010–15	0.9%	Economic freedom index	67.8

Origins of GDP	*% of total*	**Components of GDP**	*% of total*
Agriculture	1	Private consumption	51
Industry, of which:	22	Public consumption	24
manufacturing	14	Investment	23
Services	77	Exports	83
		Imports	-81

Structure of employment

	% of total		*% of labour force*
Agriculture	1.2	Unemployed 2015	8.5
Industry	21.4	Av. ann. rate 2005–15	8.0
Services	77.4		

Energy

	m TOE		
Total output	8.3	Net energy imports as % of energy use	76
Total consumption	61.2		
Consumption per head kg oil equivalent	4,699		

Inflation and finance

			av. ann. increase 2011–16
Consumer price inflation 2016	2.1%	Narrow money (M1)	8.1%
Av. ann. inflation 2011–16	3.3%	Broad money	3.60%
Treasury bill rate, Dec. 2016	-1.00%		

Exchange rates

	end 2016		*December 2016*
€ per $	0.95	Effective rates	2010 = 100
€ per sdr	1.28	– nominal	97.6
		– real	97.4

Trade

Principal exports

	$bn fob
Chemicals & related products	120.2
Machinery & transport equip.	85.8
Food, drink & tobacco	37.2
Mineral fuels & lubricants	33.2
Total incl. others	**398.1**

Principal imports

	$bn cif
Chemicals & related products	97.4
Machinery & transport equip.	90.1
Mineral fuels & lubricants	45.6
Food, drink & tobacco	31.3
Total incl. others	**375.7**

Main export destinations

	% of total
Germany	16.7
France	15.5
Netherlands	11.4
United Kingdom	8.8
EU28	71.9

Main origins of imports

	% of total
Netherlands	16.7
Germany	12.8
France	9.5
United States	8.7
EU28	62.8

Balance of payments, reserves and debt, $bn

Visible exports fob	254.8
Visible imports fob	-251.9
Trade balance	2.8
Invisibles inflows	164.1
Invisibles outflows	-157.6
Net transfers	-7.4
Current account balance	1.9
– as % of GDP	0.4
Capital balance	-4.0
Overall balance	-1.1
Change in reserves	-1.3
Level of reserves end Dec.	24.1
No. months of import cover	0.7
Official gold holdings, m oz	7.3
Aid given	1.9
– as % of GDP	0.4

Health and education

Health spending, % of GDP	10.6
Doctors per 1,000 pop.	4.9
Hospital beds per 1,000 pop.	6.5
Improved-water source access, % of pop.	100
Education spending, % of GDP	6.4
Enrolment, %: primary	105
secondary	165
tertiary	73

Society

No. of households, m	4.7
Av. no. per household	2.4
Marriages per 1,000 pop.	3.6
Divorces per 1,000 pop.	2.5
Religion, % of pop.	
Christian	64.2
Non-religious	29.0
Muslim	5.9
Other	0.6
Jewish	0.3
Hindu	<0.1
Cost of living, Dec. 2016 New York = 100	81
Cars per 1,000 pop.	496
Colour TV households, % with:	
cable	74.2
satellite	5.9
Telephone lines per 100 pop.	40.1
Mobile telephone subscribers per 100 pop.	115.7
Broadband subs per 100 pop.	36.8
Internet users, % of pop.	85.1

BRAZIL

Area, sq km	8,516,000	Capital	Brasília
Arable as % of total land	9.6	Currency	Real (R)

People

Population, m	207.8	Life expectancy: men	71.8 yrs
Pop. per sq km	24.4	women	79.1 yrs
Average annual growth in pop. 2015–20, %	0.8	Adult literacy	92.6
Pop. aged 0–24, %	39.5	Fertility rate (per woman)	1.8
Pop. aged 70 and over, %	5.0	Urban population, 2020, %	86.8
No. of men per 100 women	96.7		*per 1,000 pop.*
Human Development Index	75.4	Crude birth rate	14.0
		Crude death rate	6.3

The economy

GDP	$1,801bn	GDP per head	$8,669
GDP	R6,001bn	GDP per head in purchasing power parity (USA=100)	27.6
Av. ann. growth in real GDP 2010–15	1.0%	Economic freedom index	52.9

Origins of GDP	*% of total*	**Components of GDP**	*% of total*
Agriculture	5	Private consumption	64
Industry, of which:	22	Public consumption	20
manufacturing	12	Investment	18
Services	73	Exports	13
		Imports	-14

Structure of employment

	% of total		*% of labour force*
Agriculture	10.3	Unemployed 2015	8.5
Industry	22.2	Av. ann. rate 2005–15	9.0
Services	77.3		

Energy

	m TOE		
Total output	150.3	Net energy imports as % of energy use	12
Total consumption	320.9		
Consumption per head kg oil equivalent	1,471		

Inflation and finance

			av. ann. increase 2011–16
Consumer price inflation 2016	9.0%	Narrow money (M1)	3.9%
Av. ann. inflation 2011–16	7.8%	Broad money	11.8%
Treasury bill rate, Dec. 2016	12.27%		

Exchange rates

	end 2016		*December 2016*
R per $	3.26	Effective rates	2010 = 100
R per sdr	4.38	– nominal	68.17
R per €	3.73	– real	84.00

Trade

Principal exports	$bn fob
Primary products	87.2
Manufactured goods	72.8
Semi-manufactured goods	26.5
Total incl. others	**191.1**

Principal imports	$bn cif
Intermediate products & raw materials	81.2
Capital goods	37.7
Consumer goods	30.8
Fuels & lubricants	21.8
Total incl. others	**171.4**

Main export destinations	% of total
China	18.6
United States	12.7
Argentina	6.7
Netherlands	5.3

Main origins of imports	% of total
United States	19.0
China	16.5
Argentina	6.4
Netherlands	6.4

Balance of payments, reserves and debt, $bn

Visible exports fob	190.1
Visible imports fob	-172.4
Trade balance	17.7
Invisibles inflows	45.7
Invisibles outflows	-125.0
Net transfers	2.7
Current account balance	-58.9
– as % of GDP	-3.3
Capital balance	56.7
Overall balance	1.6
Change in reserves	-7.1
Level of reserves end Dec.	356.5
No. months of import cover	14.4
Official gold holdings, m oz	2.2
Foreign debt	543.4
– as % of GDP	30.2
– as % of total exports	227.7
Debt service ratio	37.6

Health and education

Health spending, % of GDP	8.3
Doctors per 1,000 pop.	1.9
Hospital beds per 1,000 pop.	2.3
Improved-water source access, % of pop.	98.1
Education spending, % of GDP	6.0
Enrolment, %: primary	111
secondary	102
tertiary	49

Society

No. of households, m	62.1
Av. no. per household	3.3
Marriages per 1,000 pop.	...
Divorces per 1,000 pop.	...
Religion, % of pop.	
Christian	88.9
Non-religious	7.9
Other	3.1
Hindu	<0.1
Jewish	<0.1
Muslim	<0.1
Cost of living, Dec. 2016 New York = 100	65
Cars per 1,000 pop.	162
Colour TV households, % with:	
cable	11.3
satellite	16.9
Telephone lines per 100 pop.	21.4
Mobile telephone subscribers per 100 pop.	126.6
Broadband subs per 100 pop.	12.2
Internet users, % of pop.	59.1

BULGARIA

Area, sq km	108,560	Capital	Sofia
Arable as % of total land	32.1	Currency	Lev (BGL)

People

Population, m	7.1	Life expectancy: men	71.1 yrs
Pop. per sq km	65.4	women	78.0 yrs
Average annual growth in pop. 2015–20, %	-0.8	Adult literacy	98.4
Pop. aged 0–24, %	23.8	Fertility rate (per woman)	1.5
Pop. aged 70 and over, %	13.3	Urban population, 2020, %	75.5
No. of men per 100 women	94.5		*per 1,000 pop.*
Human Development Index	79.4	Crude birth rate	9.5
		Crude death rate	15.6

The economy

GDP	$50bn	GDP per head	$7,070
GDP	BGL89bn	GDP per head in purchasing power parity (USA=100)	34.7
Av. ann. growth in real GDP 2010–15	1.5%	Economic freedom index	67.9

Origins of GDP		**Components of GDP**	
	% of total		*% of total*
Agriculture	5	Private consumption	63
Industry, of which:	28	Public consumption	16
manufacturing	...	Investment	21
Services	67	Exports	64
		Imports	-64

Structure of employment

	% of total		*% of labour force*
Agriculture	6.9	Unemployed 2015	9.1
Industry	29.9	Av. ann. rate 2005–15	9.6
Services	63.3		

Energy

	m TOE		
Total output	9.0	Net energy imports as % of energy use	37
Total consumption	19.5		
Consumption per head kg oil equivalent	2,478		

Inflation and finance

Consumer price inflation 2016	-1.6%		*av. ann. change 2011–16*
Av. ann. inflation 2011–16	2.3%	Narrow money (M1)	14.2%
Money market rate, Dec. 2016	-0.11%	Broad money	6.9%

Exchange rates

	end 2016		*December 2016*
BGL per $	1.86	Effective rates	2010 = 100
BGL per sdr	2.49	– nominal	107.60
BGL per €	1.96	– real	98.19

Trade

Principal exports	$bn fob
Raw materials	10.4
Consumer goods	6.8
Capital goods	5.4
Mineral fuels & lubricants	2.1
Total incl. others	**25.5**

Principal imports	$bn cif
Raw materials	10.7
Capital goods	7.5
Consumer goods	6.2
Mineral fuels & lubricants	3.6
Total incl. others	**29.2**

Main export destinations	% of total
Germany	12.6
Italy	9.3
Turkey	8.6
Romania	8.2
EU28	64.9

Main origins of imports	% of total
Germany	12.9
Russia	12.0
Italy	7.6
Romania	6.8
EU28	64.3

Balance of payments, reserves and debt, $bn

Visible exports fob	24.3
Visible imports fob	-27.2
Trade balance	-2.9
Invisibles inflows	8.8
Invisibles outflows	-7.8
Net transfers	1.8
Current account balance	-0.1
– as % of GDP	-0.1
Capital balance	2.7
Overall balance	4.0
Change in reserves	2.0
Level of reserves end Dec.	22.2
No. months of import cover	7.6
Official gold holdings, m oz	1.3
Foreign debt	37.5
– as % of GDP	74.7
– as % of total exports	108.0
Debt service ratio	30.3

Health and education

Health spending, % of GDP	8.4
Doctors per 1,000 pop.	3.9
Hospital beds per 1,000 pop.	6.4
Improved-water source access, % of pop.	99.4
Education spending, % of GDP	4.1
Enrolment, %: primary	97
secondary	99
tertiary	74

Society

No. of households, m	2.9
Av. no. per household	2.4
Marriages per 1,000 pop.	3.4
Divorces per 1,000 pop.	1.5
Religion, % of pop.	
Christian	82.1
Muslim	13.7
Non-religious	4.2
Hindu	<0.1
Jewish	<0.1
Other	<0.1
Cost of living, Dec. 2016 New York = 100	54
Cars per 1,000 pop.	419
Colour TV households, % with:	
cable	48.2
satellite	28.8
Telephone lines per 100 pop.	23.3
Mobile telephone subscribers per 100 pop.	129.3
Broadband subs per 100 pop.	22.7
Internet users, % of pop.	56.7

CAMEROON

Area, sq km	475,000	Capital	Yaoundé
Arable as % of total land	13.1	Currency	CFA franc (CFAfr)

People

Population, m	23.3	Life expectancy: men	55.9 yrs
Pop. per sq km	49.1	women	58.2 yrs
Average annual growth in pop. 2015–20, %	2.4	Adult literacy	75.0
Pop. aged 0–24, %	62.8	Fertility rate (per woman)	4.8
Pop. aged 70 and over, %	1.9	Urban population, 2020, %	57.1
			per 1,000 pop.
No. of men per 100 women	100.0	Crude birth rate	35.0
Human Development Index	51.8	Crude death rate	10.6

The economy

GDP	$28bn	GDP per head	$1,220
GDP	CFAfr16,807bn	GDP per head in purchasing power parity (USA=100)	5.6
Av. ann. growth in real GDP 2010–15	5.2%	Economic freedom index	51.8

Origins of GDP	*% of total*	**Components of GDP**	*% of total*
Agriculture	23	Private consumption	78
Industry, of which:	28	Public consumption	12
manufacturing	14	Investment	21
Services	49	Exports	20
		Imports	-30

Structure of employment

	% of total		*% of labour force*
Agriculture	...	Unemployed 2015	4.4
Industry	...	Av. ann. rate 2005–15	3.9
Services	...		

Energy

	m TOE		
Total output	4.5	Net energy imports as % of energy use	-28
Total consumption	3.9		
Consumption per head kg oil equivalent	334		

Inflation and finance

			av. ann. change 2011–16
Consumer price inflation 2016	2.2%	Narrow money (M1)	8.4%
Av. ann. inflation 2011–16	4.1%	Broad money	7.6%
Deposit rate, Jun. 2016	2.45%		

Exchange rates

	end 2016		*December 2016*
CFAfr per $	622.29	Effective rates	2010 = 100
CFAfr per sdr	836.56	– nominal	103.20
CFAfr per €	654.80	– real	98.16

Trade

Principal exports	$bn fob
Fuels	1.5
Cocoa beans & products	0.6
Timber	0.6
Cotton	0.1
Total incl. others	**5.2**

Principal imports	$bn cif
Manufactured products	3.2
Food	1.1
Fuels	1.1
Total incl. others	**5.6**

Main export destinations	% of total
Netherlands	16.3
India	15.6
China	12.5
Portugal	7.1

Main origins of imports	% of total
China	19.4
Nigeria	12.1
France	10.5
Belgium	4.9

Balance of payments, reserves and debt, $bn

Visible exports fob	5.2	Change in reserves	0.4
Visible imports fob	-5.6	Level of reserves end Dec.	3.5
Trade balance	-0.4	No. months of import cover	5.0
Invisibles inflows	1.7	Official gold holdings, m oz	0.0
Invisibles outflows	-2.8	Foreign debt	6.6
Net transfers	0.3	– as % of GDP	23.1
Current account balance	-1.2	– as % of total exports	91.6
– as % of GDP	-4.1	Debt service ratio	5.9
Capital balance	1.9		
Overall balance	0.7		

Health and education

Health spending, % of GDP	4.1	Education spending, % of GDP	3.0
Doctors per 1,000 pop.	...	Enrolment, %: primary	117
Hospital beds per 1,000 pop.	1.3	secondary	58
Improved-water source access, % of pop.	75.6	tertiary	18

Society

No. of households, m	4.4	Cost of living, Dec. 2016 New York = 100	...
Av. no. per household	5.3	Cars per 1,000 pop.	11
Marriages per 1,000 pop.	...	Colour TV households, % with: cable	...
Divorces per 1,000 pop.	...	satellite	2.4
Religion, % of pop.		Telephone lines per 100 pop.	4.5
Christian	70.3	Mobile telephone subscribers per 100 pop.	71.8
Muslim	18.3	Broadband subs per 100 pop.	0.1
Other	6.0	Internet users, % of pop.	20.7
Non-religious	5.3		
Hindu	<0.1		
Jewish	<0.1		

CANADA

Area, sq km[a]	9,985,000	Capital	Ottawa
Arable as % of total land	5.1	Currency	Canadian dollar (C$)

People

Population, m	35.9	Life expectancy: men	80.8 yrs
Pop. per sq km	3.6	women	84.4 yrs
Average annual growth in pop. 2015–20, %	0.9	Adult literacy	...
Pop. aged 0–24, %	28.8	Fertility rate (per woman)	1.6
Pop. aged 70 and over, %	10.8	Urban population, 2020, %	82.7
			per 1,000 pop.
No. of men per 100 women	98.4	Crude birth rate	10.5
Human Development Index	92.0	Crude death rate	7.5

The economy

GDP	$1,553bn	GDP per head	$43,254
GDP	C$1,986bn	GDP per head in purchasing power parity (USA=100)	81.4
Av. ann. growth in real GDP 2010–15	2.1%	Economic freedom index	78.5

Origins of GDP	*% of total*	**Components of GDP**	*% of total*
Agriculture	2	Private consumption	58
Industry, of which:	28	Public consumption	21
manufacturing	...	Investment	23
Services	70	Exports	31
		Imports	-33

Structure of employment

	% of total		*% of labour force*
Agriculture	1.6	Unemployed 2015	6.9
Industry	19.9	Av. ann. rate 2005–15	7.0
Services	78.4		

Energy

	m TOE		
Total output	417.8	Net energy imports as % of energy use	-68
Total consumption	364.2		
Consumption per head kg oil equivalent	7,874		

Inflation and finance

			av. ann. increase 2011–16
Consumer price inflation 2016	1.6%	Narrow money (M1)	7.6%
Av. ann. inflation 2011–16	3.4%	Broad money	8.1%
Treasury bill rate, Dec. 2016	0.47%		

Exchange rates

	end 2016		*December 2016*
C$ per $	1.34	Effective rates	2010 = 100
C$ per sdr	1.81	– nominal	83.38
C$ per €	1.41	– real	82.64

Trade

Principal exports	$bn fob
Motor vehicles & parts	68.1
Energy products	65.6
Consumer goods	54.2
Metal & mineral products	45.2
Total incl. others	**410.5**

Principal imports	$bn cif
Consumer goods	91.9
Motor vehicles & parts	78.5
Electronic & electrical equip.	49.4
Energy products	42.0
Total incl. others	**428.5**

Main export destinations	% of total
United States	76.7
China	3.9
United Kingdom	3.1
Japan	1.9
EU28	7.2

Main origins of imports	% of total
United States	53.1
China	12.2
Mexico	5.8
Germany	3.2
EU28	11.5

Balance of payments, reserves and aid, $bn

Visible exports fob	410.7
Visible imports fob	-428.8
Trade balance	-18.0
Invisibles inflows	151.3
Invisibles outflows	-183.5
Net transfers	-2.8
Current account balance	-53.1
– as % of GDP	-3.4
Capital balance	62.2
Overall balance	8.5
Change in reserves	5.1
Level of reserves end Dec.	79.8
No. months of import cover	1.6
Official gold holdings, m oz	0.1
Aid given	4.3
– as % of GDP	0.3

Health and education

Health spending, % of GDP	10.4
Doctors per 1,000 pop.	2.1
Hospital beds per 1,000 pop.	2.7
Improved-water source access, % of pop.	99.8
Education spending, % of GDP	5.3
Enrolment, %: primary	101
secondary	110
tertiary	...

Society

No. of households, m	14.0
Av. no. per household	2.6
Marriages per 1,000 pop.	...
Divorces per 1,000 pop.	...
Religion, % of pop.	
Christian	69.0
Non-religious	23.7
Other	2.8
Muslim	2.1
Hindu	1.4
Jewish	1.0
Cost of living, Dec. 2016 New York = 100	81
Cars per 1,000 pop.	612
Colour TV households, % with:	
cable	66.4
satellite	22.2
Telephone lines per 100 pop.	43.5
Mobile telephone subscribers per 100 pop.	83.0
Broadband subs per 100 pop.	36.3
Internet users, % of pop.	88.5

a Including freshwater.

CHILE

Area, sq km	743,532	Capital	Santiago
Arable as % of total land	1.7	Currency	Chilean peso (Ps)

People

Population, m	17.9	Life expectancy: men	79.8 yrs
Pop. per sq km	24.1	women	85.3 yrs
Average annual growth in pop. 2015–20, %	1.0	Adult literacy	96.6
Pop. aged 0–24, %	35.4	Fertility rate (per woman)	1.8
Pop. aged 70 and over, %	7.4	Urban population, 2020, %	90.3
No. of men per 100 women	97.4		*per 1,000 pop.*
Human Development Index	84.7	Crude birth rate	12.7
		Crude death rate	5.2

The economy

GDP	$243bn	GDP per head	$13,550
GDP	158.6trn pesos	GDP per head in purchasing power parity (USA=100)	42.5
Av. ann. growth in real GDP 2010–15	3.9%	Economic freedom index	76.5

Origins of GDP	*% of total*	**Components of GDP**	*% of total*
Agriculture	4	Private consumption	64
Industry, of which:	33	Public consumption	13
manufacturing	12	Investment	22
Services	63	Exports	30
		Imports	-30

Structure of employment

	% of total		*% of labour force*
Agriculture	9.6	Unemployed 2015	6.2
Industry	23.1	Av. ann. rate 2005–15	7.3
Services	67.3		

Energy

	m TOE		
Total output	2.3	Net energy imports as % of energy use	64
Total consumption	34.8		
Consumption per head kg oil equivalent	2,033		

Inflation and finance

			av. ann. increase 2011–16
Consumer price inflation 2016	4.0%	Narrow money (M1)	9.4%
Av. ann. inflation 2011–16	5.1%	Broad money	8.9%
Money market rate, Sep. 2016	3.50%		

Exchange rates

	end 2016		*December 2016*
Ps per $	667.29	Effective rates	2010 = 100
Ps per sdr	897.06	– nominal	98.52
Ps per €	702.16	– real	100.69

Trade

Principal exports	$bn fob
Copper	30.1
Fresh fruit	4.5
Cellulose & paper products	3.2
Total incl. others	**62.3**

Principal imports	$bn cif
Intermediate goods	32.2
Consumer goods	18.0
Capital goods	12.3
Total incl. others	**63.0**

Main export destinations	% of total
China	26.2
United States	13.2
Japan	8.5
South Korea	6.5

Main origins of imports	% of total
China	23.2
United States	18.7
Brazil	7.7
Argentina	4.0

Balance of payments, reserves and debt, $bn

Visible exports fob	62.2	Change in reserves	-1.8
Visible imports fob	-58.7	Level of reserves end Dec.	38.6
Trade balance	3.5	No. months of import cover	5.4
Invisibles inflows	17.1	Official gold holdings, m oz	0.0
Invisibles outflows	-27.1	Foreign debt	156.2
Net transfers	1.8	– as % of GDP	64.9
Current account balance	-4.8	– as % of total exports	201.1
– as % of GDP	-2.0	Debt service ratio	33.1
Capital balance	5.5		
Overall balance	0.2		

Health and education

Health spending, % of GDP	7.8	Education spending, % of GDP	4.8
Doctors per 1,000 pop.	1.0	Enrolment, %: primary	102
Hospital beds per 1,000 pop.	2.1	secondary	101
Improved-water source access, % of pop.	99.0	tertiary	89

Society

No. of households, m	6.2	Cost of living, Dec. 2016 New York = 100	65
Av. no. per household	2.9	Cars per 1,000 pop.	168
Marriages per 1,000 pop.	3.5	Colour TV households, % with: cable	34.2
Divorces per 1,000 pop.	0.1	satellite	5.2
Religion, % of pop.		Telephone lines per 100 pop.	19.2
Christian	89.4	Mobile telephone subscribers per 100 pop.	129.5
Non-religious	8.6	Broadband subs per 100 pop.	15.2
Other	1.9	Internet users, % of pop.	64.3
Jewish	0.1		
Hindu	<0.1		
Muslim	<0.1		

CHINA

Area, sq km	9,563,000	Capital	Beijing
Arable as % of total land	11.3	Currency	Yuan

People

Population, m	1,376.0	Life expectancy: men	75.3 yrs
Pop. per sq km	143.9	women	78.1 yrs
Average annual growth in pop. 2015–20, %	0.4	Adult literacy	96.4
Pop. aged 0–24, %	30.7	Fertility rate (per woman)	1.6
Pop. aged 70 and over, %	5.8	Urban population, 2020, %	61.0
No. of men per 100 women	106.3		*per 1,000 pop.*
Human Development Index	73.8	Crude birth rate	11.4
		Crude death rate	7.4

The economy

GDP	$11,226bn	GDP per head	$8,159
GDP	Yuan 69,911bn	GDP per head in purchasing power parity (USA=100)	25.5
Av. ann. growth in real GDP 2010–15	7.9%	Economic freedom index	57.4

Origins of GDP	*% of total*	**Components of GDP**	*% of total*
Agriculture	9	Private consumption	37
Industry, of which:	41	Public consumption	14
manufacturing	30	Investment	45
Services	50	Exports	22
		Imports	-18

Structure of employment

	% of total		*% of labour force*
Agriculture	28.3	Unemployed 2015	4.6
Industry	29.3	Av. ann. rate 2005–15	4.3
Services	42.4		

Energy

	m TOE		
Total output	2,395.7	Net energy imports as % of energy use	15
Total consumption	3,072.7		
Consumption per head kg oil equivalent	2,237		

Inflation and finance

			av. ann. increase 2011–16
Consumer price inflation 2016	2.1%	Narrow money (M1)	10.9%
Av. ann. inflation 2011–16	4.1%	Broad money	12.7%
Treasury bill rate, Dec. 2016	0.67%		

Exchange rates

	end 2016		*December 2016*
Yuan per $	6.95	Effective rates	2010 = 100
Yuan per sdr	9.34	– nominal	115.39
Yuan per €	7.31	– real	122.64

Trade

Principal exports	$bn fob
Telecoms equipment	296.5
Electrical goods	292.2
Office machinery	190.1
Clothing & apparel	174.4
Total incl. others	**2,273.5**

Principal imports	$bn cif
Electrical machinery	351.0
Petroleum products	161.0
Metal ores & scrap	110.4
Professional instruments	80.3
Total incl. others	**1,679.6**

Main export destinations	% of total
United States	18.1
Hong Kong	14.6
Japan	6.0
South Korea	4.5
EU28	15.6

Main origins of imports	% of total
South Korea	10.4
United States	8.6
Japan	8.5
Taiwan	8.5
EU28	12.4

Balance of payments, reserves and debt, $bn

Visible exports fob	2,142.8
Visible imports fob	-1,575.8
Trade balance	567.0
Invisibles inflows	514.3
Invisibles outflows	-742.1
Net transfers	-8.7
Current account balance	330.6
– as % of GDP	3.0
Capital balance	-485.3
Overall balance	-342.9
Change in reserves	-494.8
Level of reserves end Dec.	3,405.3
No. months of import cover	17.6
Official gold holdings, m oz	56.7
Foreign debt	1,418.3
– as % of GDP	12.6
– as % of total exports	52.5
Debt service ratio	4.6

Health and education

Health spending, % of GDP	5.5
Doctors per 1,000 pop.	1.9
Hospital beds per 1,000 pop.	3.8
Improved-water source access, % of pop.	95.5
Education spending, % of GDP	...
Enrolment, %: primary	104
secondary	94
tertiary	43

Society

No. of households, m	453.0
Av. no. per household	3.0
Marriages per 1,000 pop.	9.6
Divorces per 1,000 pop.	1.8
Religion, % of pop.	
Non-religious	52.2
Other	22.7
Buddhist	18.2
Christian	5.1
Muslim	1.8
Jewish	<0.1
Cost of living, Dec. 2016 New York = 100	79
Cars per 1,000 pop.	83
Colour TV households, % with:	
cable	50.0
satellite	...
Telephone lines per 100 pop.	16.5
Mobile telephone subscribers per 100 pop.	92.2
Broadband subs per 100 pop.	19.8
Internet users, % of pop.	50.3

Note: Data exclude Special Administrative Regions, ie, Hong Kong and Macau.

COLOMBIA

Area, sq km	1,142,000	Capital	Bogotá
Arable as % of total land	1.5	Currency	Colombian peso (peso)

People

Population, m	48.2	Life expectancy: men	71.2 yrs
Pop. per sq km	42.2	women	78.3 yrs
Average annual growth in pop. 2015–20, %	0.8	Adult literacy	94.6
Pop. aged 0–24, %	41.4	Fertility rate (per woman)	2.0
Pop. aged 70 and over, %	4.3	Urban population, 2020, %	77.8
No. of men per 100 women	97.0		*per 1,000 pop.*
Human Development Index	72.7	Crude birth rate	14.8
		Crude death rate	6.1

The economy

GDP	$292bn	GDP per head	$6,048
GDP	799trn pesos	GDP per head in purchasing power parity (USA=100)	24.7
Av. ann. growth in real GDP 2010–15	4.6%	Economic freedom index	69.7

Origins of GDP	*% of total*	Components of GDP	*% of total*
Agriculture	7	Private consumption	64
Industry, of which:	34	Public consumption	18
manufacturing	12	Investment	28
Services	59	Exports	15
		Imports	-24

Structure of employment

	% of total		*% of labour force*
Agriculture	15.8	Unemployed 2015	9.0
Industry	19.6	Av. ann. rate 2005–15	10.8
Services	64.6		

Energy

	m TOE		
Total output	116.8	Net energy imports as % of energy use	-274
Total consumption	41.7		
Consumption per head kg oil equivalent	712		

Inflation and finance

			av. ann. increase 2011–16
Consumer price inflation 2016	7.6%	Narrow money (M1)	6.0%
Av. ann. inflation 2011–16	5.0%	Broad money	10.6%
Money market rate, Dec. 2016	7.65%		

Exchange rates

	end 2016		*December 2016*
Peso per $	3,000.71	Effective rates	2010 = 100
Peso per sdr	4,033.94	– nominal	83.92
Peso per €	3,157.50	– real	68.51

Trade

Principal exports

	$bn fob
Petroleum & products	14.2
Coal	4.6
Coffee	2.5
Nickel	0.4
Total incl. others	**35.7**

Principal imports

	$bn cif
Intermediate goods & raw materials	23.3
Capital goods	18.6
Consumer goods	12.1
Total incl. others	**54.1**

Main export destinations

	% of total
United States	27.5
Panama	7.2
China	5.2
Spain	4.4

Main origins of imports

	% of total
United States	28.8
China	18.6
Mexico	7.1
Germany	4.2

Balance of payments, reserves and debt, $bn

Visible exports fob	38.1
Visible imports fob	-52.0
Trade balance	-14.0
Invisibles inflows	11.9
Invisibles outflows	-22.0
Net transfers	5.3
Current account balance	-18.8
– as % of GDP	-6.4
Capital balance	18.7
Overall balance	0.4
Change in reserves	-0.6
Level of reserves end Dec.	46.2
No. months of import cover	7.5
Official gold holdings, m oz	0.1
Foreign debt	111.0
– as % of GDP	38.0
– as % of total exports	203.4
Debt service ratio	25.6

Health and education

Health spending, % of GDP	7.2
Doctors per 1,000 pop.	1.5
Hospital beds per 1,000 pop.	1.5
Improved-water source access, % of pop.	91.4
Education spending, % of GDP	4.5
Enrolment, %: primary	114
secondary	98
tertiary	56

Society

No. of households, m	13.3
Av. no. per household	3.6
Marriages per 1,000 pop.	...
Divorces per 1,000 pop.	...
Religion, % of pop.	
Christian	92.5
Non-religious	6.6
Other	0.8
Hindu	<0.1
Jewish	<0.1
Muslim	<0.1
Cost of living, Dec. 2016 New York = 100	61
Cars per 1,000 pop.	62
Colour TV households, % with:	
cable	57.0
satellite	7.4
Telephone lines per 100 pop.	14.4
Mobile telephone subscribers per 100 pop.	115.7
Broadband subs per 100 pop.	11.2
Internet users, % of pop.	55.9

CZECH REPUBLIC

Area, sq km	77,210	Capital	Prague
Arable as % of total land	40.7	Currency	Koruna (Kc)

People

Population, m	10.5	Life expectancy: men	76.3 yrs
Pop. per sq km	136.0	women	81.9 yrs
Average annual growth in pop. 2015–20, %	0.1	Adult literacy	...
Pop. aged 0–24, %	25.1	Fertility rate (per woman)	1.4
Pop. aged 70 and over, %	11.6	Urban population, 2020, %	73.1
No. of men per 100 women	96.6		*per 1,000 pop.*
Human Development Index	87.8	Crude birth rate	10.0
		Crude death rate	10.6

The economy

GDP	$185bn	GDP per head	$17,634
GDP	Kc4,555bn	GDP per head in purchasing power parity (USA=100)	57.4
Av. ann. growth in real GDP 2010–15	1.6%	Economic freedom index	73.3

Origins of GDP	*% of total*	**Components of GDP**	*% of total*
Agriculture	3	Private consumption	47
Industry, of which:	38	Public consumption	20
manufacturing	27	Investment	27
Services	60	Exports	83
		Imports	-77

Structure of employment

	% of total		*% of labour force*
Agriculture	2.9	Unemployed 2015	5.1
Industry	38.0	Av. ann. rate 2005–15	6.4
Services	59.0		

Energy

	m TOE		
Total output	27.8	Net energy imports as % of energy use	29
Total consumption	40.7		
Consumption per head kg oil equivalent	3,915		

Inflation and finance

			av. ann. increase 2011–16
Consumer price inflation 2016	0.6%	Narrow money (M1)	9.7%
Av. ann. inflation 2011–16	3.4%	Broad money	4.0%
Treasury bill rate, Dec. 2016	-1.19%		

Exchange rates

	end 2016		*December 2016*
Kc per $	25.64	Effective rates	2010 = 100
Kc per sdr	34.47	– nominal	91.10
Kc per €	26.98	– real	91.49

Trade

Principal exports

	$bn fob
Machinery & transport equip.	87.5
Semi-manufactures	25.0
Miscellaneous manufactured goods	19.4
Chemicals	9.8
Total incl. others	**157.9**

Principal imports

	$bn cif
Machinery & transport equip.	64.6
Semi-manufactures	24.1
Chemicals	15.9
Miscellaneous manufactured goods	15.7
Total incl. others	**141.4**

Main export destinations

	% of total
Germany	32.1
Slovakia	9.0
Poland	5.9
United Kingdom	5.3
EU28	83.3

Main origins of imports

	% of total
Germany	29.9
Poland	9.0
China	8.3
Slovakia	6.5
EU28	77.3

Balance of payments, reserves and debt, $bn

Visible exports fob	128.2
Visible imports fob	-120.5
Trade balance	7.6
Invisibles inflows	30.2
Invisibles outflows	-37.4
Net transfers	0.0
Current account balance	0.5
– as % of GDP	0.2
Capital balance	11.3
Overall balance	14.3
Change in reserves	10.0
Level of reserves end Dec.	64.5
No. months of import cover	4.9
Official gold holdings, m oz	0.3
Foreign debt	126.3
– as % of GDP	68.2
– as % of total exports	77.1
Debt service ratio	10.0

Health and education

Health spending, % of GDP	7.4
Doctors per 1,000 pop.	3.6
Hospital beds per 1,000 pop.	6.8
Improved-water source access, % of pop.	100
Education spending, % of GDP	...
Enrolment, %: primary	99
secondary	104
tertiary	65

Society

No. of households, m	4.4
Av. no. per household	2.3
Marriages per 1,000 pop.	4.3
Divorces per 1,000 pop.	2.5
Religion, % of pop.	
Non-religious	76.4
Christian	23.3
Other	0.2
Hindu	<0.1
Jewish	<0.1
Muslim	<0.1
Cost of living, Dec. 2016 New York = 100	62
Cars per 1,000 pop.	461
Colour TV households, % with:	
cable	24.5
satellite	27.0
Telephone lines per 100 pop.	17.6
Mobile telephone subscribers per 100 pop.	123.2
Broadband subs per 100 pop.	27.3
Internet users, % of pop.	81.3

DENMARK

Area, sq km	42,262	Capital	Copenhagen
Arable as % of total land	57.5	Currency	Danish krone (DKr)

People

Population, m	5.7	Life expectancy: men	78.9 yrs
Pop. per sq km	134.9	women	82.3 yrs
Average annual growth in pop. 2015–20, %	0.4	Adult literacy	...
Pop. aged 0–24, %	30.0	Fertility rate (per woman)	1.7
Pop. aged 70 and over, %	12.3	Urban population, 2020, %	88.5
No. of men per 100 women	98.6		*per 1,000 pop.*
Human Development Index	92.5	Crude birth rate	10.7
		Crude death rate	9.6

The economy

GDP	$301bn	GDP per head	$52,861
GDP	DKr2,027bn	GDP per head in purchasing power parity (USA=100)	83.7
Av. ann. growth in real GDP 2010–15	0.6%	Economic freedom index	75.1

Origins of GDP	*% of total*	**Components of GDP**	*% of total*
Agriculture	1	Private consumption	47
Industry, of which:	23	Public consumption	26
manufacturing	15	Investment	20
Services	76	Exports	55
		Imports	-48

Structure of employment

	% of total		*% of labour force*
Agriculture	2.5	Unemployed 2015	6.2
Industry	19.2	Av. ann. rate 2005–15	5.8
Services	78.0		

Energy

	m TOE		
Total output	13.1	Net energy imports as % of energy use	1
Total consumption	18.0		
Consumption per head kg oil equivalent	2,873		

Inflation and finance

			av. ann. increase 2011–16
Consumer price inflation 2016	0.4%	Narrow money (M1)	7.6%
Av. ann. inflation 2011–16	3.1%	Broad money	4.0%
Treasury bill rate, Dec. 2016	-0.49%		

Exchange rates

	end 2016		*December 2016*
DKr per $	7.05	Effective rates	2010 = 100
DKr per sdr	9.48	– nominal	98.41
DKr per €	7.42	– real	95.59

Trade

Principal exports

	$bn fob
Machinery & transport equip.	25.1
Chemicals & related products	19.0
Food, drink & tobacco	17.3
Mineral fuels & lubricants	5.7
Total incl. others	**94.6**

Principal imports

	$bn cif
Machinery & transport equip.	27.9
Food, drink & tobacco	11.7
Chemicals & related products	10.7
Mineral fuels & lubricants	5.6
Total incl. others	**85.3**

Main export destinations

	% of total
Germany	18.1
Sweden	11.7
United States	8.5
United Kingdom	6.4
EU28	61.3

Main origins of imports

	% of total
Germany	20.5
Sweden	12.3
Netherlands	8.2
China	7.3
EU28	69.5

Balance of payments, reserves and aid, $bn

Visible exports fob	102.6
Visible imports fob	-87.5
Trade balance	15.1
Invisibles inflows	93.0
Invisibles outflows	-75.6
Net transfers	-4.8
Current account balance	27.6
– as % of GDP	9.2
Capital balance	-24.7
Overall balance	-3.1
Change in reserves	-10.2
Level of reserves end Dec.	65.2
No. months of import cover	4.8
Official gold holdings, m oz	2.1
Aid given	2.6
– as % of GDP	0.9

Health and education

Health spending, % of GDP	10.8
Doctors per 1,000 pop.	3.5
Hospital beds per 1,000 pop.	3.5
Improved-water source access, % of pop.	100
Education spending, % of GDP	8.6
Enrolment, %: primary	101
secondary	130
tertiary	82

Society

No. of households, m	2.4
Av. no. per household	2.4
Marriages per 1,000 pop.	5.0
Divorces per 1,000 pop.	3.4
Religion, % of pop.	
Christian	83.5
Non-religious	11.8
Muslim	4.1
Hindu	0.4
Other	0.2
Jewish	<0.1
Cost of living, Dec. 2016 New York = 100	100
Cars per 1,000 pop.	417
Colour TV households, % with:	
cable	65.3
satellite	11.8
Telephone lines per 100 pop.	29.9
Mobile telephone subscribers per 100 pop.	128.3
Broadband subs per 100 pop.	42.5
Internet users, % of pop.	96.3

EGYPT

Area, sq km	1,001,000	Capital	Cairo
Arable as % of total land	2.7	Currency	Egyptian pound (£E)

People

Population, m	91.5	Life expectancy: men	69.6 yrs
Pop. per sq km	91.4	women	74.1 yrs
Average annual growth in pop. 2015–20, %	1.9	Adult literacy	75.8
Pop. aged 0–24, %	50.5	Fertility rate (per woman)	2.8
Pop. aged 70 and over, %	3.0	Urban population, 2020, %	43.8
No. of men per 100 women	102.1		*per 1,000 pop.*
Human Development Index	69.1	Crude birth rate	25.1
		Crude death rate	5.9

The economy

GDP	$332bn	GDP per head	$3,629
GDP	£E2,444bn	GDP per head in purchasing power parity (USA=100)	20.9
Av. ann. growth in real GDP 2010–15	2.5%	Economic freedom index	52.6

Origins of GDP	*% of total*	**Components of GDP**	*% of total*
Agriculture	11	Private consumption	82
Industry, of which:	36	Public consumption	12
manufacturing	17	Investment	14
Services	52	Exports	13
		Imports	-22

Structure of employment

	% of total		*% of labour force*
Agriculture	25.8	Unemployed 2015	12.8
Industry	25.1	Av. ann. rate 2005–15	11.0
Services	49.1		

Energy

	m TOE		
Total output	81.7	Net energy imports as % of energy use	-7
Total consumption	89.6		
Consumption per head kg oil equivalent	835		

Inflation and finance

			av. ann. increase 2011–16
Consumer price inflation 2016	10.2%	Narrow money (M1)	19.6%
Av. ann. inflation 2011–16	9.7%	Broad money	20.7%
Treasury bill rate, Dec. 2016	19.03%		

Exchange rates

	end 2016		*December 2016*
£E per $	18.13	Effective rates	2010 = 100
£E per sdr	24.37	– nominal	...
£E per €	19.08	– real	...

Trade

Principal exports

	$bn fob
Petroleum & products	8.9
Finished goods incl. textiles	2.0
Chemicals	1.9
Food	1.8
Total incl. others	**19.0**

Principal imports

	$bn cif
Petroleum & products	12.4
Machinery & equip.	6.9
Vehicles	5.9
Chemicals	5.6
Total incl. others	**57.6**

Main export destinations

	% of total
Saudi Arabia	9.1
Italy	7.5
Turkey	5.8
United Arab Emirates	5.1

Main origins of imports

	% of total
China	13.0
Germany	7.7
United States	5.9
Turkey	4.5

Balance of payments, reserves and debt, $bn

Visible exports fob	19.0
Visible imports fob	-50.1
Trade balance	-31.0
Invisibles inflows	18.8
Invisibles outflows	-22.8
Net transfers	18.2
Current account balance	-16.8
– as % of GDP	-5.1
Capital balance	21.1
Overall balance	-0.4
Change in reserves	0.9
Level of reserves end Dec.	15.9
No. months of import cover	2.6
Official gold holdings, m oz	2.4
Foreign debt	46.6
– as % of GDP	15.9
– as % of total exports	82.9
Debt service ratio	8.9

Health and education

Health spending, % of GDP	5.6
Doctors per 1,000 pop.	2.8
Hospital beds per 1,000 pop.	0.5
Improved-water source access, % of pop.	99.4
Education spending, % of GDP	...
Enrolment, %: primary	104
secondary	86
tertiary	36

Society

No. of households, m	23.4
Av. no. per household	3.9
Marriages per 1,000 pop.	11.0
Divorces per 1,000 pop.	2.1
Religion, % of pop.	
Muslim	94.9
Christian	5.1
Hindu	<0.1
Jewish	<0.1
Non-religious	<0.1
Other	<0.1
Cost of living, Dec. 2016 New York = 100	59
Cars per 1,000 pop.	47
Colour TV households, % with:	
cable	...
satellite	71.6
Telephone lines per 100 pop.	7.4
Mobile telephone subscribers per 100 pop.	111.0
Broadband subs per 100 pop.	4.5
Internet users, % of pop.	37.8

FINLAND

Area, sq km	303,890	Capital	Helsinki
Arable as % of total land	7.3	Currency	Euro (€)

People

Population, m	5.5	Life expectancy: men	78.8 yrs
Pop. per sq km	18.1	women	84.1 yrs
Average annual growth in pop. 2015–20, %	0.3	Adult literacy	...
Pop. aged 0–24, %	28.2	Fertility rate (per woman)	1.8
Pop. aged 70 and over, %	13.1	Urban population, 2020, %	84.9
No. of men per 100 women	96.9		*per 1,000 pop.*
Human Development Index	89.5	Crude birth rate	10.7
		Crude death rate	9.9

The economy

GDP	$232bn	GDP per head	$42,269
GDP	€210bn	GDP per head in purchasing power parity (USA=100)	73.1
Av. ann. growth in real GDP 2010–15	0.0%	Economic freedom index	74.0

Origins of GDP	*% of total*	**Components of GDP**	*% of total*
Agriculture	2	Private consumption	55
Industry, of which:	27	Public consumption	24
manufacturing	17	Investment	21
Services	71	Exports	37
		Imports	-37

Structure of employment

	% of total		*% of labour force*
Agriculture	4.2	Unemployed 2015	9.4
Industry	21.6	Av. ann. rate 2005–15	8.0
Services	73.8		

Energy

	m TOE		
Total output	5.8	Net energy imports as % of energy use	46
Total consumption	29.0		
Consumption per head kg oil equivalent	6,213		

Inflation and finance

			av. ann. increase 2011–16
Consumer price inflation 2016	0.4%	Narrow money (M1)	8.1%
Av. ann. inflation 2011–16	3.6%	Broad money	3.6%
Money market rate, Dec. 2016	-0.32%		

Exchange rates

	end 2016		*December 2016*
€ per $	0.95	Effective rates	2010 = 100
€ per sdr	1.28	– nominal	99.71
		– real	96.37

Trade

Principal exports

	$bn fob
Machinery & transport equip.	19.0
Chemicals & related products	6.3
Raw materials	5.3
Mineral fuels & lubricants	4.3
Total incl. others	**59.7**

Principal imports

	$bn cif
Machinery & transport equip.	20.6
Mineral fuels & lubricants	8.6
Chemicals & related products	7.7
Food, drink & tobacco	4.8
Total incl. others	**57.5**

Main export destinations

	% of total
Germany	13.9
Sweden	10.1
United States	7.0
Netherlands	6.6
EU28	58.9

Main origins of imports

	% of total
Germany	17.8
Sweden	16.9
Russia	11.5
Netherlands	9.5
EU28	73.0

Balance of payments, reserves and aid, $bn

Visible exports fob	59.6
Visible imports fob	-57.5
Trade balance	2.2
Invisibles inflows	42.1
Invisibles outflows	-43.1
Net transfers	-2.6
Current account balance	-1.4
– as % of GDP	-0.6
Capital balance	2.4
Overall balance	-0.2
Change in reserves	-0.7
Level of reserves end Dec.	10.0
No. months of import cover	1.2
Official gold holdings, m oz	1.6
Aid given	1.3
– as % of GDP	0.6

Health and education

Health spending, % of GDP	9.7
Doctors per 1,000 pop.	2.9
Hospital beds per 1,000 pop.	5.5
Improved-water source access, % of pop.	100
Education spending, % of GDP	7.2
Enrolment, %: primary	102
secondary	149
tertiary	87

Society

No. of households, m	2.6
Av. no. per household	2.1
Marriages per 1,000 pop.	4.5
Divorces per 1,000 pop.	2.5
Religion, % of pop.	
Christian	81.6
Non-religious	17.6
Muslim	0.8
Hindu	<0.1
Jewish	<0.1
Other	<0.1
Cost of living, Dec. 2016 New York = 100	92
Cars per 1,000 pop.	592
Colour TV households, % with:	
cable	68.5
satellite	11.1
Telephone lines per 100 pop.	9.8
Mobile telephone subscribers per 100 pop.	135.4
Broadband subs per 100 pop.	31.7
Internet users, % of pop.	92.7

FRANCE

Area, sq km	549,000	Capital	Paris
Arable as % of total land	33.5	Currency	Euro (€)

People

Population, m	64.4	Life expectancy: men	80.0 yrs
Pop. per sq km	117.3	women	85.6 yrs
Average annual growth in pop. 2015–20, %	0.4	Adult literacy	...
Pop. aged 0–24, %	30.1	Fertility rate (per woman)	2.1
Pop. aged 70 and over, %	13.2	Urban population, 2020, %	80.6
No. of men per 100 women	94.8		*per 1,000 pop.*
Human Development Index	89.7	Crude birth rate	11.9
		Crude death rate	9.1

The economy

GDP	$2,420bn	GDP per head	$37,580
GDP	€2,181bn	GDP per head in purchasing power parity (USA=100)	73.9
Av. ann. growth in real GDP 2010–15	0.9%	Economic freedom index	63.3

Origins of GDP	*% of total*	**Components of GDP**	*% of total*
Agriculture	2	Private consumption	55
Industry, of which:	20	Public consumption	24
manufacturing	11	Investment	22
Services	79	Exports	30
		Imports	-31

Structure of employment

	% of total		*% of labour force*
Agriculture	2.7	Unemployed 2015	10.4
Industry	20.1	Av. ann. rate 2005–15	9.3
Services	75.9		

Energy

	m TOE		
Total output	109.4	Net energy imports as % of energy use	43
Total consumption	254.2		
Consumption per head kg oil equivalent	3,661		

Inflation and finance

			av. ann. increase 2011–16
Consumer price inflation 2016	0.3%	Narrow money (M1)	8.1%
Av. ann. inflation 2011–16	3.1%	Broad money	3.6%
Treasury bill rate, Dec. 2016	-0.85%		

Exchange rates

	end 2016		*December 2016*
€ per $	0.95	Effective rates	2010 = 100
€ per sdr	1.28	– nominal	96.57
		– real	92.80

Trade

Principal exports

	$bn fob
Machinery & transport equip.	197.8
Chemicals & related products	93.9
Food, drink and tobacco	60.9
Mineral fuels & lubricants	16.3
Total incl. others	**505.4**

Principal imports

	$bn cif
Machinery & transport equip.	204.6
Chemicals & related products	79.9
Mineral fuels & lubricants	59.7
Food, drink and tobacco	51.0
Total incl. others	**555.5**

Main export destinations

	% of total
Germany	15.8
Spain	7.3
United States	7.2
Italy	7.1
EU28	58.8

Main origins of imports

	% of total
Germany	20.1
Belgium	11.2
Italy	7.9
Netherlands	7.8
EU28	68.5

Balance of payments, reserves and aid, $bn

Visible exports fob	510.8
Visible imports fob	-537.5
Trade balance	-26.7
Invisibles inflows	419.8
Invisibles outflows	-352.2
Net transfers	-45.7
Current account balance	-4.9
– as % of GDP	-0.2
Capital balance	18.6
Overall balance	8.0
Change in reserves	-5.8
Level of reserves end Dec.	138.2
No. months of import cover	1.9
Official gold holdings, m oz	78.3
Aid given	9.0
– as % of GDP	0.4

Health and education

Health spending, % of GDP	11.5
Doctors per 1,000 pop.	3.2
Hospital beds per 1,000 pop.	6.4
Improved-water source access, % of pop.	100
Education spending, % of GDP	5.5
Enrolment, %: primary	105
secondary	111
tertiary	64

Society

No. of households, m	29.3
Av. no. per household	2.2
Marriages per 1,000 pop.	3.7
Divorces per 1,000 pop.	1.9
Religion, % of pop.	
Christian	63.0
Non-religious	28.0
Muslim	7.5
Other	1.0
Jewish	0.5
Hindu	<0.1
Cost of living, Dec. 2016 New York = 100	107
Cars per 1,000 pop.	492
Colour TV households, % with:	
cable	13.1
satellite	34.1
Telephone lines per 100 pop.	59.9
Mobile telephone subscribers per 100 pop.	102.6
Broadband subs per 100 pop.	41.3
Internet users, % of pop.	84.7

GERMANY

Area, sq km	357,000	Capital	Berlin
Arable as % of total land	34.1	Currency	Euro (€)

People

Population, m	80.7	Life expectancy: men	79.3 yrs
Pop. per sq km	226.1	women	83.8 yrs
Average annual growth in pop. 2015–20, %	-0.1	Adult literacy	...
Pop. aged 0–24, %	23.3	Fertility rate (per woman)	1.4
Pop. aged 70 and over, %	16.1	Urban population, 2020, %	76.4
			per 1,000 pop.
No. of men per 100 women	96.6	Crude birth rate	8.7
Human Development Index	92.6	Crude death rate	11.3

The economy

GDP	$3,365bn	GDP per head	$41,701
GDP	€3,033bn	GDP per head in purchasing power parity (USA=100)	85.3
Av. ann. growth in real GDP 2010–15	1.6%	Economic freedom index	73.8

Origins of GDP	*% of total*	**Components of GDP**	*% of total*
Agriculture	1	Private consumption	54
Industry, of which:	30	Public consumption	19
manufacturing	23	Investment	19
Services	69	Exports	47
		Imports	-39

Structure of employment

	% of total		*% of labour force*
Agriculture	1.4	Unemployed 2015	4.6
Industry	27.7	Av. ann. rate 2005–15	7.1
Services	70.9		

Energy

	m TOE		
Total output	72.7	Net energy imports as % of energy use	61
Total consumption	321.8		
Consumption per head kg oil equivalent	3,779		

Inflation and finance

			av. ann. increase 2011–16
Consumer price inflation 2016	0.4%	Narrow money (M1)	8.1%
Av. ann. inflation 2011–16	3.2%	Broad money	3.6%
Deposit rate, Dec. 2016	0.23%		

Exchange rates

	end 2016		*December 2016*
€ per $	0.95	Effective rates	2010 = 100
€ per sdr	1.28	– nominal	98.05
		– real	94.33

Trade

Principal exports

	$bn fob
Machinery & transport equip.	658.6
Chemicals & related products	210.8
Food, drink and tobacco	71.3
Mineral fuels & lubricants	32.3
Total incl. others	**1,320.7**

Principal imports

	$bn cif
Machinery & transport equip.	387.5
Chemicals & related products	145.2
Mineral fuels & lubricants	98.6
Food, drink and tobacco	79.4
Total incl. others	**1,051.6**

Main export destinations

	% of total
United States	9.6
France	8.6
United Kingdom	7.5
Netherlands	6.7
EU28	57.9

Main origins of imports

	% of total
Netherlands	13.6
France	7.6
China	7.3
Belgium	6.0
EU28	65.6

Balance of payments, reserves and aid, $bn

Visible exports fob	1,305.7
Visible imports fob	-1,017.8
Trade balance	287.9
Invisibles inflows	480.5
Invisibles outflows	-444.4
Net transfers	-44.0
Current account balance	280.0
– as % of GDP	8.3
Capital balance	-252.2
Overall balance	-2.4
Change in reserves	-19.8
Level of reserves end Dec.	173.7
No. months of import cover	1.4
Official gold holdings, m oz	108.7
Aid given	17.9
– as % of GDP	0.5

Health and education

Health spending, % of GDP	11.3
Doctors per 1,000 pop.	3.9
Hospital beds per 1,000 pop.	8.2
Improved-water source access, % of pop.	100
Education spending, % of GDP	4.9
Enrolment, %: primary	105
secondary	103
tertiary	68

Society

No. of households, m	41.6
Av. no. per household	1.9
Marriages per 1,000 pop.	4.8
Divorces per 1,000 pop.	2.1
Religion, % of pop.	
Christian	68.7
Non-religious	24.7
Muslim	5.8
Other	0.5
Jewish	0.3
Hindu	<0.1
Cost of living, Dec. 2016 New York = 100	77
Cars per 1,000 pop.	537
Colour TV households, % with:	
cable	46.0
satellite	45.1
Telephone lines per 100 pop.	54.9
Mobile telephone subscribers per 100 pop.	116.7
Broadband subs per 100 pop.	37.2
Internet users, % of pop.	87.6

GREECE

Area, sq km	128,900	Capital	Athens
Arable as % of total land	20.2	Currency	Euro (€)

People

Population, m	11.0	Life expectancy: men	78.8
Pop. per sq km	85.3	women	84.3
Average annual growth in pop. 2015–20, %	-0.2	Adult literacy	95.3
Pop. aged 0–24, %	24.8	Fertility rate (per woman)	1.4
Pop. aged 70 and over, %	15.4	Urban population, 2020, %	79.5
No. of men per 100 women	95.3		*per 1,000 pop.*
Human Development Index	86.6	Crude birth rate	8.0
		Crude death rate	11.3

The economy

GDP	$195bn	GDP per head	$17,723
GDP	€176bn	GDP per head in purchasing power parity (USA=100)	46.3
Av. ann. growth in real GDP 2010–15	-3.9%	Economic freedom index	55.0

Origins of GDP	*% of total*	**Components of GDP**	*% of total*
Agriculture	4	Private consumption	70
Industry, of which:	16	Public consumption	20
manufacturing	9	Investment	10
Services	80	Exports	32
		Imports	-32

Structure of employment

	% of total		*% of labour force*
Agriculture	12.9	Unemployed 2015	24.9
Industry	14.9	Av. ann. rate 2005–15	16.2
Services	72.2		

Energy

	m TOE		
Total output	5.9	Net energy imports as % of energy use	62
Total consumption	26.3		
Consumption per head kg oil equivalent	2,124		

Inflation and finance

			av. ann. increase 2011–16
Consumer price inflation 2016	-0.1%	Narrow money (M1)	8.1%
Av. ann. inflation 2011–16	1.8%	Broad money	3.6%
Treasury bill rate, Dec. 2016	-0.08%		

Exchange rates

	end 2016		*December 2016*
€ per $	0.95	Effective rates	2010 = 100
€ per sdr	1.28	– nominal	98.42
		– real	89.30

Trade

Principal exports

	$bn fob
Mineral fuels & lubricants	8.4
Food, drink and tobacco	5.1
Chemicals & related products	3.0
Machinery & transport equip.	2.9
Total incl. others	**28.7**

Principal imports

	$bn cif
Mineral fuels & lubricants	12.6
Machinery & transport equip.	9.7
Chemicals & related products	7.6
Food, drink and tobacco	6.3
Total incl. others	**48.4**

Main export destinations

	% of total
Italy	11.3
Germany	7.3
Turkey	6.6
Cyprus	6.0
EU28	54.2

Main origins of imports

	% of total
Germany	10.8
Italy	8.3
Russia	7.8
Iraq	6.9
EU28	52.9

Balance of payments, reserves and debt, $bn

Visible exports fob	27.5
Visible imports fob	-46.6
Trade balance	-19.1
Invisibles inflows	39.3
Invisibles outflows	-19.4
Net transfers	-0.6
Current account balance	0.2
– as % of GDP	0.1
Capital balance	9.1
Overall balance	10.6
Change in reserves	-0.2
Level of reserves end Dec.	6.0
No. months of import cover	1.1
Official gold holdings, m oz	3.6
Aid given	0.2
– as % of GDP	0.1

Health and education

Health spending, % of GDP	8.1
Doctors per 1,000 pop.	6.2
Hospital beds per 1,000 pop.	...
Improved-water source access, % of pop.	100
Education spending, % of GDP	...
Enrolment, %: primary	98
secondary	107
tertiary	114

Society

No. of households, m	4.4
Av. no. per household	2.5
Marriages per 1,000 pop.	4.9
Divorces per 1,000 pop.	1.5
Religion, % of pop.	
Christian	88.1
Non-religious	6.1
Muslim	5.3
Other	0.3
Hindu	0.1
Jewish	<0.1
Cost of living, Dec. 2016 New York = 100	63
Cars per 1,000 pop.	460
Colour TV households, % with:	
cable	0.9
satellite	13.5
Telephone lines per 100 pop.	47.3
Mobile telephone subscribers per 100 pop.	113.0
Broadband subs per 100 pop.	30.9
Internet users, % of pop.	66.8

HONG KONG

Area, sq km	1,050	Capital	Victoria
Arable as % of total land	3.0	Currency	Hong Kong dollar (HK$)

People

Population, m	7.3	Life expectancy: men	81.7
Pop. per sq km	6,952.4	women	87.4
Average annual growth in pop. 2015–20, %	0.7	Adult literacy	...
Pop. aged 0–24, %	23.2	Fertility rate (per woman)	1.2
Pop. aged 70 and over, %	10.2	Urban population, 2020, %	100.0
No. of men per 100 women	88.5		*per 1,000 pop.*
Human Development Index	91.7	Crude birth rate	9.8
		Crude death rate	6.6

The economy

GDP	$309bn	GDP per head	$42,384
GDP	HK$2,398bn	GDP per head in purchasing power parity (USA=100)	101.7
Av. ann. growth in real GDP 2010–15	2.9%	Economic freedom index	89.8

Origins of GDP	*% of total*	**Components of GDP**	*% of total*
Agriculture	0	Private consumption	66
Industry, of which:	7	Public consumption	10
manufacturing	1	Investment	22
Services	92	Exports	202
		Imports	-199

Structure of employment

	% of total		*% of labour force*
Agriculture	...	Unemployed 2015	3.3
Industry	11.4	Av. ann. rate 2005–15	4.0
Services	79.4		

Energy

	m TOE		
Total output	...	Net energy imports as % of energy use	99
Total consumption	29.7		
Consumption per head kg oil equivalent	1,967		

Inflation and finance

			av. ann. increase 2011–16
Consumer price inflation 2016	2.5%	Narrow money (M1)	14.5%
Av. ann. inflation 2011–16	5.5%	Broad money	9.2%
Treasury bill rate, Dec. 2016	0.67%		

Exchange rates

	end 2016		*December 2016*
HK$ per $	7.75	Effective rates	2010 = 100
HK$ per sdr	10.42	– nominal	109.39
HK$ per €	8.15	– real	...

Trade

Principal exports[a]	$bn fob	Principal imports[a]	$bn cif
Capital goods	192.2	Capital goods & raw materials	193.7
Semi-finished goods	159.8	Raw materials & semi-manufactures	182.9
Consumer goods	100.7	Consumer goods	111.6
Foodstuffs	6.3	Foodstuffs	22.3
Total incl. others	**465.5**	Total incl. others	**522.6**

Main export destinations	% of total	Main origins of imports	% of total
China	53.7	China	49.0
United States	9.5	Taiwan	6.8
Japan	3.4	Japan	6.4
India	2.8	Singapore	6.1

Balance of payments, reserves and debt, $bn

Visible exports fob	501.7	Change in reserves	30.3
Visible imports fob	-524.6	Level of reserves end Dec.	358.8
Trade balance	-22.9	No. months of import cover	5.7
Invisibles inflows	268.8	Official gold holdings, m oz	0.1
Invisibles outflows	-232.8	Foreign debt	491.9
Net transfers	-2.9	– as % of GDP	159.0
Current account balance	10.3	– as % of total exports	63.7
– as % of GDP	3.3	Debt service ratio	6.3
Capital balance	19.8		
Overall balance	36.4		

Health and education

Health spending, % of GDP	...	Education spending, % of GDP	3.3
Doctors per 1,000 pop.	...	Enrolment, %: primary	111
Hospital beds per 1,000 pop.	...	secondary	101
Improved-water source access, % of pop.	...	tertiary	68

Society

No. of households, m	2.4	Cost of living, Dec. 2016 New York = 100	114
Av. no. per household	3.0	Cars per 1,000 pop.	70
Marriages per 1,000 pop.	7.8	Colour TV households, % with: cable	94.4
Divorces per 1,000 pop.	...	satellite	0.1
Religion, % of pop.		Telephone lines per 100 pop.	59.2
Non-religious	56.1	Mobile telephone subscribers per 100 pop.	228.7
Christian	14.3	Broadband subs per 100 pop.	32.1
Other	14.2	Internet users, % of pop.	84.9
Buddhist	13.2		
Muslim	1.8		
Hindu	0.4		

a Including re-exports.

Note: Hong Kong became a Special Administrative Region of China on July 1 1997.

HUNGARY

Area, sq km	90,530	Capital	Budapest
Arable as % of total land	48.6	Currency	Forint (Ft)

People

Population, m	9.9	Life expectancy: men	71.9 yrs
Pop. per sq km	109.4	women	79.1 yrs
Average annual growth in pop. 2015–20, %	-0.4	Adult literacy	99.4
Pop. aged 0–24, %	25.4	Fertility rate (per woman)	1.4
Pop. aged 70 and over, %	12.4	Urban population, 2020, %	73.4
No. of men per 100 women	90.8		*per 1,000 pop.*
Human Development Index	83.6	Crude birth rate	9.4
		Crude death rate	13.5

The economy

GDP	$122bn	GDP per head	$12,289
GDP	Ft33,999bn	GDP per head in purchasing power parity (USA=100)	47.1
Av. ann. growth in real GDP 2010–15	1.7%	Economic freedom index	65.8

Origins of GDP	*% of total*	**Components of GDP**	*% of total*
Agriculture	4	Private consumption	49
Industry, of which:	32	Public consumption	20
manufacturing	25	Investment	22
Services	64	Exports	91
		Imports	-82

Structure of employment

	% of total		*% of labour force*
Agriculture	4.9	Unemployed 2015	6.8
Industry	30.3	Av. ann. rate 2005–15	8.9
Services	64.7		

Energy

	m TOE		
Total output	7.7	Net energy imports as % of energy use	56
Total consumption	23.7		
Consumption per head kg oil equivalent	2,314		

Inflation and finance

			av. ann. increase 2011–16
Consumer price inflation 2016	0.4%	Narrow money (M1)	17.3%
Av. ann. inflation 2011–16	3.7%	Broad money	4.0%
Treasury bill rate, Dec. 2016	0.16%		

Exchange rates

	end 2016		*December 2016*
Ft per $	293.69	Effective rates	2010 = 100
Ft per sdr	394.82	– nominal	87.96
Ft per €	309.04	– real	89.68

Trade

Trade

Principal exports

	$bn fob
Machinery & equipment	57.4
Manufactured goods	31.2
Food, drink & tobacco	7.3
Raw materials	2.3
Total incl. others	**100.3**

Principal imports

	$bn cif
Machinery & equipment	45.0
Manufactured goods	32.4
Fuels & energy	7.4
Food, drink & tobacco	4.7
Total incl. others	**90.7**

Main export destinations

	% of total
Germany	27.5
Romania	5.4
Slovakia	5.0
Austria	4.9
EU28	81.3

Main origins of imports

	% of total
Germany	26.4
Austria	6.7
China	6.3
Poland	5.5
EU28	76.6

Balance of payments, reserves and debt, $bn

Visible exports fob	88.3
Visible imports fob	-83.4
Trade balance	4.9
Invisibles inflows	34.0
Invisibles outflows	-33.7
Net transfers	-1.2
Current account balance	4.0
– as % of GDP	3.3
Capital balance	-7.2
Overall balance	-5.4
Change in reserves	-8.9
Level of reserves end Dec.	33.1
No. months of import cover	3.4
Official gold holdings, m oz	0.1
Foreign debt	127.4
– as % of GDP	104.8
– as % of total exports	104.1
Debt service ratio	25.9

Health and education

Health spending, % of GDP	7.4
Doctors per 1,000 pop.	3.1
Hospital beds per 1,000 pop.	7.2
Improved-water source access, % of pop.	100
Education spending, % of GDP	4.2
Enrolment, %: primary	102
secondary	105
tertiary	51

Society

No. of households, m	4.2
Av. no. per household	2.4
Marriages per 1,000 pop.	3.9
Divorces per 1,000 pop.	2.0
Religion, % of pop.	
Christian	81.0
Non-religious	18.6
Other	0.2
Jewish	0.1
Hindu	<0.1
Muslim	<0.1
Cost of living, Dec. 2016 New York = 100	56
Cars per 1,000 pop.	314
Colour TV households, % with:	
cable	56.4
satellite	28.5
Telephone lines per 100 pop.	31.2
Mobile telephone subscribers per 100 pop.	118.9
Broadband subs per 100 pop.	27.4
Internet users, % of pop.	72.8

INDIA

Area, sq km	3,287,000	Capital	New Delhi
Arable as % of total land	52.6	Currency	Indian rupee (Rs)

People

Population, m	1,311.1	Life expectancy: men	67.7 yrs
Pop. per sq km	398.9	women	70.6 yrs
Average annual growth in pop. 2015–20, %	1.2	Adult literacy	72.2
Pop. aged 0–24, %	47.2	Fertility rate (per woman)	2.5
Pop. aged 70 and over, %	3.4	Urban population, 2020, %	34.8
No. of men per 100 women	107.6		*per 1,000 pop.*
Human Development Index	62.4	Crude birth rate	19.1
		Crude death rate	7.3

The economy

GDP	$2,088bn	GDP per head	$1,593
GDP	Rs136trn	GDP per head in purchasing power parity (USA=100)	10.9
Av. ann. growth in real GDP 2010–15	6.7%	Economic freedom index	52.6

Origins of GDP	*% of total*	**Components of GDP**	*% of total*
Agriculture	17	Private consumption	59
Industry, of which:	30	Public consumption	10
manufacturing	17	Investment	33
Services	53	Exports	20
		Imports	-22

Structure of employment

	% of total		*% of labour force*
Agriculture	49.7	Unemployed 2015	3.5
Industry	21.5	Av. ann. rate 2005–15	3.8
Services	28.7		

Energy

	m TOE		
Total output	354.6	Net energy imports as % of energy use	34
Total consumption	622.5		
Consumption per head kg oil equivalent	637		

Inflation and finance

			av. ann. increase 2011–16
Consumer price inflation 2016	5.5%	Narrow money (M1)	3.3%
Av. ann. inflation 2011–16	8.4%	Broad money	10.8%
Money market rate, Dec. 2016	6.00%		

Exchange rates

	end 2016		*December 2016*
Rs per $	67.95	Effective rates	2010 = 100
Rs per sdr	91.35	– nominal	...
Rs per €	71.50	– real	...

Trade

Principal exports	$bn fob
Engineering products	60.6
Gems & jewellery	39.5
Petroleum & products	30.4
Agricultural products	26.4
Total incl. others	**262.0**

Principal imports	$bn cif
Petroleum & products	82.9
Electronic goods	40.0
Gold & silver	35.3
Machinery	29.5
Total incl. others	**380.4**

Main export destinations	% of total
United States	15.4
United Arab Emirates	11.6
Hong Kong	4.7
China	3.7

Main origins of imports	% of total
China	16.2
Saudi Arabia	5.6
Switzerland	5.5
United States	5.4

Balance of payments, reserves and debt, $bn

Visible exports fob	272.4
Visible imports fob	-409.2
Trade balance	-136.9
Invisibles inflows	170.8
Invisibles outflows	-120.5
Net transfers	64.2
Current account balance	-22.5
– as % of GDP	-1.1
Capital balance	67.7
Overall balance	44.1
Change in reserves	28.2
Level of reserves end Dec.	353.3
No. months of import cover	8.0
Official gold holdings, m oz	17.9
Foreign debt	479.6
– as % of GDP	23.0
– as % of total exports	93.7
Debt service ratio	9.4

Health and education

Health spending, % of GDP	4.7
Doctors per 1,000 pop.	0.7
Hospital beds per 1,000 pop.	0.7
Improved-water source access, % of pop.	94.1
Education spending, % of GDP	3.8
Enrolment, %: primary	108
secondary	74
tertiary	26

Society

No. of households, m	268.6
Av. no. per household	4.9
Marriages per 1,000 pop.	...
Divorces per 1,000 pop.	...
Religion, % of pop.	
Hindu	79.5
Muslim	14.4
Other	3.6
Christian	2.5
Jewish	<0.1
Non-religious	<0.1
Cost of living, Dec. 2016 New York = 100	47
Cars per 1,000 pop.	17
Colour TV households, % with:	
cable	62.5
satellite	17.1
Telephone lines per 100 pop.	2.0
Mobile telephone subscribers per 100 pop.	78.1
Broadband subs per 100 pop.	1.3
Internet users, % of pop.	26.0

INDONESIA

Area, sq km	1,911,000	Capital	Jakarta
Arable as % of total land	13.0	Currency	Rupiah (Rp)

People

Population, m	257.6	Life expectancy: men	67.4 yrs
Pop. per sq km	134.8	women	71.7 yrs
Average annual growth in pop. 2015–20, %	1.1	Adult literacy	95.4
Pop. aged 0–24, %	44.8	Fertility rate (per woman)	2.2
Pop. aged 70 and over, %	3.1	Urban population, 2020, %	57.2
			per 1,000 pop.
No. of men per 100 women	101.4	Crude birth rate	18.5
Human Development Index	68.9	Crude death rate	7.2

The economy

GDP	$861bn	GDP per head	$3,343
GDP	Rs11,531trn	GDP per head in purchasing power parity (USA=100)	19.7
Av. ann. growth in real GDP 2010–15	5.5%	Economic freedom index	61.9

Origins of GDP	*% of total*	**Components of GDP**	*% of total*
Agriculture	14	Private consumption	55
Industry, of which:	40	Public consumption	10
manufacturing	21	Investment	35
Services	46	Exports	21
		Imports	-21

Structure of employment

	% of total		*% of labour force*
Agriculture	32.9	Unemployed 2015	6.0
Industry	22.2	Av. ann. rate 2005–15	7.8
Services	44.9		

Energy

	m TOE		
Total output	380.2	Net energy imports as % of energy use	-103
Total consumption	184.6		
Consumption per head kg oil equivalent	886		

Inflation and finance

			av. ann. increase 2011–16
Consumer price inflation 2016	3.7%	Narrow money (M1)	11.4%
Av. ann. inflation 2011–16	7.0%	Broad money	11.7%
Money market rate, Nov. 2016	4.17%		

Exchange rates

	end 2016		*December 2016*
Rp per $	13,436	Effective rates	2010 = 100
Rp per sdr	18,062	– nominal	...
Rp per €	14,138	– real	...

Trade

Principal exports

	$bn fob
Manufactured goods	106.2
Mining & other sector products	34.4
Agricultural goods	5.8
Unclassified exports	1.3
Total incl. others	**150.4**

Principal imports

	$bn cif
Raw materials & auxiliary materials	98.0
Capital goods	24.9
Consumer goods	18.5
Total incl. others	**142.7**

Main export destinations

	% of total
Japan	12.0
United States	10.8
China	10.0
Singapore	8.4

Main origins of imports

	% of total
China	20.6
Singapore	12.6
Japan	9.3
Malaysia	6.0

Balance of payments, reserves and debt, $bn

Visible exports fob	149.1
Visible imports fob	-135.1
Trade balance	14.0
Invisibles inflows	25.0
Invisibles outflows	-62.1
Net transfers	5.5
Current account balance	-17.5
– as % of GDP	-2.0
Capital balance	16.9
Overall balance	-1.1
Change in reserves	-5.9
Level of reserves end Dec.	105.9
No. months of import cover	6.4
Official gold holdings, m oz	2.5
Foreign debt	308.5
– as % of GDP	35.8
– as % of total exports	167.8
Debt service ratio	30.3

Health and education

Health spending, % of GDP	2.8
Doctors per 1,000 pop.	0.2
Hospital beds per 1,000 pop.	0.9
Improved-water source access, % of pop.	87.4
Education spending, % of GDP	3.3
Enrolment, %: primary	106
secondary	82
tertiary	31

Society

No. of households, m	65.3
Av. no. per household	3.9
Marriages per 1,000 pop.	...
Divorces per 1,000 pop.	...
Religion, % of pop.	
Muslim	87.2
Christian	9.9
Hindu	1.7
Other	1.1
Jewish	<0.1
Non-religious	<0.1
Cost of living, Dec. 2016 New York = 100	66
Cars per 1,000 pop.	50
Colour TV households, % with:	
cable	6.0
satellite	25.5
Telephone lines per 100 pop.	8.8
Mobile telephone subscribers per 100 pop.	132.3
Broadband subs per 100 pop.	1.1
Internet users, % of pop.	22.0

IRAN

Area, sq km	1,745,000	Capital	Tehran
Arable as % of total land	9.0	Currency	Rial (IR)

People

Population, m	79.1	Life expectancy: men	74.7 yrs
Pop. per sq km	45.3	women	77.1 yrs
Average annual growth in pop. 2015–20, %	1.1	Adult literacy	87.2
Pop. aged 0–24, %	39.5	Fertility rate (per woman)	1.8
Pop. aged 70 and over, %	3.2	Urban population, 2020, %	75.7
No. of men per 100 women	101.4		*per 1,000 pop.*
Human Development Index	77.4	Crude birth rate	15.6
		Crude death rate	4.6

The economy

GDP	$374bn	GDP per head	$4,732
GDP	IR11,096trn	GDP per head in purchasing power parity (USA=100)	30.4
Av. ann. growth in real GDP 2010–15	-0.1%	Economic freedom index	50.5

Origins of GDP	*% of total*	**Components of GDP**	*% of total*
Agriculture	11	Private consumption	50
Industry, of which:	33	Public consumption	12
manufacturing	...	Investment	36
Services	56	Exports	20
		Imports	-19

Structure of employment

	% of total		*% of labour force*
Agriculture	18.0	Unemployed 2015	11.1
Industry	32.5	Av. ann. rate 2005–15	11.5
Services	49.4		

Energy

	m TOE		
Total output	334.0	Net energy imports as % of energy use	-33
Total consumption	264.7		
Consumption per head kg oil equivalent	3,034		

Inflation and finance

			av. ann. increase 2011–16
Consumer price inflation 2016	7.4%	Narrow money (M1)	14.9%
Av. ann. inflation 2011–16	20.6%	Broad money	29.5%
Deposit rate, Dec. 2016	12.90%		

Exchange rates

	end 2016		*December 2016*
IR per $	32,376	Effective rates	2010 = 100
IR per sdr	43,524	– nominal	39.56
IR per €	34,067	– real	109.43

Trade

Principal exports	$bn fob
Oil & gas	33.6
Petrochemicals[a]	9.8
Fresh & dry fruits[a]	1.5
Carpets[a]	0.4
Total incl. others	**64.6**

Principal imports	$bn cif
Machinery & transport equip.[a]	14.1
Intermediate goods[a]	8.2
Chemicals[a]	6.2
Total incl. others	**52.4**

Main export destinations	% of total
China	38.1
India	14.8
Turkey	14.5
Japan	7.7

Main origins of imports	% of total
United Arab Emirates	27.6
China	15.4
Turkey	6.2
South Korea	4.9

Balance of payments[b], reserves and debt, $bn

Visible exports fob	64.6
Visible imports fob	-52.4
Trade balance	12.2
Invisibles inflows	12.3
Invisibles outflows	-16.0
Net transfers	0.5
Current account balance	9.0
– as % of GDP	2.4
Capital balance	-2.5
Overall balance	2.2
Change in reserves	...
Level of reserves end Dec.	...
No. months of import cover	...
Official gold holdings, m oz	...
Foreign debt	6.3
– as % of GDP	1.5
– as % of total exports	8.1
Debt service ratio	1.1

Health and education

Health spending, % of GDP	6.9
Doctors per 1,000 pop.	...
Hospital beds per 1,000 pop.	0.1
Improved-water source access, % of pop.	96.2
Education spending, % of GDP	2.9
Enrolment, %: primary	109
secondary	89
tertiary	72

Society

No. of households, m	24.3
Av. no. per household	3.3
Marriages per 1,000 pop.	9.3
Divorces per 1,000 pop.	2.1
Religion, % of pop.	
Muslim	99.5
Christian	0.2
Other	0.2
Non-religious	0.1
Hindu	<0.1
Jewish	<0.1
Cost of living, Dec. 2016 New York = 100	50
Cars per 1,000 pop.	153
Colour TV households, % with:	
cable	...
satellite	37.0
Telephone lines per 100 pop.	38.3
Mobile telephone subscribers per 100 pop.	93.4
Broadband subs per 100 pop.	10.9
Internet users, % of pop.	45.3

a Estimate. b Iranian year ending March 19th 2016.

IRELAND

Area, sq km	69,797	Capital	Dublin
Arable as % of total land	15.4	Currency	Euro (€)

People

Population, m	4.7	Life expectancy: men	79.5 yrs
Pop. per sq km	67.3	women	83.5 yrs
Average annual growth in pop. 2015–20, %	0.8	Adult literacy	...
Pop. aged 0–24, %	32.9	Fertility rate (per woman)	2.0
Pop. aged 70 and over, %	8.6	Urban population, 2020, %	64.8
No. of men per 100 women	99.6		*per 1,000 pop.*
Human Development Index	92.3	Crude birth rate	13.3
		Crude death rate	6.6

The economy

GDP	$283bn	GDP per head	$60,303
GDP	€256bn	GDP per head in purchasing power parity (USA=100)	115.7
Av. ann. growth in real GDP 2010–15	6.5%	Economic freedom index	76.7

Origins of GDP	*% of total*	**Components of GDP**	*% of total*
Agriculture	1	Private consumption	34
Industry, of which:	42	Public consumption	13
manufacturing	37	Investment	22
Services	57	Exports	124
		Imports	-92

Structure of employment

	% of total		*% of labour force*
Agriculture	5.6	Unemployed 2015	9.4
Industry	19.0	Av. ann. rate 2005–15	9.9
Services	75.0		

Energy

	m TOE		
Total output	0.1	Net energy imports as % of energy use	84
Total consumption	14.1		
Consumption per head kg oil equivalent	2,766		

Inflation and finance

			av. ann. increase 2011–16
Consumer price inflation 2016	0.3%	Narrow money (M1)	8.1%
Av. ann. inflation 2011–16	2.8%	Broad money	3.6%
Money market rate, Dec. 2016	-0.37%		

Exchange rates

	end 2016		*December 2016*
€ per $	0.95	Effective rates	2010 = 100
€ per sdr	1.28	– nominal	93.23
		– real	88.06

Trade

Principal exports

	$bn fob
Chemicals & related products	71.2
Machinery & transport equip.	18.4
Food, drink and tobacco	12.3
Raw materials	2.0
Total incl. others	**124.7**

Principal imports

	$bn cif
Machinery & transport equip.	30.2
Chemicals & related products	15.3
Food, drink and tobacco	8.4
Mineral fuels & lubricants	5.7
Total incl. others	**77.7**

Main export destinations

	% of total
United States	23.8
United Kingdom	13.6
Belgium	12.9
Germany	6.5
EU28	53.1

Main origins of imports

	% of total
United Kingdom	31.2
United States	14.5
France	11.0
Germany	9.0
EU28	66.1

Balance of payments, reserves and aid, $bn

Visible exports fob	216.9
Visible imports fob	-94.3
Trade balance	122.6
Invisibles inflows	203.2
Invisibles outflows	-293.3
Net transfers	-3.5
Current account balance	29.0
– as % of GDP	10.2
Capital balance	-14.9
Overall balance	11.8
Change in reserves	0.5
Level of reserves end Dec.	2.2
No. months of import cover	0.1
Official gold holdings, m oz	0.2
Aid given	0.7
– as % of GDP	0.3

Health and education

Health spending, % of GDP	7.8
Doctors per 1,000 pop.	2.7
Hospital beds per 1,000 pop.	2.9
Improved-water source access, % of pop.	97.9
Education spending, % of GDP	5.3
Enrolment, %: primary	102
secondary	127
tertiary	78

Society

No. of households, m	1.7
Av. no. per household	2.8
Marriages per 1,000 pop.	4.8
Divorces per 1,000 pop.	0.6
Religion, % of pop.	
Christian	92.0
Non-religious	6.2
Muslim	1.1
Other	0.4
Hindu	0.2
Jewish	<0.1
Cost of living, Dec. 2016 New York = 100	88
Cars per 1,000 pop.	411
Colour TV households, % with:	
cable	31.7
satellite	47.6
Telephone lines per 100 pop.	40.9
Mobile telephone subscribers per 100 pop.	103.7
Broadband subs per 100 pop.	27.7
Internet users, % of pop.	80.1

ISRAEL

Area, sq km	22,072	Capital	Jerusalem[a]
Arable as % of total land	13.9	Currency	New Shekel (NIS)

People

Population, m	8.1	Life expectancy: men	81.3 yrs
Pop. per sq km	367.0	women	84.6 yrs
Average annual growth in pop. 2015–20, %	1.6	Adult literacy	...
Pop. aged 0–24, %	42.7	Fertility rate (per woman)	2.7
Pop. aged 70 and over, %	7.4	Urban population, 2020, %	52.7
No. of men per 100 women	98.4		*per 1,000 pop.*
Human Development Index	89.9	Crude birth rate	19.6
		Crude death rate	5.2

The economy

GDP	$299bn	GDP per head	$36,965
GDP	NIS1,164bn	GDP per head in purchasing power parity (USA=100)	62.8
Av. ann. growth in real GDP 2010–15	3.5%	Economic freedom index	69.7

Origins of GDP	*% of total*	**Components of GDP**	*% of total*
Agriculture	2	Private consumption	55
Industry, of which:	27	Public consumption	22
manufacturing	20	Investment	20
Services	69	Exports	31
		Imports	-28

Structure of employment

	% of total		*% of labour force*
Agriculture	1.0	Unemployed 2015	5.3
Industry	17.4	Av. ann. rate 2005–15	8.0
Services	79.8		

Energy

	m TOE		
Total output	7.2	Net energy imports as % of energy use	67
Total consumption	23.2		
Consumption per head kg oil equivalent	2,763		

Inflation and finance

			av. ann. increase 2011–16
Consumer price inflation 2016	-0.6%	Narrow money (M1)	22.9%
Av. ann. inflation 2011–16	2.9%	Broad money	9.2%
Treasury bill rate, Dec. 2016	0.15%		

Exchange rates

	end 2016		*December 2016*
NIS per $	3.85	Effective rates	2010 = 100
NIS per sdr	5.17	– nominal	115.8
NIS per €	4.05	– real	107.3

Trade

Principal exports	$bn fob
Chemicals & chemical products	14.0
Communications, medical & scientific equipment	8.2
Polished diamonds	7.2
Electronic components & computers	7.1
Total incl. others	**53.5**

Principal imports	$bn cif
Fuel	7.4
Diamonds	6.3
Machinery & equipment	5.7
Chemicals	4.6
Total incl. others	**61.3**

Main export destinations	% of total
United States	33.9
Hong Kong	9.9
United Kingdom	7.5
China	6.1

Main origins of imports	% of total
United States	13.2
China	9.4
Switzerland	7.2
Germany	6.2

Balance of payments, reserves and debt, $bn

Visible exports fob	56.3
Visible imports fob	-59.7
Trade balance	-3.4
Invisibles inflows	45.1
Invisibles outflows	-37.1
Net transfers	9.0
Current account balance	13.6
– as % of GDP	4.6
Capital balance	-6.4
Overall balance	7.3
Change in reserves	4.5
Level of reserves end Dec.	90.6
No. months of import cover	11.2
Official gold holdings, m oz	0.0
Foreign debt	89.1
– as % of GDP	29.8
– as % of total exports	87.0
Debt service ratio	16.8

Health and education

Health spending, % of GDP	7.8
Doctors per 1,000 pop.	3.3
Hospital beds per 1,000 pop.	3.3
Improved-water source access, % of pop.	100
Education spending, % of GDP	5.9
Enrolment, %: primary	104
secondary	102
tertiary	66

Society

No. of households, m	2.3
Av. no. per household	3.5
Marriages per 1,000 pop.	6.5
Divorces per 1,000 pop.	1.8
Religion, % of pop.	
Jewish	75.6
Muslim	18.6
Non-religious	3.1
Christian	2.0
Other	0.6
Hindu	<0.1
Cost of living, Dec. 2016 New York = 100	99
Cars per 1,000 pop.	317
Colour TV households, % with:	
cable	77.8
satellite	19.2
Telephone lines per 100 pop.	43.1
Mobile telephone subscribers per 100 pop.	133.5
Broadband subs per 100 pop.	27.4
Internet users, % of pop.	77.4

a Sovereignty over the city is disputed.

ITALY

Area, sq km	301,000	Capital	Rome
Arable as % of total land	22.9	Currency	Euro (€)

People

Population, m	59.8	Life expectancy: men	81.3 yrs
Pop. per sq km	198.7	women	86.0 yrs
Average annual growth in pop. 2015–20, %	0.0	Adult literacy	99.0
Pop. aged 0–24, %	23.3	Fertility rate (per woman)	1.4
Pop. aged 70 and over, %	16.3	Urban population, 2020, %	69.8
			per 1,000 pop.
No. of men per 100 women	94.6	Crude birth rate	8.3
Human Development Index	88.7	Crude death rate	10.2

The economy

GDP	$1,826bn	GDP per head	$30,532
GDP	€1,645bn	GDP per head in purchasing power parity (USA=100)	65.2
Av. ann. growth in real GDP 2010–15	-0.7%	Economic freedom index	62.5

Origins of GDP		**Components of GDP**	
	% of total		*% of total*
Agriculture	2	Private consumption	61
Industry, of which:	24	Public consumption	19
manufacturing	16	Investment	17
Services	74	Exports	30
		Imports	-27

Structure of employment

	% of total		*% of labour force*
Agriculture	3.8	Unemployed 2015	11.9
Industry	26.6	Av. ann. rate 2005–15	9.0
Services	69.7		

Energy

	m TOE		
Total output	12.5	Net energy imports as % of energy use	75
Total consumption	160.3		
Consumption per head kg oil equivalent	2,414		

Inflation and finance

Consumer price inflation 2016	-0.1%		*av. ann. increase 2011–16*
Av. ann. inflation 2011–16	3.3%	Narrow money (M1)	8.1%
Treasury bill rate, Dec. 2016	-0.27%	Broad money	3.6%

Exchange rates

	end 2016		*December 2016*
€ per $	0.95	Effective rates	2010 = 100
€ per sdr	1.28	– nominal	98.10
		– real	94.92

Trade

Principal exports

	$bn fob
Machinery & transport equip.	166.9
Chemicals & related products	55.9
Food, drink and tobacco	37.1
Mineral fuels & lubricants	15.7
Total incl. others	**457.0**

Principal imports

	$bn cif
Machinery & transport equip.	111.6
Chemicals & related products	65.4
Mineral fuels & lubricants	52.3
Food, drink and tobacco	39.3
Total incl. others	**410.9**

Main export destinations

	% of total
Germany	12.3
France	10.4
United States	8.7
United Kingdom	5.4
EU28	54.8

Main origins of imports

	% of total
Germany	15.5
France	8.7
China	7.6
Netherlands	5.6
EU28	58.7

Balance of payments, reserves and aid, $bn

Visible exports fob	449.3
Visible imports fob	-391.4
Trade balance	57.9
Invisibles inflows	157.0
Invisibles outflows	-169.0
Net transfers	-16.5
Current account balance	29.3
– as % of GDP	1.6
Capital balance	-24.4
Overall balance	0.6
Change in reserves	-12.2
Level of reserves end Dec.	130.6
No. months of import cover	2.8
Official gold holdings, m oz	78.8
Aid given	4.0
– as % of GDP	0.2

Health and education

Health spending, % of GDP	9.2
Doctors per 1,000 pop.	3.8
Hospital beds per 1,000 pop.	3.4
Improved-water source access, % of pop.	100
Education spending, % of GDP	4.2
Enrolment, %: primary	102
secondary	103
tertiary	63

Society

No. of households, m	27.3
Av. no. per household	2.2
Marriages per 1,000 pop.	3.1
Divorces per 1,000 pop.	0.9
Religion, % of pop.	
Christian	83.3
Non-religious	12.4
Muslim	3.7
Other	0.4
Hindu	0.1
Jewish	<0.1
Cost of living, Dec. 2016 New York = 100	82
Cars per 1,000 pop.	607
Colour TV households, % with:	
cable	1.1
satellite	29.0
Telephone lines per 100 pop.	33.1
Mobile telephone subscribers per 100 pop.	142.1
Broadband subs per 100 pop.	24.4
Internet users, % of pop.	65.6

IVORY COAST

Area, sq km	322,463	Capital	Yamoussoukro
Arable as % of total land	9.1	Currency	CFA franc (CFAfr)

People

Population, m	22.7	Life expectancy: men	52.0 yrs
Pop. per sq km	70.4	women	53.7 yrs
Average annual growth in pop. 2015–20, %	2.4	Adult literacy	43.3
Pop. aged 0–24, %	62.8	Fertility rate (per woman)	3.5
Pop. aged 70 and over, %	1.7	Urban population, 2020, %	57.5
			per 1,000 pop.
No. of men per 100 women	103.5	Crude birth rate	36.2
Human Development Index	47.4	Crude death rate	12.8

The economy

GDP	$33bn	GDP per head	$1,443
GDP	CFAfr19,368bn	GDP per head in purchasing power parity (USA=100)	6.3
Av. ann. growth in real GDP 2010–15	6.2%	Economic freedom index	63.0

Origins of GDP		**Components of GDP**	
	% of total		*% of total*
Agriculture	23	Private consumption	62
Industry, of which:	29	Public consumption	14
manufacturing	14	Investment	21
Services	49	Exports	39
		Imports	-36

Structure of employment

	% of total		*% of labour force*
Agriculture	48.3	Unemployed 2015	9.3
Industry	6.2	Av. ann. rate 2005–15	9.3
Services	45.5		

Energy

	m TOE		
Total output	3.7	Net energy imports as % of energy use	7
Total consumption	4.1		
Consumption per head kg oil equivalent	626		

Inflation and finance

Consumer price inflation 2016	1.0%		*av. ann. increase 2011–16*
Av. ann. inflation 2011–16	3.4%	Narrow money (M1)	12.7%
Money market rate, Dec. 2016	4.87%	Broad money	12.1%

Exchange rates

	end 2016		*December 2016*
CFAfr per $	622.29	Effective rates	2010 = 100
CFAfr per sdr	856.56	– nominal	100.28
CFAfr per €	654.80	– real	96.29

Trade

Principal exports	$bn fob
Cocoa beans & butter	5.1
Petroleum products	1.9
Coffee beans & products	1.6
Gold	0.8
Total incl. others	**11.9**

Principal imports	$bn cif
Fuels & lubricants	2.1
Capital equip.	2.0
Foodstuffs	1.9
Raw materials & intermediate goods	1.8
Total incl. others	**9.8**

Main export destinations	% of total
Netherlands	12.0
United States	8.1
Belgium	6.5
France	6.4

Main origins of imports	% of total
Nigeria	14.8
France	13.5
China	12.6
United States	4.3

Balance of payments, reserves and debt, $bn

Visible exports fob	11.7
Visible imports fob	-8.6
Trade balance	3.2
Invisibles inflows	1.0
Invisibles outflows	-4.0
Net transfers	-0.3
Current account balance	-0.2
– as % of GDP	-0.6
Capital balance	0.7
Overall balance	0.4
Change in reserves	0.2
Level of reserves end Dec.	4.7
No. months of import cover	4.5
Official gold holdings, m oz	0.0
Foreign debt	10.0
– as % of GDP	31.6
– as % of total exports	81.7
Debt service ratio	6.7

Health and education

Health spending, % of GDP	5.1
Doctors per 1,000 pop.	0.1
Hospital beds per 1,000 pop.	...
Improved-water source access, % of pop.	81.9
Education spending, % of GDP	4.7
Enrolment, %: primary	94
secondary	44
tertiary	9

Society

No. of households, m	3.7
Av. no. per household	6.1
Marriages per 1,000 pop.	...
Divorces per 1,000 pop.	...
Religion, % of pop.	...
Cost of living, Dec. 2016 New York = 100	59
Cars per 1,000 pop.	20
Colour TV households, % with: cable	...
satellite	...
Telephone lines per 100 pop.	1.3
Mobile telephone subscribers per 100 pop.	119.3
Broadband subs per 100 pop.	0.5
Internet users, % of pop.	21.0

JAPAN

Area, sq km	377,930	Capital	Tokyo
Arable as % of total land	11.6	Currency	Yen (¥)

People

Population, m	126.6	Life expectancy: men	80.8 yrs
Pop. per sq km	335.0	women	87.3 yrs
Average annual growth in pop. 2015–20, %	-0.2	Adult literacy	...
Pop. aged 0–24, %	22.4	Fertility rate (per woman)	1.4
Pop. aged 70 and over, %	18.9	Urban population, 2020, %	95.3
No. of men per 100 women	94.7		*per 1,000 pop.*
Human Development Index	90.3	Crude birth rate	8.1
		Crude death rate	10.9

The economy

GDP	$4,382bn	GDP per head	$34,616
GDP	¥530trn	GDP per head in purchasing power parity (USA=100)	72.1
Av. ann. growth in real GDP 2010–15	0.6%	Economic freedom index	69.6

Origins of GDP	*% of total*	**Components of GDP**	*% of total*
Agriculture	1	Private consumption	57
Industry, of which:	30	Public consumption	20
manufacturing	...	Investment	24
Services	69	Exports	18
		Imports	-18

Structure of employment

	% of total		*% of labour force*
Agriculture	3.6	Unemployed 2015	3.4
Industry	25.5	Av. ann. rate 2005–15	4.2
Services	69.4		

Energy

	m TOE		
Total output	5.4	Net energy imports as % of energy use	94
Total consumption	476.7		
Consumption per head kg oil equivalent	3,475		

Inflation and finance

			av. ann. increase 2011–16
Consumer price inflation 2016	-0.2%	Narrow money (M1)	4.9%
Av. ann. inflation 2011–16	3.1%	Broad money	2.9%
Treasury bill rate, Dec. 2016	-0.41%		

Exchange rates

	end 2016		*December 2016*
¥ per $	116.80	Effective rates	2010 = 100
¥ per sdr	157.02	– nominal	83.20
¥ per €	122.90	– real	76.08

Trade

Principal exports

	$bn fob
Capital equipment	315.4
Industrial supplies	150.8
Consumer durable goods	104.5
Consumer non-durable goods	4.6
Total incl. others	**624.9**

Principal imports

	$bn cif
Industrial supplies	299.0
Capital equipment	179.1
Food & direct consumer goods	58.1
Consumer durable goods	48.9
Total incl. others	**648.1**

Main export destinations

	% of total
United States	20.2
China	17.5
South Korea	7.0
Taiwan	5.9

Main origins of imports

	% of total
China	24.8
United States	10.5
Australia	5.4
South Korea	4.1

Balance of payments, reserves and aid, $bn

Visible exports fob	622.0
Visible imports fob	-629.4
Trade balance	-7.3
Invisibles inflows	409.3
Invisibles outflows	-251.6
Net transfers	-16.3
Current account balance	134.1
– as % of GDP	3.1
Capital balance	-175.7
Overall balance	5.1
Change in reserves	-27.6
Level of reserves end Dec.	1,233.1
No. months of import cover	16.8
Official gold holdings, m oz	24.6
Aid given	9.2
– as % of GDP	0.2

Health and education

Health spending, % of GDP	10.2
Doctors per 1,000 pop.	2.3
Hospital beds per 1,000 pop.	13.7
Improved-water source access, % of pop.	100
Education spending, % of GDP	3.8
Enrolment, %: primary	101
secondary	102
tertiary	63

Society

No. of households, m	53.0
Av. no. per household	2.4
Marriages per 1,000 pop.	5.1
Divorces per 1,000 pop.	1.7
Religion, % of pop.	
Non-religious	57.0
Buddhist	36.2
Other	5.0
Christian	1.6
Muslim	0.2
Jewish	<0.1
Cost of living, Dec. 2016 New York = 100	110
Cars per 1,000 pop.	478
Colour TV households, % with:	
cable	52.7
satellite	42.3
Telephone lines per 100 pop.	50.2
Mobile telephone subscribers per 100 pop.	126.5
Broadband subs per 100 pop.	30.7
Internet users, % of pop.	91.1

KENYA

Area, sq km	580,000	Capital	Nairobi
Arable as % of total land	10.2	Currency	Kenyan shilling (KSh)

People

Population, m	46.1	Life expectancy: men	61.1 yrs
Pop. per sq km	79.5	women	65.5 yrs
Average annual growth in pop. 2015–20, %	2.5	Adult literacy	78.0
Pop. aged 0–24, %	61.4	Fertility rate (per woman)	3.3
Pop. aged 70 and over, %	1.6	Urban population, 2020, %	27.9
No. of men per 100 women	99.9		*per 1,000 pop.*
Human Development Index	55.5	Crude birth rate	32.8
		Crude death rate	7.6

The economy

GDP	$64bn	GDP per head	$1,380
GDP	KSh6,224bn	GDP per head in purchasing power parity (USA=100)	5.5
Av. ann. growth in real GDP 2010–15	5.5%	Economic freedom index	53.5

Origins of GDP	*% of total*	**Components of GDP**	*% of total*
Agriculture	33	Private consumption	78
Industry, of which:	20	Public consumption	14
manufacturing	11	Investment	21
Services	48	Exports	16
		Imports	-29

Structure of employment

	% of total		*% of labour force*
Agriculture	...	Unemployed 2015	11.3
Industry	...	Av. ann. rate 2005–15	11.8
Services	...		

Energy

	m TOE		
Total output	...	Net energy imports as % of energy use	17
Total consumption	6.7		
Consumption per head kg oil equivalent	527		

Inflation and finance

			av. ann. increase 2011–16
Consumer price inflation 2016	6.2%	Narrow money (M1)	16.0%
Av. ann. inflation 2011–16	8.1%	Broad money	12.3%
Treasury bill rate, Dec. 2016	8.44%		

Exchange rates

	end 2016		*December 2016*
KSh per $	116.80	Effective rates	2010 = 100
KSh per sdr	157.02	– nominal	83.20
KSh per €	122.90	– real	76.08

Trade

Principal exports

	$bn fob
Tea	1.3
Horticultural products	1.2
Coffee	0.4
Fish products	0.1
Total incl. others	**6.5**

Principal imports

	$bn cif
Industrial supplies	5.0
Machinery & other capital equip.	3.2
Transport equipment	2.0
Food & beverages	1.2
Total incl. others	**15.6**

Main export destinations

	% of total
Uganda	11.4
Tanzania	8.6
United States	7.5
Netherlands	7.1

Main origins of imports

	% of total
India	20.8
China	11.9
United Arab Emirates	6.8
United Kingdom	6.7

Balance of payments[a], reserves[a] and debt, $bn

Visible exports fob	6.2
Visible imports fob	-17.6
Trade balance	-11.4
Invisibles inflows	5.1
Invisibles outflows	-3.8
Net transfers	3.8
Current account balance	-6.3
– as % of GDP	-10.0
Capital balance	6.9
Overall balance	1.4
Change in reserves	1.3
Level of reserves end Dec.	7.9
No. months of import cover	4.4
Official gold holdings, m oz	0.0
Foreign debt	19.1
– as % of GDP	30.2
– as % of total exports	155.6
Debt service ratio	6.1

Health and education

Health spending, % of GDP	5.7
Doctors per 1,000 pop.	0.2
Hospital beds per 1,000 pop.	1.4
Improved-water source access, % of pop.	63.2
Education spending, % of GDP	5.4
Enrolment, %: primary	109
secondary	68
tertiary	...

Society

No. of households, m	10.5
Av. no. per household	4.3
Marriages per 1,000 pop.	...
Divorces per 1,000 pop.	...
Religion, % of pop.	
Christian	84.8
Muslim	9.7
Other	3.0
Non-religious	2.5
Hindu	0.1
Jewish	<0.1
Cost of living, Dec. 2016 New York = 100	69
Cars per 1,000 pop.	17
Colour TV households, % with:	
cable	2.4
satellite	3.4
Telephone lines per 100 pop.	0.2
Mobile telephone subscribers per 100 pop.	80.7
Broadband subs per 100 pop.	0.3
Internet users, % of pop.	45.6

a 2014

MALAYSIA

Area, sq km	331,000	Capital	Kuala Lumpur
Arable as % of total land	2.9	Currency	Malaysian dollar/ringgit (M$)

People

Population, m	30.3	Life expectancy: men	73.0 yrs
Pop. per sq km	91.5	women	77.7 yrs
Average annual growth in pop. 2015–20, %	1.3	Adult literacy	94.6
Pop. aged 0–24, %	43.2	Fertility rate (per woman)	2.6
Pop. aged 70 and over, %	3.4	Urban population, 2020, %	77.7
No. of men per 100 women	98.2		*per 1,000 pop.*
Human Development Index	78.9	Crude birth rate	16.6
		Crude death rate	5.2

The economy

GDP	$296bn	GDP per head	$9,778
GDP	M$1,157bn	GDP per head in purchasing power parity (USA=100)	48.1
Av. ann. growth in real GDP 2010–15	5.3%	Economic freedom index	73.8

Origins of GDP	*% of total*	**Components of GDP**	*% of total*
Agriculture	8	Private consumption	54
Industry, of which:	36	Public consumption	13
manufacturing	23	Investment	25
Services	55	Exports	71
		Imports	-63

Structure of employment

	% of total		*% of labour force*
Agriculture	12.5	Unemployed 2015	3.1
Industry	27.5	Av. ann. rate 2005–15	3.2
Services	60.0		

Energy

	m TOE		
Total output	95.2	Net energy imports as % of energy use	-6
Total consumption	87.0		
Consumption per head kg oil equivalent	3,000		

Inflation and finance

			av. ann. increase 2011–16
Consumer price inflation 2016	2.1%	Narrow money (M1)	8.1%
Av. ann. inflation 2011–16	4.1%	Broad money	5.6%
Treasury bill rate, Dec. 2016	3.12%		

Exchange rates

	end 2016		*December 2016*
M$ per $	4.49	Effective rates	2010 = 100
M$ per SDR	6.03	– nominal	81.98
M$ per €	4.72	– real	84.58

Trade

Principal exports

	$bn fob
Machinery & transport equip.	83.5
Mineral fuels	32.9
Manufactured goods	19.2
Chemicals	15.5
Total incl. others	**199.2**

Principal imports

	$bn cif
Machinery & transport equip.	76.1
Manufactured goods	23.0
Mineral fuels	21.7
Chemicals	17.9
Total incl. others	**176.0**

Main export destinations

	% of total
Singapore	14.0
China	13.0
Japan	9.5
United States	9.5

Main origins of imports

	% of total
China	18.8
Singapore	12.0
United States	8.1
Japan	7.8

Balance of payments, reserves and debt, $bn

Visible exports fob	175.7
Visible imports fob	-147.7
Trade balance	28.1
Invisibles inflows	47.3
Invisibles outflows	-60.7
Net transfers	-5.6
Current account balance	9.0
– as % of GDP	3.0
Capital balance	-13.6
Overall balance	0.3
Change in reserves	-20.7
Level of reserves end Dec.	95.3
No. months of import cover	5.5
Official gold holdings, m oz	1.2
Foreign debt	191.0
– as % of GDP	64.4
– as % of total exports	85.0
Debt service ratio	6.0

Health and education

Health spending, % of GDP	4.2
Doctors per 1,000 pop.	1.2
Hospital beds per 1,000 pop.	1.9
Improved-water source access, % of pop.	98.2
Education spending, % of GDP	5.0
Enrolment, %: primary	102
secondary	78
tertiary	26

Society

No. of households, m	7.3
Av. no. per household	4.2
Marriages per 1,000 pop.	...
Divorces per 1,000 pop.	...
Religion, % of pop.	
Muslim	63.7
Buddhist	17.7
Christian	9.4
Hindu	6.0
Other	2.5
Non-religious	0.7
Cost of living, Dec. 2016 New York = 100	61
Cars per 1,000 pop.	365
Colour TV households, % with:	
cable	12.7
satellite	56.2
Telephone lines per 100 pop.	14.6
Mobile telephone subscribers per 100 pop.	143.9
Broadband subs per 100 pop.	10.0
Internet users, % of pop.	71.1

MEXICO

Area, sq km	1,964,375	Capital	Mexico City
Arable as % of total land	11.8	Currency	Mexican peso (PS)

People

Population, m	127.0	Life expectancy: men	75.2 yrs
Pop. per sq km	64.7	women	79.9 yrs
Average annual growth in pop. 2015–20, %	1.2	Adult literacy	94.5
Pop. aged 0–24, %	45.9	Fertility rate (per woman)	2.3
Pop. aged 70 and over, %	4.3	Urban population, 2020, %	80.6
No. of men per 100 women	99.0		*per 1,000 pop.*
Human Development Index	76.2	Crude birth rate	17.7
		Crude death rate	4.9

The economy

GDP	$1,151bn	GDP per head	$9,063
GDP	PS18,242bn	GDP per head in purchasing power parity (USA=100)	31.4
Av. ann. growth in real GDP 2010–15	2.8%	Economic freedom index	63.6

Origins of GDP	*% of total*	**Components of GDP**	*% of total*
Agriculture	4	Private consumption	67
Industry, of which:	33	Public consumption	12
manufacturing	18	Investment	23
Services	64	Exports	35
		Imports	-37

Structure of employment

	% of total		*% of labour force*
Agriculture	13.5	Unemployed 2015	4.3
Industry	24.9	Av. ann. rate 2005–15	4.5
Services	61.1		

Energy

	m TOE		
Total output	195.9	Net energy imports as % of energy use	-11
Total consumption	187.9		
Consumption per head kg oil equivalent	1,499		

Inflation and finance

			av. ann. increase 2011–16
Consumer price inflation 2016	2.8%	Narrow money (M1)	13.2%
Av. ann. inflation 2011–16	5.3%	Broad money	10.2%
Treasury bill rate, Dec. 2016	5.61%		

Exchange rates

	end 2016		*December 2016*
PS per $	20.73	Effective rates	2010 = 100
PS per sdr	27.87	– nominal	66.1
PS per €	21.81	– real	73.8

Trade

Principal exports	$bn fob
Manufactured goods	340.0
Crude oil & products	23.2
Agricultural products	13.0
Mining products	4.5
Total	**380.6**

Principal imports	$bn cif
Intermediate goods	297.3
Consumer goods	56.3
Capital goods	41.7
Total	**395.2**

Main export destinations	% of total
United States	81.2
Canada	2.8
China	1.3
Colombia	1.0

Main origins of imports	% of total
United States	50.1
China	18.8
Japan	4.7
South Korea	3.9

Balance of payments, reserves and debt, $bn

Visible exports fob	381.0
Visible imports fob	-395.6
Trade balance	-14.5
Invisibles inflows	30.8
Invisibles outflows	-73.9
Net transfers	24.3
Current account balance	-33.3
– as % of GDP	-2.9
Capital balance	35.2
Overall balance	-15.4
Change in reserves	-18.1
Level of reserves end Dec.	177.6
No. months of import cover	4.5
Official gold holdings, m oz	3.9
Foreign debt	426.3
– as % of GDP	37.0
– as % of total exports	97.6
Debt service ratio	12.4

Health and education

Health spending, % of GDP	6.3
Doctors per 1,000 pop.	2.1
Hospital beds per 1,000 pop.	1.5
Improved-water source access, % of pop.	96.1
Education spending, % of GDP	5.2
Enrolment, %: primary	103
secondary	91
tertiary	30

Society

No. of households, m	32.8
Av. no. per household	3.9
Marriages per 1,000 pop.	4.8
Divorces per 1,000 pop.	0.9
Religion, % of pop.	
Christian	95.1
Non-religious	4.7
Hindu	<0.1
Jewish	<0.1
Muslim	<0.1
Other	<0.1
Cost of living, Dec. 2016 New York = 100	66
Cars per 1,000 pop.	206
Colour TV households, % with:	
cable	21.4
satellite	23.5
Telephone lines per 100 pop.	15.9
Mobile telephone subscribers per 100 pop.	86.0
Broadband subs per 100 pop.	11.6
Internet users, % of pop.	57.4

MOROCCO

Area, sq km	447,400	Capital	Rabat
Arable as % of total land	18.2	Currency	Dirham (Dh)

People

Population, m	34.4	Life expectancy: men	73.8 yrs
Pop. per sq km	76.9	women	76.0 yrs
Average annual growth in pop. 2015–20, %	1.2	Adult literacy	71.7
Pop. aged 0–24, %	44.9	Fertility rate (per woman)	2.4
Pop. aged 70 and over, %	4.1	Urban population, 2020, %	62.6
No. of men per 100 women	97.7		*per 1,000 pop.*
Human Development Index	64.7	Crude birth rate	19.1
		Crude death rate	5.7

The economy

GDP	$101bn	GDP per head	$2,924
GDP	Dh982bn	GDP per head in purchasing power parity (USA=100)	14.2
Av. ann. growth in real GDP 2010–15	4.0%	Economic freedom index	61.5

Origins of GDP	*% of total*	**Components of GDP**	*% of total*
Agriculture	14	Private consumption	58
Industry, of which:	29	Public consumption	19
manufacturing	18	Investment	30
Services	56	Exports	34
		Imports	-42

Structure of employment

	% of total		*% of labour force*
Agriculture	37.2	Unemployed 2015	9.7
Industry	17.7	Av. ann. rate 2005–15	9.5
Services	44.9		

Energy

	m TOE		
Total output	0.1	Net energy imports as % of energy use	91
Total consumption	20.5		
Consumption per head kg oil equivalent	560		

Inflation and finance

			av. ann. increase 2011–16
Consumer price inflation 2016	1.3%	Narrow money (M1)	5.1%
Av. ann. inflation 2011–16	3.3%	Broad money	4.8%
Money market rate, Dec. 2016	2.25%		

Exchange rates

	end 2016		*December 2016*
Dh per $	10.10	Effective rates	2010 = 100
Dh per sdr	13.57	– nominal	105.62
Dh per €	10.63	– real	100.95

Trade

Principal exports

	$bn fob
Electric cables & wires	2.3
Clothing & textiles	2.1
Fertilisers & chemicals	1.9
Phosphoric acid	1.7
Total incl. others	**22.4**

Principal imports

	$bn cif
Capital goods	9.6
Semi-finished goods	8.8
Consumer goods	7.2
Fuel & lubricants	6.8
Total incl. others	**38.2**

Main export destinations

	% of total
Spain	22.1
France	19.7
India	4.9
United States	4.3

Main origins of imports

	% of total
Spain	13.9
France	12.4
China	8.5
United States	6.5

Balance of payments, reserves and debt, $bn

Visible exports fob	18.6
Visible imports fob	-33.3
Trade balance	-14.7
Invisibles inflows	15.2
Invisibles outflows	-10.3
Net transfers	7.6
Current account balance	-2.2
– as % of GDP	-2.1
Capital balance	5.8
Overall balance	4.3
Change in reserves	2.5
Level of reserves end Dec.	23.0
No. months of import cover	6.3
Official gold holdings, m oz	0.7
Foreign debt	43.0
– as % of GDP	42.6
– as % of total exports	105.6
Debt service ratio	8.7

Health and education

Health spending, % of GDP	5.9
Doctors per 1,000 pop.	0.6
Hospital beds per 1,000 pop.	0.9
Improved-water source access, % of pop.	85.4
Education spending, % of GDP	...
Enrolment, %: primary	115
secondary	69
tertiary	28

Society

No. of households, m	7.5
Av. no. per household	4.6
Marriages per 1,000 pop.	...
Divorces per 1,000 pop.	...
Religion, % of pop.	
Muslim	99.9
Christian	<0.1
Hindu	<0.1
Jewish	<0.1
Non-religious	<0.1
Other	<0.1
Cost of living, Dec. 2016 New York = 100	57
Cars per 1,000 pop.	72
Colour TV households, % with:	
cable	...
satellite	92.0
Telephone lines per 100 pop.	6.5
Mobile telephone subscribers per 100 pop.	126.9
Broadband subs per 100 pop.	3.4
Internet users, % of pop.	57.1

NETHERLANDS

Area, sq km[a]	37,354	Capital	Amsterdam
Arable as % of total land	31.0	Currency	Euro (€)

People

Population, m	16.9	Life expectancy: men	80.3 yrs
Pop. per sq km	452.4	women	83.7 yrs
Average annual growth in pop. 2015–20, %	0.3	Adult literacy	...
Pop. aged 0–24, %	28.4	Fertility rate (per woman)	1.8
Pop. aged 70 and over, %	12.0	Urban population, 2020, %	92.8
No. of men per 100 women	98.5		*per 1,000 pop.*
Human Development Index	92.4	Crude birth rate	10.5
		Crude death rate	8.8

The economy

GDP	$751bn	GDP per head	$44,420
GDP	€677bn	GDP per head in purchasing power parity (USA=100)	88.7
Av. ann. growth in real GDP 2010–15	0.8%	Economic freedom index	75.8

Origins of GDP

	% of total
Agriculture	2
Industry, of which:	20
manufacturing	12
Services	78

Components of GDP

	% of total
Private consumption	45
Public consumption	25
Investment	19
Exports	82
Imports	-72

Structure of employment

	% of total		*% of labour force*
Agriculture	2.1	Unemployed 2015	6.9
Industry	15.2	Av. ann. rate 2005–15	5.0
Services	74.9		

Energy

	m TOE		
Total output	58.4	Net energy imports as % of energy use	20
Total consumption	96.2		
Consumption per head kg oil equivalent	4,326		

Inflation and finance

			av. ann. increase 2011–16
Consumer price inflation 2016	0.1%	Narrow money (M1)	8.1%
Av. ann. inflation 2011–16	3.5%	Broad money	3.6%
Deposit rate, Dec. 2016	1.75%		

Exchange rates

	end 2016		*December 2016*
€ per $	0.95	Effective rates	2010 = 100
€ per sdr	1.28	– nominal	97.35
		– real	96.69

Trade

Principal exports

	$bn fob
Machinery & transport equip.	183.2
Chemicals & related products	95.7
Mineral fuels & lubricants	74.3
Food, drink & tobacco	73.5
Total incl. others	**474.1**

Principal imports

	$bn cif
Machinery & transport equip.	171.3
Mineral fuels & lubricants	82.3
Chemicals & related products	67.5
Food, drink & tobacco	50.8
Total incl. others	**425.0**

Main export destinations

	% of total
Germany	29.5
Belgium	13.4
United Kingdom	11.2
France	10.1
EU28	75.7

Main origins of imports

	% of total
Germany	17.8
China	17.4
Belgium	10.0
United States	9.6
EU28	45.9

Balance of payments, reserves and aid, $bn

Visible exports fob	474.1
Visible imports fob	-389.6
Trade balance	84.5
Invisibles inflows	400.2
Invisibles outflows	-406.4
Net transfers	-12.2
Current account balance	66.2
– as % of GDP	8.8
Capital balance	-63.2
Overall balance	-0.5
Change in reserves	-4.8
Level of reserves end Dec.	38.2
No. months of import cover	0.6
Official gold holdings, m oz	19.7
Aid given	5.7
– as % of GDP	0.8

Health and education

Health spending, % of GDP	10.9
Doctors per 1,000 pop.	2.9
Hospital beds per 1,000 pop.	...
Improved-water source access, % of pop.	100
Education spending, % of GDP	5.6
Enrolment, %: primary	104
secondary	132
tertiary	79

Society

No. of households, m	7.7
Av. no. per household	2.2
Marriages per 1,000 pop.	3.9
Divorces per 1,000 pop.	2.1
Religion, % of pop.	
Christian	50.6
Non-religious	42.1
Muslim	6.0
Other	0.6
Hindu	0.5
Jewish	0.2
Cost of living, Dec. 2016 New York = 100	75
Cars per 1,000 pop.	488
Colour TV households, % with:	
cable	69.3
satellite	7.2
Telephone lines per 100 pop.	41.3
Mobile telephone subscribers per 100 pop.	123.5
Broadband subs per 100 pop.	41.7
Internet users, % of pop.	93.1

a Includes water.

NEW ZEALAND

Area, sq km	268,107	Capital	Wellington
Arable as % of total land	2.2	Currency	New Zealand dollar (NZ$)

People

Population, m	4.5	Life expectancy: men	80.8 yrs
Pop. per sq km	16.8	women	84.0 yrs
Average annual growth in pop. 2015–20, %	0.9	Adult literacy	...
Pop. aged 0–24, %	34.1	Fertility rate (per woman)	2.0
Pop. aged 70 and over, %	9.8	Urban population, 2020, %	86.5
No. of men per 100 women	95.6		*per 1,000 pop.*
Human Development Index	91.5	Crude birth rate	12.9
		Crude death rate	6.9

The economy

GDP	$173bn	GDP per head	$38,501
GDP	NZ$247bn	GDP per head in purchasing power parity (USA=100)	66.6
Av. ann. growth in real GDP 2010–15	2.5%	Economic freedom index	83.7

Origins of GDP	*% of total*	**Components of GDP**	*% of total*
Agriculture	4	Private consumption	58
Industry, of which:	26	Public consumption	19
manufacturing	...	Investment	23
Services	70	Exports	28
		Imports	-27

Structure of employment

	% of total		*% of labour force*
Agriculture	6.1	Unemployed 2015	5.4
Industry	21.9	Av. ann. rate 2005–15	5.1
Services	71.5		

Energy

	m TOE		
Total output	9.5	Net energy imports as % of energy use	17
Total consumption	22.5		
Consumption per head kg oil equivalent	4,560		

Inflation and finance

			av. ann. increase 2011–16
Consumer price inflation 2016	0.7%	Narrow money (M1)	8.2%
Av. ann. inflation 2011–16	3.1%	Broad money	6.3%
Treasury bill rate, Dec. 2016	1.79%		

Exchange rates

	end 2016		*December 2016*
NZ$ per $	1.44	Effective rates	2010 = 100
NZ$ per sdr	1.93	– nominal	116.96
NZ$ per €	1.52	– real	114.34

Trade

Principal exports	$bn fob
Dairy produce	8.1
Meat	4.8
Forestry products	2.5
Wool	0.6
Total incl. others	**34.4**

Principal imports	$bn cif
Machinery & electrical equip.	7.9
Transport equipment	6.4
Mineral fuels	3.7
Total incl. others	**36.6**

Main export destinations	% of total
China	17.5
Australia	16.9
United States	11.8
Japan	6.0

Main origins of imports	% of total
China	19.5
Australia	11.9
United States	11.7
Japan	6.6

Balance of payments, reserves and aid, $bn

Visible exports fob	34.4
Visible imports fob	-35.8
Trade balance	-1.4
Invisibles inflows	19.7
Invisibles outflows	-23.6
Net transfers	-0.3
Current account balance	-5.5
– as % of GDP	-3.2
Capital balance	-1.9
Overall balance	-0.5
Change in reserves	-1.2
Level of reserves end Dec.	14.7
No. months of import cover	3.0
Official gold holdings, m oz	0.0
Aid given	0.4
– as % of GDP	0.3

Health and education

Health spending, % of GDP	11.0
Doctors per 1,000 pop.	...
Hospital beds per 1,000 pop.	2.3
Improved-water source access, % of pop.	100
Education spending, % of GDP	6.4
Enrolment, %: primary	99
secondary	118
tertiary	81

Society

No. of households, m	1.5
Av. no. per household	3.0
Marriages per 1,000 pop.	4.5
Divorces per 1,000 pop.	1.8
Religion, % of pop.	
Christian	57.0
Non-religious	36.6
Other	2.8
Hindu	2.1
Muslim	1.2
Jewish	0.2
Cost of living, Dec. 2016 New York = 100	92
Cars per 1,000 pop.	648
Colour TV households, % with:	
cable	5.9
satellite	40.7
Telephone lines per 100 pop.	40.2
Mobile telephone subscribers per 100 pop.	121.8
Broadband subs per 100 pop.	31.6
Internet users, % of pop.	88.2

NIGERIA

Area, sq km	923,768	Capital	Abuja
Arable as % of total land	37.3	Currency	Naira (N)

People

Population, m	182.2	Life expectancy: men	53.3 yrs
Pop. per sq km	197.2	women	54.0 yrs
Average annual growth in pop. 2015–20, %	2.5	Adult literacy	59.6
Pop. aged 0–24, %	63.0	Fertility rate (per woman)	5.2
Pop. aged 70 and over, %	1.4	Urban population, 2020, %	51.7
No. of men per 100 women	103.8		*per 1,000 pop.*
Human Development Index	52.7	Crude birth rate	37.9
		Crude death rate	12.2

The economy

GDP	$494bn	GDP per head	$2,710
GDP	N95,178bn	GDP per head in purchasing power parity (USA=100)	10.7
Av. ann. growth in real GDP 2010–15	4.7%	Economic freedom index	57.1

Origins of GDP	*% of total*	**Components of GDP**	*% of total*
Agriculture	21	Private consumption	78
Industry, of which:	20	Public consumption	7
manufacturing	10	Investment	15
Services	59	Exports	11
		Imports	-11

Structure of employment

	% of total		*% of labour force*
Agriculture	...	Unemployed 2015	4.3
Industry	...	Av. ann. rate 2005–15	6.7
Services	...		

Energy

	m TOE		
Total output	170.6	Net energy imports as % of energy use	-93
Total consumption	33.2		
Consumption per head kg oil equivalent	759		

Inflation and finance

			av. ann. increase 2011–16
Consumer price inflation 2016	15.4%	Narrow money (M1)	5.9%
Av. ann. inflation 2011–16	9.9%	Broad money	9.4%
Treasury bill rate, Dec. 2016	13.96%		

Exchange rates

	end 2016		*December 2016*
N per $	305.00	Effective rates	2010 = 100
N per sdr	410.02	– nominal	61.11
N per €	320.94	– real	101.61

Trade

Principal exports	$bn fob
Crude oil	35.4
Gas	6.8
Food, drink & tobacco	0.9
Vegetable products	0.5
Total incl. others	**49.8**

Principal imports[a]	$bn cif
Machinery & transport equip.	11.3
Mineral fuels	6.4
Food & live animals	5.2
Manufactured goods	4.8
Total incl. others	**34.8**

Main export destinations	% of total
India	40.5
Brazil	11.2
Netherlands	8.2
Spain	7.5

Main origins of imports	% of total
China	21.8
United States	12.2
Belgium	5.8
United Kingdom	4.4

Balance of payments, reserves and debt, $bn

Visible exports fob	46.9	Change in reserves	-6.2
Visible imports fob	-53.4	Level of reserves end Dec.	31.3
Trade balance	-6.6	No. months of import cover	4.3
Invisibles inflows	4.2	Official gold holdings, m oz	0.7
Invisibles outflows	-34.0	Foreign debt	29.0
Net transfers	20.6	– as % of GDP	5.9
Current account balance	-15.8	– as % of total exports	40.9
– as % of GDP	-3.2	Debt service ratio	2.1
Capital balance	-7.0		
Overall balance	-6.0		

Health and education

Health spending, % of GDP	3.7	Education spending, % of GDP	...
Doctors per 1,000 pop.	0.4	Enrolment, %: primary	94
Hospital beds per 1,000 pop.	...	secondary	56
Improved-water source access, % of pop.	68.5	tertiary	...

Society

No. of households, m	38.3	Cost of living, Dec. 2016 New York = 100	39
Av. no. per household	4.8	Cars per 1,000 pop.	16
Marriages per 1,000 pop.	...	Colour TV households, % with:	
Divorces per 1,000 pop.	...	cable	1.9
Religion, % of pop.		satellite	...
Christian	49.3	Telephone lines per 100 pop.	0.1
Muslim	48.8	Mobile telephone subscribers per 100 pop.	82.2
Other	1.4	Broadband subs per 100 pop.	0.0
Non-religious	0.4	Internet users, % of pop.	47.4
Hindu	<0.1		
Jewish	<0.1		

a 2012

NORWAY

Area, sq km	385,000	Capital	Oslo
Arable as % of total land	2.2	Currency	Norwegian krone (Nkr)

People

Population, m	5.2	Life expectancy: men	80.2 yrs
Pop. per sq km	13.5	women	84.0 yrs
Average annual growth in pop. 2015–20, %	1.1	Adult literacy	...
Pop. aged 0–24, %	31.1	Fertility rate (per woman)	1.9
Pop. aged 70 and over, %	10.6	Urban population, 2020, %	81.7
			per 1,000 pop.
No. of men per 100 women	101.5	Crude birth rate	11.9
Human Development Index	94.9	Crude death rate	7.9

The economy

GDP	$387bn	GDP per head	$74,342
GDP	Nkr3,117bn	GDP per head in purchasing power parity (USA=100)	122.2
Av. ann. growth in real GDP 2010–15	1.7%	Economic freedom index	74.0

Origins of GDP	*% of total*	**Components of GDP**	*% of total*
Agriculture	2	Private consumption	43
Industry, of which:	35	Public consumption	23
manufacturing	8	Investment	28
Services	64	Exports	37
		Imports	-32

Structure of employment

	% of total		*% of labour force*
Agriculture	2.0	Unemployed 2015	4.3
Industry	20.1	Av. ann. rate 2005–15	3.7
Services	77.7		

Energy

	m TOE		
Total output	195.3	Net energy imports as % of energy use	-583
Total consumption	47.8		
Consumption per head kg oil equivalent	5,596		

Inflation and finance

			av. ann. increase 2011–16
Consumer price inflation 2016	3.2%	Narrow money (M1)	17.4%
Av. ann. inflation 2011–16	3.7%	Broad money	4.5%
Central bank policy rate Dec. 2016	0.50%		

Exchange rates

	end 2016		*December 2016*
Nkr per $	8.62	Effective rates	2010 = 100
Nkr per sdr	11.59	– nominal	86.05
Nkr per €	9.07	– real	88.80

Trade

Principal exports

	$bn fob
Mineral fuels & lubricants	60.0
Machinery & transport equip.	12.3
Food & beverages	9.6
Manufactured goods	9.6
Total incl. others	**103.9**

Principal imports

	$bn cif
Machinery & transport equip.	31.1
Miscellaneous manufactured goods	12.2
Manufactured goods	10.8
Chemicals & mineral products	7.4
Total incl. others	**76.4**

Main export destinations

	% of total
United Kingdom	22.1
Germany	17.8
Netherlands	10.1
France	6.6
EU28	79.4

Main origins of imports

	% of total
Sweden	11.5
Germany	11.3
China	10.4
United Kingdom	6.7
EU28	60.9

Balance of payments, reserves and aid, $bn

Visible exports fob	103.4
Visible imports fob	-75.4
Trade balance	27.9
Invisibles inflows	83.0
Invisibles outflows	-70.3
Net transfers	-6.9
Current account balance	33.7
– as % of GDP	8.7
Capital balance	-17.3
Overall balance	-5.0
Change in reserves	-7.3
Level of reserves end Dec.	57.5
No. months of import cover	4.7
Official gold holdings, m oz	0.0
Aid given	4.3
– as % of GDP	1.1

Health and education

Health spending, % of GDP	9.4
Doctors per 1,000 pop.	4.3
Hospital beds per 1,000 pop.	3.3
Improved-water source access, % of pop.	100
Education spending, % of GDP	7.4
Enrolment, %: primary	100
secondary	113
tertiary	77

Society

No. of households, m	2.3
Av. no. per household	2.3
Marriages per 1,000 pop.	4.6
Divorces per 1,000 pop.	1.9
Religion, % of pop.	
Christian	84.7
Non-religious	10.1
Muslim	3.7
Other	0.9
Hindu	0.5
Jewish	<0.1
Cost of living, Dec. 2016 New York = 100	99
Cars per 1,000 pop.	498
Colour TV households, % with:	
cable	44.5
satellite	38.5
Telephone lines per 100 pop.	18.4
Mobile telephone subscribers per 100 pop.	111.1
Broadband subs per 100 pop.	39.7
Internet users, % of pop.	96.8

PAKISTAN

Area, sq km	796,095	Capital	Islamabad
Arable as % of total land	39.5	Currency	Pakistan rupee (PRs)

People

Population, m	188.9	Life expectancy: men	65.8 yrs
Pop. per sq km	237.3	women	67.8 yrs
Average annual growth in pop. 2015–20, %	2.0	Adult literacy	56.4
Pop. aged 0–24, %	54.9	Fertility rate (per woman)	2.8
Pop. aged 70 and over, %	2.8	Urban population, 2020, %	41.2
No. of men per 100 women	105.6		*per 1,000 pop.*
Human Development Index	55.0	Crude birth rate	27.6
		Crude death rate	7.2

The economy

GDP	$271bn	GDP per head	$1,435
GDP	PRs27,493bn	GDP per head in purchasing power parity (USA=100)	8.8
Av. ann. growth in real GDP 2010–15	3.8%	Economic freedom index	52.8

Origins of GDP	*% of total*	**Components of GDP**	*% of total*
Agriculture	25	Private consumption	80
Industry, of which:	20	Public consumption	11
manufacturing	13	Investment	15
Services	55	Exports	11
		Imports	-17

Structure of employment

	% of total		*% of labour force*
Agriculture	43.5	Unemployed 2015	5.9
Industry	22.5	Av. ann. rate 2005–15	5.9
Services	34.0		

Energy

	m TOE		
Total output	37.4	Net energy imports as % of energy use	24
Total consumption	66.3		
Consumption per head kg oil equivalent	486		

Inflation and finance

			av. ann. increase 2011–16
Consumer price inflation 2016	2.9%	Narrow money (M1)	16.6%
Av. ann. inflation 2011–16	8.7%	Broad money	13.6%
Treasury bill rate, Dec. 2016	5.98%		

Exchange rates

	end 2016		*December 2016*
PRs per $	104.81	Effective rates	2010 = 100
PRs per sdr	140.90	– nominal	95.05
PRs per €	110.29	– real	127.49

Trade

Principal exports	$bn fob
Cotton fabrics	2.2
Knitwear	2.1
Rice	1.8
Cotton yard & thread	1.6
Total incl. others	**21.9**

Principal imports	$bn cif
Petroleum products	6.5
Crude oil	3.7
Palm oil	1.8
Telecoms equipment	1.4
Total incl. others	**43.9**

Main export destinations	% of total
United States	16.7
China	8.8
Afghanistan	7.9
United Kingdom	7.2

Main origins of imports	% of total
China	25.1
United Arab Emirates	13.1
Saudi Arabia	6.8
Indonesia	4.7

Balance of payments, reserves and debt, $bn

Visible exports fob	22.7
Visible imports fob	-39.3
Trade balance	-16.6
Invisibles inflows	6.4
Invisibles outflows	-13.6
Net transfers	22.1
Current account balance	-1.6
– as % of GDP	-0.6
Capital balance	6.0
Overall balance	3.9
Change in reserves	5.7
Level of reserves end Dec.	20.0
No. months of import cover	4.5
Official gold holdings, m oz	2.1
Foreign debt	65.5
– as % of GDP	24.2
– as % of total exports	135.1
Debt service ratio	7.7

Health and education

Health spending, % of GDP	2.6
Doctors per 1,000 pop.	0.8
Hospital beds per 1,000 pop.	0.6
Improved-water source access, % of pop.	91.4
Education spending, % of GDP	2.7
Enrolment, %: primary	93
secondary	45
tertiary	10

Society

No. of households, m	28.1
Av. no. per household	6.7
Marriages per 1,000 pop.	...
Divorces per 1,000 pop.	...
Religion, % of pop.	
Muslim	96.4
Hindu	1.9
Christian	1.6
Jewish	<0.1
Non-religious	<0.1
Other	<0.1
Cost of living, Dec. 2016 New York = 100	44
Cars per 1,000 pop.	13
Colour TV households, % with:	
cable	1.3
satellite	15.4
Telephone lines per 100 pop.	1.9
Mobile telephone subscribers per 100 pop.	66.9
Broadband subs per 100 pop.	1.0
Internet users, % of pop.	18.0

PERU

Area, sq km	1,285,216	Capital	Lima
Arable as % of total land	3.2	Currency	Nuevo Sol (new Sol)

People

Population, m	31.4	Life expectancy: men	72.9 yrs
Pop. per sq km	24.4	women	78.1 yrs
Average annual growth in pop. 2015–20, %	1.2	Adult literacy	94.4
Pop. aged 0–24, %	45.7	Fertility rate (per woman)	2.2
Pop. aged 70 and over, %	4.5	Urban population, 2020, %	80.1
No. of men per 100 women	99.8		*per 1,000 pop.*
Human Development Index	74.0	Crude birth rate	18.7
		Crude death rate	5.6

The economy

GDP	$192bn	GDP per head	$6,127
GDP	New Soles 613bn	GDP per head in purchasing power parity (USA=100)	21.9
Av. ann. growth in real GDP 2010–15	4.8%	Economic freedom index	68.9

Origins of GDP

	% of total
Agriculture	8
Industry, of which:	33
manufacturing	15
Services	59

Components of GDP

	% of total
Private consumption	65
Public consumption	13
Investment	24
Exports	21
Imports	-24

Structure of employment

	% of total		*% of labour force*
Agriculture	...	Unemployed 2015	4.4
Industry	22.8	Av. ann. rate 2005–15	5.2
Services	76.1		

Energy

	m TOE		
Total output	22.9	Net energy imports as % of energy use	0.15
Total consumption	26.4		
Consumption per head kg oil equivalent	768		

Inflation and finance

			av. ann. increase 2011–16
Consumer price inflation 2016	3.6%	Narrow money (M1)	8.6%
Av. ann. inflation 2011–16	5.0%	Broad money	10.0%
Money market rate, Dec. 2016	4.37%		

Exchange rates

	end 2016		*December 2016*
New Soles per $	3.36	Effective rates	2010 = 100
New Soles per sdr	4.51	– nominal	...
New Soles per €	3.54	– real	...

Trade

Principal exports	$bn fob
Copper	8.2
Gold	6.7
Zinc	1.5
Fishmeal	1.4
Total incl. others	**34.2**

Principal imports	$bn cif
Intermediate goods	15.9
Capital goods	12.0
Consumer goods	8.8
Total incl. others	**37.4**

Main export destinations	% of total
China	21.5
United States	14.8
Switzerland	7.8
Canada	6.8

Main origins of imports	% of total
China	24.4
United States	22.2
Brazil	5.4
Mexico	4.8

Balance of payments, reserves and debt, $bn

Visible exports fob	34.2
Visible imports fob	-37.0
Trade balance	-2.8
Invisibles inflows	6.9
Invisibles outflows	-16.6
Net transfers	3.3
Current account balance	-9.2
– as % of GDP	-4.8
Capital balance	10.1
Overall balance	-0.8
Change in reserves	-0.9
Level of reserves end Dec.	61.6
No. months of import cover	13.8
Official gold holdings, m oz	1.1
Foreign debt	65.9
– as % of GDP	34.3
– as % of total exports	150.4
Debt service ratio	10.8

Health and education

Health spending, % of GDP	5.5
Doctors per 1,000 pop.	1.1
Hospital beds per 1,000 pop.	1.5
Improved-water source access, % of pop.	86.7
Education spending, % of GDP	3.9
Enrolment, %: primary	102
secondary	96
tertiary	...

Society

No. of households, m	7.8
Av. no. per household	4.0
Marriages per 1,000 pop.	3.1
Divorces per 1,000 pop.	0.4
Religion, % of pop.	
Christian	95.5
Non-religious	3.0
Other	1.5
Hindu	<0.1
Jewish	<0.1
Muslim	<0.1
Cost of living, Dec. 2016 New York = 100	65
Cars per 1,000 pop.	45
Colour TV households, % with:	
cable	32.5
satellite	0.2
Telephone lines per 100 pop.	9.3
Mobile telephone subscribers per 100 pop.	109.9
Broadband subs per 100 pop.	6.4
Internet users, % of pop.	40.9

PHILIPPINES

Area, sq km	300,000	Capital	Manila
Arable as % of total land	18.7	Currency	Philippine peso (P)

People

Population, m	100.7	Life expectancy: men	65.4 yrs
Pop. per sq km	335.7	women	72.4 yrs
Average annual growth in pop. 2015–20, %	1.5	Adult literacy	96.6
Pop. aged 0–24, %	51.5	Fertility rate (per woman)	3.1
Pop. aged 70 and over, %	2.6	Urban population, 2020, %	44.3
No. of men per 100 women	101.9		*per 1,000 pop.*
Human Development Index	68.2	Crude birth rate	22.7
		Crude death rate	6.8

The economy

GDP	$292bn	GDP per head	$2,904
GDP	P13,307bn	GDP per head in purchasing power parity (USA=100)	13.2
Av. ann. growth in real GDP 2010–15	5.9%	Economic freedom index	65.6

Origins of GDP	*% of total*	**Components of GDP**	*% of total*
Agriculture	10	Private consumption	75
Industry, of which:	31	Public consumption	11
manufacturing	20	Investment	21
Services	59	Exports	28
		Imports	-35

Structure of employment

	% of total		*% of labour force*
Agriculture	29.2	Unemployed 2015	6.3
Industry	16.2	Av. ann. rate 2005–15	7.2
Services	54.7		

Energy

	m TOE		
Total output	9.7	Net energy imports as % of energy use	46
Total consumption	34.8		
Consumption per head kg oil equivalent	481		

Inflation and finance

			av. ann. increase 2011–16
Consumer price inflation 2016	2.0%	Narrow money (M1)	15.5%
Av. ann. inflation 2011–16	4.7%	Broad money	14.0%
Treasury bill rate, Dec. 2016	1.56%		

Exchange rates

	end 2016		*December 2016*
P per $	49.81	Effective rates	2010 = 100
P per sdr	66.97	– nominal	103.14
P per €	52.41	– real	112.11

Trade

Principal exports	$bn fob
Electrical & electronic equip.	28.6
Machinery & transport equip.	5.2
Agricultural products	3.7
Mineral products	2.9
Total incl. others	**58.6**

Principal imports	$bn cif
Raw materials & intermediate goods	30.5
Capital goods	19.6
Consumer goods	11.4
Mineral fuels & lubricants	9.2
Total incl. others	**74.8**

Main export destinations	% of total
Japan	21.1
United States	15.0
China	10.9
Hong Kong	10.6

Main origins of imports	% of total
China	15.9
United States	10.6
Japan	9.4
Taiwan	7.7

Balance of payments, reserves and debt, $bn

Visible exports fob	43.2
Visible imports fob	-66.5
Trade balance	-23.3
Invisibles inflows	38.6
Invisibles outflows	-31.3
Net transfers	23.3
Current account balance	7.3
– as % of GDP	2.5
Capital balance	-2.2
Overall balance	2.6
Change in reserves	1.0
Level of reserves end Dec.	80.6
No. months of import cover	9.9
Official gold holdings, m oz	6.3
Foreign debt	77.7
– as % of GDP	26.6
– as % of total exports	69.5
Debt service ratio	7.2

Health and education

Health spending, % of GDP	4.7
Doctors per 1,000 pop.	...
Hospital beds per 1,000 pop.	1.0
Improved-water source access, % of pop.	91.8
Education spending, % of GDP	...
Enrolment, %: primary	117
secondary	88
tertiary	36

Society

No. of households, m	22.9
Av. no. per household	4.4
Marriages per 1,000 pop.	...
Divorces per 1,000 pop.	...
Religion, % of pop.	
Christian	92.6
Muslim	5.5
Other	1.7
Non-religious	0.1
Hindu	<0.1
Jewish	<0.1
Cost of living, Dec. 2016 New York = 100	63
Cars per 1,000 pop.	31
Colour TV households, % with:	
cable	52.5
satellite	0.6
Telephone lines per 100 pop.	3.2
Mobile telephone subscribers per 100 pop.	116.0
Broadband subs per 100 pop.	4.8
Internet users, % of pop.	40.7

POLAND

Area, sq km	312,888	Capital	Warsaw
Arable as % of total land	35.7	Currency	Zloty (Zl)

People

Population, m	38.6	Life expectancy: men	74.1 yrs
Pop. per sq km	123.4	women	81.8 yrs
Average annual growth in pop. 2015–20, %	-0.1	Adult literacy	99.8
Pop. aged 0–24, %	26.5	Fertility rate (per woman)	1.3
Pop. aged 70 and over, %	10.2	Urban population, 2020, %	60.7
No. of men per 100 women	93.7		*per 1,000 pop.*
Human Development Index	85.5	Crude birth rate	9.5
		Crude death rate	10.4

The economy

GDP	$477bn	GDP per head	$12,359
GDP	Zl1,798bn	GDP per head in purchasing power parity (USA=100)	46.8
Av. ann. growth in real GDP 2010–15	2.9%	Economic freedom index	68.3

Origins of GDP	*% of total*	**Components of GDP**	*% of total*
Agriculture	3	Private consumption	58
Industry, of which:	34	Public consumption	18
manufacturing	20	Investment	20
Services	63	Exports	50
		Imports	-46

Structure of employment

	% of total		*% of labour force*
Agriculture	11.5	Unemployed 2015	7.5
Industry	30.4	Av. ann. rate 2005–15	10.2
Services	57.8		

Energy

	m TOE		
Total output	54.7	Net energy imports as % of energy use	28
Total consumption	98.0		
Consumption per head kg oil equivalent	2,473		

Inflation and finance

			av. ann. increase 2011–16
Consumer price inflation 2016	-0.6%	Narrow money (M1)	11.7%
Av. ann. inflation 2011–16	3.0%	Broad money	7.5%
Money market rate, Dec. 2016	1.47%		

Exchange rates

	end 2016		*December 2016*
Zl per $	4.18	Effective rates	2010 = 100
Zl per sdr	5.62	– nominal	91.51
Zl per €	4.40	– real	88.18

Trade

Principal exports

	$bn fob
Machinery & transport equip.	77.0
Manufactured goods	37.6
Foodstuffs & live animals	21.4
Total incl. others	**199.4**

Principal imports

	$bn cif
Machinery & transport equip.	71.0
Manufactured goods	34.0
Chemicals & mineral products	27.4
Total incl. others	**195.2**

Main export destinations

	% of total
Germany	27.1
United Kingdom	6.7
Czech Republic	6.6
France	5.5
EU28	79.3

Main origins of imports

	% of total
Germany	27.8
China	7.4
Russia	7.2
Netherlands	5.9
EU28	70.7

Balance of payments, reserves and debt, $bn

Visible exports fob	191.0
Visible imports fob	-188.6
Trade balance	2.5
Invisibles inflows	57.5
Invisibles outflows	-62.0
Net transfers	-1.0
Current account balance	-2.9
– as % of GDP	-0.6
Capital balance	10.9
Overall balance	1.1
Change in reserves	-5.5
Level of reserves end Dec.	94.9
No. months of import cover	4.5
Official gold holdings, m oz	3.3
Foreign debt	331.4
– as % of GDP	69.5
– as % of total exports	131.2
Debt service ratio	12.2

Health and education

Health spending, % of GDP	6.4
Doctors per 1,000 pop.	2.2
Hospital beds per 1,000 pop.	6.5
Improved-water source access, % of pop.	98.3
Education spending, % of GDP	4.9
Enrolment, %: primary	101
secondary	109
tertiary	71

Society

No. of households, m	14.1
Av. no. per household	2.7
Marriages per 1,000 pop.	5.0
Divorces per 1,000 pop.	1.7
Religion, % of pop.	
Christian	94.3
Non-religious	5.6
Hindu	<0.1
Jewish	<0.1
Muslim	<0.1
Other	<0.1
Cost of living, Dec. 2016 New York = 100	58
Cars per 1,000 pop.	523
Colour TV households, % with:	
cable	33.8
satellite	62.8
Telephone lines per 100 pop.	23.7
Mobile telephone subscribers per 100 pop.	142.7
Broadband subs per 100 pop.	19.0
Internet users, % of pop.	68.0

PORTUGAL

Area, sq km	92,225	Capital	Lisbon
Arable as % of total land	12.4	Currency	Euro (€)

People

Population, m	10.3	Life expectancy: men	78.8 yrs
Pop. per sq km	111.7	women	84.4 yrs
Average annual growth in pop. 2015–20, %	-0.4	Adult literacy	95.4
Pop. aged 0–24, %	24.5	Fertility rate (per woman)	1.5
Pop. aged 70 and over, %	15.0	Urban population, 2020, %	66.1
No. of men per 100 women	89.9		*per 1,000 pop.*
Human Development Index	84.3	Crude birth rate	7.6
		Crude death rate	10.7

The economy

GDP	$199bn	GDP per head	$19,342
GDP	€180bn	GDP per head in purchasing power parity (USA=100)	50.4
Av. ann. growth in real GDP 2010–15	-0.9%	Economic freedom index	62.6

Origins of GDP	*% of total*	**Components of GDP**	*% of total*
Agriculture	2	Private consumption	66
Industry, of which:	22	Public consumption	18
manufacturing	14	Investment	15
Services	75	Exports	41
		Imports	-40

Structure of employment

	% of total		*% of labour force*
Agriculture	7.5	Unemployed 2015	12.4
Industry	24.4	Av. ann. rate 2005–15	11.1
Services	68.1		

Energy

	m TOE		
Total output	...	Net energy imports as % of energy use	72
Total consumption	25.6		
Consumption per head kg oil equivalent	2,035		

Inflation and finance

			av. ann. increase 2011–16
Consumer price inflation 2016	0.7%	Narrow money (M1)	8.1%
Av. ann. inflation 2011–16	3.0%	Broad money	3.6%
Deposit rate, Dec. 2016	0.32%		

Exchange rates

	end 2016		*December 2016*
€ per $	0.95	Effective rates	2010 = 100
€ per sdr	1.28	– nominal	98.14
		– real	97.21

Trade

Principal exports

	$bn fob
Machinery & transport equip.	14.3
Food, drink & tobacco	6.2
Chemicals & related products	4.9
Mineral fuels & lubricants	4.3
Total incl. others	**55.3**

Principal imports

	$bn cif
Machinery & transport equip.	18.6
Chemicals & related products	9.5
Food, drink & tobacco	8.8
Mineral fuels & lubricants	8.8
Total incl. others	**66.9**

Main export destinations

	% of total
Spain	25.0
France	12.1
Germany	11.8
United Kingdom	6.7
EU28	72.8

Main origins of imports

	% of total
Spain	33.0
Germany	12.9
France	7.4
Italy	5.4
EU28	76.5

Balance of payments, reserves and debt, $bn

Visible exports fob	54.5
Visible imports fob	-64.7
Trade balance	-10.3
Invisibles inflows	37.0
Invisibles outflows	-28.3
Net transfers	1.7
Current account balance	0.1
– as % of GDP	0.1
Capital balance	11.0
Overall balance	10.8
Change in reserves	-0.3
Level of reserves end Dec.	19.4
No. months of import cover	2.5
Official gold holdings, m oz	12.3
Aid given	0.3
– as % of GDP	0.2

Health and education

Health spending, % of GDP	9.5
Doctors per 1,000 pop.	4.1
Hospital beds per 1,000 pop.	3.4
Improved-water source access, % of pop.	100
Education spending, % of GDP	5.3
Enrolment, %: primary	109
secondary	116
tertiary	66

Society

No. of households, m	4.1
Av. no. per household	2.5
Marriages per 1,000 pop.	3.0
Divorces per 1,000 pop.	2.2
Religion, % of pop.	
Christian	93.8
Non-religious	4.4
Other	1.0
Muslim	0.6
Hindu	0.1
Jewish	<0.1
Cost of living, Dec. 2016 New York = 100	64
Cars per 1,000 pop.	421
Colour TV households, % with:	
cable	56.1
satellite	20.1
Telephone lines per 100 pop.	44.1
Mobile telephone subscribers per 100 pop.	110.4
Broadband subs per 100 pop.	29.6
Internet users, % of pop.	68.6

ROMANIA

Area, sq km	238,391	Capital	Bucharest
Arable as % of total land	38.2	Currency	Leu (RON)

People

Population, m	19.5	Life expectancy: men	71.6 yrs
Pop. per sq km	81.8	women	78.7 yrs
Average annual growth in pop. 2015–20, %	-0.7	Adult literacy	98.8
Pop. aged 0–24, %	26.0	Fertility rate (per woman)	1.3
Pop. aged 70 and over, %	11.8	Urban population, 2020, %	55.6
No. of men per 100 women	93.9		*per 1,000 pop.*
Human Development Index	80.2	Crude birth rate	9.0
		Crude death rate	13.7

The economy

GDP	$178bn	GDP per head	$9,104
GDP	RON711bn	GDP per head in purchasing power parity (USA=100)	38.1
Av. ann. growth in real GDP 2010–15	2.4%	Economic freedom index	69.7

Origins of GDP	*% of total*	**Components of GDP**	*% of total*
Agriculture	5	Private consumption	61
Industry, of which:	35	Public consumption	14
manufacturing	24	Investment	26
Services	60	Exports	41
		Imports	-42

Structure of employment

	% of total		*% of labour force*
Agriculture	25.6	Unemployed 2015	6.8
Industry	28.5	Av. ann. rate 2005–15	6.8
Services	46.0		

Energy

	m TOE		
Total output	21.3	Net energy imports as % of energy use	17
Total consumption	33.2		
Consumption per head kg oil equivalent	1,592		

Inflation and finance

			av. ann. increase 2011–16
Consumer price inflation 2016	-1.5%	Narrow money (M1)	16.0%
Av. ann. inflation 2011–16	3.9%	Broad money	7.8%
Treasury bill rate, Dec. 2016	2.43%		

Exchange rates

	end 2016		*December 2016*
Lei per $	4.30	Effective rates	2010 = 100
Lei per sdr	5.79	– nominal	94.81
Lei per €	4.52	– real	94.98

Trade

Principal exports

	$bn fob
Machinery & transport equip.	26.9
Basic metals & products	5.2
Textiles & apparel	4.4
Minerals, fuels & lubricants	2.7
Total incl. others	**60.6**

Principal imports

	$bn cif
Machinery & transport equip.	26.3
Chemical products	7.0
Minerals, fuels & lubricants	4.9
Textiles & products	4.7
Total incl. others	**69.9**

Main export destinations

	% of total
Germany	19.7
Italy	12.5
France	6.8
Hungary	5.4
EU28	73.7

Main origins of imports

	% of total
Germany	19.8
Italy	10.9
Hungary	7.9
France	5.6
EU28	77.1

Balance of payments, reserves and debt, $bn

Visible exports fob	54.5
Visible imports fob	-63.1
Trade balance	-8.6
Invisibles inflows	21.1
Invisibles outflows	-17.7
Net transfers	3.1
Current account balance	-2.2
– as % of GDP	-1.2
Capital balance	2.7
Overall balance	0.9
Change in reserves	-4.5
Level of reserves end Dec.	38.7
No. months of import cover	5.7
Official gold holdings, m oz	3.3
Foreign debt	96.0
– as % of GDP	53.9
– as % of total exports	121.9
Debt service ratio	30.1

Health and education

Health spending, % of GDP	5.6
Doctors per 1,000 pop.	2.4
Hospital beds per 1,000 pop.	6.1
Improved-water source access, % of pop.	100
Education spending, % of GDP	2.9
Enrolment, %: primary	90
secondary	92
tertiary	53

Society

No. of households, m	7.0
Av. no. per household	2.8
Marriages per 1,000 pop.	5.9
Divorces per 1,000 pop.	1.4
Religion, % of pop.	
Christian	99.5
Muslim	0.3
Non-religious	0.1
Hindu	<0.1
Jewish	<0.1
Other	<0.1
Cost of living, Dec. 2016 New York = 100	47
Cars per 1,000 pop.	227
Colour TV households, % with:	
cable	45.9
satellite	37.4
Telephone lines per 100 pop.	19.8
Mobile telephone subscribers per 100 pop.	107.1
Broadband subs per 100 pop.	19.8
Internet users, % of pop.	55.8

RUSSIA

Area, sq km	17,098,246	Capital	Moscow
Arable as % of total land	7.5	Currency	Rouble (Rb)

People

Population, m	143.5	Life expectancy: men	64.7 yrs
Pop. per sq km	8.4	women	76.1 yrs
Average annual growth in pop. 2015–20, %	-0.1	Adult literacy	99.7
Pop. aged 0–24, %	27.4	Fertility rate (per woman)	1.6
Pop. aged 70 and over, %	9.3	Urban population, 2020, %	74.6
No. of men per 100 women	86.8		*per 1,000 pop.*
Human Development Index	80.4	Crude birth rate	12.3
		Crude death rate	14.3

The economy

GDP	$1,366bn	GDP per head	$9,518
GDP	Rb83,233bn	GDP per head in purchasing power parity (USA=100)	46.7
Av. ann. growth in real GDP 2010–15	1.1%	Economic freedom index	57.1

Origins of GDP	*% of total*	**Components of GDP**	*% of total*
Agriculture	5	Private consumption	52
Industry, of which:	33	Public consumption	19
manufacturing	14	Investment	21
Services	63	Exports	30
		Imports	-21

Structure of employment

	% of total		*% of labour force*
Agriculture	6.7	Unemployed 2015	5.6
Industry	27.2	Av. ann. rate 2005–15	6.4
Services	66.1		

Energy

	m TOE		
Total output	1,350.3	Net energy imports as % of energy use	-84
Total consumption	772.0		
Consumption per head kg oil equivalent	4,943		

Inflation and finance

			av. ann. increase 2011–16
Consumer price inflation 2016	7.2%	Narrow money (M1)	6.7%
Av. ann. inflation 2011–16	9.4%	Broad money	12.3%
Money market rate, Dec. 2016	10.16%		

Exchange rates

	end 2016		*December 2016*
Rb per $	60.66	Effective rates	2010 = 100
Rb per sdr	81.54	– nominal	68.80
Rb per €	63.83	– real	90.83

Trade

Principal exports[a]	$bn fob
Fuels	350.8
Ores & metals	52.3
Chemicals	29.2
Machinery & equipment	26.4
Total incl.others	**497.8**

Principal imports[a]	$bn cif
Machinery & equipment	136.3
Chemicals	46.5
Food & agricultural products	39.9
Metals	20.5
Total incl.others	**286.7**

Main export destinations	% of total
Netherlands	11.9
China	8.3
Germany	7.4
Italy	6.5
EU28	39.8

Main origins of imports	% of total
China	19.1
Germany	11.2
United States	6.3
Belarus	5.1
EU28	35.8

Balance of payments, reserves and debt, $bn

Visible exports fob	341.5	Change in reserves	-18.2
Visible imports fob	-193.0	Level of reserves end Dec.	368.0
Trade balance	148.5	No. months of import cover	12.4
Invisibles inflows	89.0	Official gold holdings, m oz	45.5
Invisibles outflows	-162.8	Foreign debt	467.7
Net transfers	-5.7	– as % of GDP	34.2
Current account balance	68.9	– as % of total exports	106.9
– as % of GDP	5.0	Debt service ratio	23.0
Capital balance	-70.3		
Overall balance	1.7		

Health and education

Health spending, % of GDP	7.1	Education spending, % of GDP	4.3
Doctors per 1,000 pop.	4.3	Enrolment, %: primary	99
Hospital beds per 1,000 pop.	...	secondary	101
Improved-water source access, % of pop.	96.9	tertiary	79

Society

No. of households, m	56.5	Cost of living, Dec. 2016 New York = 100	90
Av. no. per household	2.5	Cars per 1,000 pop.	304
Marriages per 1,000 pop.	8.5	Colour TV households, % with: cable	32.9
Divorces per 1,000 pop.	4.5	satellite	24.7
Religion, % of pop.		Telephone lines per 100 pop.	25.0
Christian	73.3	Mobile telephone subscribers per 100 pop.	160.0
Non-religious	16.2	Broadband subs per 100 pop.	18.9
Muslim	10.0	Internet users, % of pop.	70.1
Jewish	0.2		
Hindu	<0.1		
Other	<0.1		

a 2014

SAUDI ARABIA

Area, sq km	2,150,000	Capital	Riyadh
Arable as % of total land	1.6	Currency	Riyal (SR)

People

Population, m	31.5	Life expectancy: men	73.5 yrs
Pop. per sq km	14.7	women	76.3 yrs
Average annual growth in pop. 2015–20, %	1.7	Adult literacy	94.8
Pop. aged 0–24, %	42.2	Fertility rate (per woman)	2.1
Pop. aged 70 and over, %	1.7	Urban population, 2020, %	84.1
No. of men per 100 women	130.1		*per 1,000 pop.*
Human Development Index	84.7	Crude birth rate	18.5
		Crude death rate	3.5

The economy

GDP	$652bn	GDP per head	$20,691
GDP	SR2,444bn	GDP per head in purchasing power parity (USA=100)	96.5
Av. ann. growth in real GDP 2010–15	5.0%	Economic freedom index	64.4

Origins of GDP	*% of total*	**Components of GDP**	*% of total*
Agriculture	2	Private consumption	41
Industry, of which:	46	Public consumption	30
manufacturing	12	Investment	35
Services	52	Exports	34
		Imports	-39

Structure of employment

	% of total		*% of labour force*
Agriculture	6.1	Unemployed 2015	5.6
Industry	22.7	Av. ann. rate 2005–15	5.7
Services	71.2		

Energy

	m TOE		
Total output	689.7	Net energy imports as % of energy use	-192
Total consumption	255.2		
Consumption per head kg oil equivalent	6,913		

Inflation and finance

			av. ann. increase 2011–16
Consumer price inflation 2016	4.0%	Narrow money (M1)	8.5%
Av. ann. inflation 2011–16	4.6%	Broad money	7.9%
Treasury bill rate, Dec. 2016	0.87%		

Exchange rates

	end 2016		*December 2016*
SR per $	3.75	Effective rates	2010 = 100
SR per sdr	5.04	– nominal	123.53
SR per €	3.95	– real	127.57

Trade

Principal exports

	$bn fob
Crude oil	128.0
Refined petroleum products	27.9
Total incl. others	**203.5**

Principal imports

	$bn cif
Machinery & transport equip.	79.7
Foodstuffs	24.5
Chemical & metal products	14.7
Total incl. others	**174.6**

Main export destinations

	% of total
China	14.1
Japan	11.7
United States	10.3
India	9.9

Main origins of imports

	% of total
China	14.5
United States	13.3
Germany	7.1
Japan	5.9

Balance of payments, reserves and aid, $bn

Visible exports fob	203.5
Visible imports fob	-159.3
Trade balance	44.3
Invisibles inflows	40.1
Invisibles outflows	-96.3
Net transfers	-44.7
Current account balance	-56.7
– as % of GDP	-8.7
Capital balance	-43.9
Overall balance	-115.4
Change in reserves	-117.5
Level of reserves end Dec.	627.0
No. months of import cover	29.4
Official gold holdings, m oz	10.4
Foreign debt	171.5
– as % of GDP	26.3
– as % of total exports	70.4
Debt service ratio	5.4

Health and education

Health spending, % of GDP	4.7
Doctors per 1,000 pop.	2.5
Hospital beds per 1,000 pop.	2.1
Improved-water source access, % of pop.	97.0
Education spending, % of GDP	...
Enrolment, %: primary	109
secondary	108
tertiary	63

Society

No. of households, m	5.0
Av. no. per household	6.3
Marriages per 1,000 pop.	...
Divorces per 1,000 pop.	...
Religion, % of pop.	
Muslim	93.0
Christian	4.4
Hindu	1.1
Other	0.9
Non-religious	0.7
Jewish	<0.1
Cost of living, Dec. 2016 New York = 100	54
Cars per 1,000 pop.	140
Colour TV households, % with:	
cable	0.3
satellite	99.5
Telephone lines per 100 pop.	12.5
Mobile telephone subscribers per 100 pop.	176.6
Broadband subs per 100 pop.	11.9
Internet users, % of pop.	69.6

SINGAPORE

Area, sq km	718	Capital	Singapore
Arable as % of total land	0.8	Currency	Singapore dollar (S$)

People

Population, m	5.6	Life expectancy: men	80.6 yrs
Pop. per sq km	7,799.4	women	86.7 yrs
Average annual growth in pop. 2015–20, %	1.4	Adult literacy	96.8
Pop. aged 0–24, %	28.7	Fertility rate (per woman)	1.0
Pop. aged 70 and over, %	7.1	Urban population, 2020, %	100.0
No. of men per 100 women	97.4		*per 1,000 pop.*
Human Development Index	92.5	Crude birth rate	8.7
		Crude death rate	5.1

The economy

GDP	$297bn	GDP per head	$53,006
GDP	S$408bn	GDP per head in purchasing power parity (USA=100)	151.9
Av. ann. growth in real GDP 2010–15	4.0%	Economic freedom index	88.6

Origins of GDP	*% of total*	**Components of GDP**	*% of total*
Agriculture	0	Private consumption	36
Industry, of which:	26	Public consumption	10
manufacturing	20	Investment	26
Services	74	Exports	176
		Imports	-150

Structure of employment

	% of total		*% of labour force*
Agriculture	1.0	Unemployed 2015	1.7
Industry	16.3	Av. ann. rate 2005–15	3.5
Services	82.7		

Energy

	m TOE		
Total output	...	Net energy imports as % of energy use	99
Total consumption	82.3		
Consumption per head kg oil equivalent	5,122		

Inflation and finance

			av. ann. increase 2011–16
Consumer price inflation 2016	-0.3%	Narrow money (M1)	5.8%
Av. ann. inflation 2011–16	3.8%	Broad money	4.9%
Money market rate, Dec. 2016	0.46%		

Exchange rates

	end 2016		*December 2016*
S$ per $	1.45	Effective rates	2010 = 100
S$ per sdr	1.94	– nominal	109.86
S$ per €	1.53	– real	108.01

Trade

Principal exports

	$bn fob
Mineral fuels	59.5
Electronic components & parts	48.5
Chemicals & chemical products	47.7
Manufactured products	30.5
Total incl.others	**357.8**

Principal imports

	$bn cif
Machinery & transport equip.	141.5
Mineral fuels	64.6
Misc. manufactured articles	26.0
Manufactured products	20.5
Total incl.others	**307.7**

Main export destinations

	% of total
China	13.5
Hong Kong	11.3
Malaysia	10.6
Indonesia	8.1

Main origins of imports

	% of total
China	13.7
Malaysia	10.8
United States	10.8
Taiwan	8.0

Balance of payments, reserves and debt, $bn

Visible exports fob	379.6
Visible imports fob	-296.7
Trade balance	82.8
Invisibles inflows	211.5
Invisibles outflows	-230.6
Net transfers	-10.0
Current account balance	53.8
– as % of GDP	18.1
Capital balance	-51.5
Overall balance	1.1
Change in reserves	-9.7
Level of reserves end Dec.	251.9
No. months of import cover	5.7
Official gold holdings, m oz	4.1
Foreign debt	465.5
– as % of GDP	156.8
– as % of total exports	78.7
Debt service ratio	7.3

Health and education

Health spending, % of GDP	4.9
Doctors per 1,000 pop.	2.0
Hospital beds per 1,000 pop.	2.0
Improved-water source access, % of pop.	100
Education spending, % of GDP	2.9
Enrolment, %: primary	...
secondary	...
tertiary	70

Society

No. of households, m	1.6
Av. no. per household	3.5
Marriages per 1,000 pop.	7.3
Divorces per 1,000 pop.	1.8
Religion, % of pop.	
Buddhist	33.9
Christian	18.2
Non-religious	16.4
Muslim	14.3
Other	12.0
Hindu	5.2
Cost of living, Dec. 2016 New York = 100	120
Cars per 1,000 pop.	118
Colour TV households, % with:	
cable	55.8
satellite	...
Telephone lines per 100 pop.	35.9
Mobile telephone subscribers per 100 pop.	146.5
Broadband subs per 100 pop.	26.4
Internet users, % of pop.	82.1

SLOVAKIA

Area, sq km	49,035	Capital	Bratislava
Arable as % of total land	29.0	Currency	Euro (€)

People

Population, m	5.4	Life expectancy: men	73.0 yrs
Pop. per sq km	110.1	women	80.3 yrs
Average annual growth in pop. 2015–20, %	0.0	Adult literacy	...
Pop. aged 0–24, %	27.0	Fertility rate (per woman)	1.4
Pop. aged 70 and over, %	9.0	Urban population, 2020, %	53.2
No. of men per 100 women	94.1		*per 1,000 pop.*
Human Development Index	84.5	Crude birth rate	10.4
		Crude death rate	10.2

The economy

GDP	$87bn	GDP per head	$16,169
GDP	€79bn	GDP per head in purchasing power parity (USA=100)	53.7
Av. ann. growth in real GDP 2010–15	2.4%	Economic freedom index	65.7

Origins of GDP	*% of total*	**Components of GDP**	*% of total*
Agriculture	4	Private consumption	55
Industry, of which:	35	Public consumption	19
manufacturing	22	Investment	23
Services	62	Exports	93
		Imports	-91

Structure of employment

	% of total		*% of labour force*
Agriculture	3.2	Unemployed 2015	11.5
Industry	36.1	Av. ann. rate 2005–15	13.0
Services	60.7		

Energy

	m TOE		
Total output	4.9	Net energy imports as % of energy use	59
Total consumption	17.0		
Consumption per head kg oil equivalent	2,943		

Inflation and finance

			av. ann. increase 2011–16
Consumer price inflation 2016	-0.2%	Narrow money (M1)	8.1%
Av. ann. inflation 2011–16	3.3%	Broad money	3.6%
Deposit rate, Dec. 2016	1.90%		

Exchange rates

	end 2016		*December 2016*
€ per $	0.95	Effective rates	2010 = 100
€ per sdr	1.28	– nominal	99.91
		– real	97.52

Trade

Principal exports

	$bn fob
Machinery & transport equip.	44.4
Chemicals & related products	3.6
Mineral fuels & lubricants	2.8
Food, drink & tobacco	2.7
Total incl. others	**75.3**

Principal imports

	$bn cif
Machinery & transport equip.	34.6
Chemicals & related products	6.4
Mineral fuels & lubricants	5.8
Food, drink & tobacco	3.9
Total incl. others	**83.4**

Main export destinations

	% of total
Germany	22.4
Czech Republic	12.5
Poland	8.5
Austria	6.0
EU28	85.5

Main origins of imports

	% of total
Germany	16.9
Czech Republic	15.2
Austria	8.1
Poland	5.6
EU28	78.7

Balance of payments, reserves and debt, $bn

Visible exports fob	73.3
Visible imports fob	-71.0
Trade balance	2.2
Invisibles inflows	12.3
Invisibles outflows	-13.0
Net transfers	-1.4
Current account balance	0.2
– as % of GDP	0.2
Capital balance	2.4
Overall balance	0.3
Change in reserves	0.3
Level of reserves end Dec.	2.9
No. months of import cover	0.4
Official gold holdings, m oz	1.0
Aid given	0.09
– as % of GDP	0.1

Health and education

Health spending, % of GDP	8.1
Doctors per 1,000 pop.	3.3
Hospital beds per 1,000 pop.	6.0
Improved-water source access, % of pop.	100
Education spending, % of GDP	...
Enrolment, %: primary	101
secondary	92
tertiary	53

Society

No. of households, m	1.8
Av. no. per household	3.0
Marriages per 1,000 pop.	4.9
Divorces per 1,000 pop.	1.9
Religion, % of pop.	
Christian	85.3
Non-religious	14.3
Muslim	0.2
Other	0.1
Hindu	<0.1
Jewish	<0.1
Cost of living, Dec. 2016 New York = 100	...
Cars per 1,000 pop.	355
Colour TV households, % with:	
cable	43.0
satellite	49.6
Telephone lines per 100 pop.	15.9
Mobile telephone subscribers per 100 pop.	122.9
Broadband subs per 100 pop.	23.3
Internet users, % of pop.	77.6

SLOVENIA

Area, sq km	20,273	Capital	Ljubljana
Arable as % of total land	9.1	Currency	Euro (€)

People

Population, m	2.1	Life expectancy: men	78.1 yrs
Pop. per sq km	103.6	women	83.9 yrs
Average annual growth in pop. 2015–20, %	0.1	Adult literacy	99.7
Pop. aged 0–24, %	24.4	Fertility rate (per woman)	1.3
Pop. aged 70 and over, %	13.0	Urban population, 2020, %	49.8
No. of men per 100 women	98.3		*per 1,000 pop.*
Human Development Index	89.0	Crude birth rate	10.1
		Crude death rate	10.0

The economy

GDP	$43bn	GDP per head	$20,380
GDP	€39bn	GDP per head in purchasing power parity (USA=100)	54.2
Av. ann. growth in real GDP 2010–15	0.4%	Economic freedom index	59.2

Origins of GDP	*% of total*	**Components of GDP**	*% of total*
Agriculture	2	Private consumption	52
Industry, of which:	33	Public consumption	19
manufacturing	23	Investment	20
Services	65	Exports	78
		Imports	-69

Structure of employment

	% of total		*% of labour force*
Agriculture	7.0	Unemployed 2015	9.0
Industry	31.6	Av. ann. rate 2005–15	7.3
Services	60.2		

Energy

	m TOE		
Total output	2.2	Net energy imports as % of energy use	44
Total consumption	7.0		
Consumption per head kg oil equivalent	3,136		

Inflation and finance

			av. ann. increase 2011–16
Consumer price inflation 2016	-0.3%	Narrow money (M1)	8.1%
Av. ann. inflation 2011–16	3.1%	Broad money	3.6%
Money market rate, Dec. 2016	-0.37%		

Exchange rates

	end 2016		*December 2016*
€ per $	0.95	Effective rates	2010 = 100
€ per sdr	1.28	– nominal	...
		– real	...

Trade

Principal exports

	$bn fob
Machinery & transport equip.	12.4
Manufactures	9.9
Chemicals	5.0
Miscellaneous manufactures	4.6
Total incl. others	**32.0**

Principal imports

	$bn cif
Machinery & transport equip.	10.1
Manufactures	8.5
Chemicals	4.2
Mineral fuels & lubricants	2.8
Total incl. others	**29.7**

Main export destinations

	% of total
Germany	19.0
Italy	10.6
Austria	8.0
Croatia	6.7
EU28	76.0

Main origins of imports

	% of total
Germany	16.5
Italy	13.8
Austria	10.2
China	5.4
EU28	70.0

Balance of payments, reserves and debt, $bn

Visible exports fob	26.7
Visible imports fob	-25.0
Trade balance	1.7
Invisibles inflows	8.5
Invisibles outflows	-7.3
Net transfers	-0.6
Current account balance	2.2
– as % of GDP	5.2
Capital balance	-1.7
Overall balance	-0.1
Change in reserves	-0.2
Level of reserves end Dec.	0.9
No. months of import cover	0.3
Official gold holdings, m oz	0.1
Aid given	0.06
– as % of GDP	0.2

Health and education

Health spending, % of GDP	9.2
Doctors per 1,000 pop.	2.5
Hospital beds per 1,000 pop.	4.6
Improved-water source access, % of pop.	99.5
Education spending, % of GDP	5.5
Enrolment, %: primary	99
secondary	111
tertiary	83

Society

No. of households, m	0.9
Av. no. per household	2.3
Marriages per 1,000 pop.	3.2
Divorces per 1,000 pop.	1.2
Religion, % of pop.	
Christian	78.4
Non-religious	18.0
Muslim	3.6
Hindu	<0.1
Jewish	<0.1
Other	<0.1
Cost of living, Dec. 2016 New York = 100	...
Cars per 1,000 pop.	513
Colour TV households, % with:	
cable	70.7
satellite	9.1
Telephone lines per 100 pop.	36.2
Mobile telephone subscribers per 100 pop.	113.2
Broadband subs per 100 pop.	27.6
Internet users, % of pop.	73.1

SOUTH AFRICA

Area, sq km	1,219,000	Capital	Pretoria
Arable as % of total land	10.3	Currency	Rand (R)

People

Population, m	54.5	Life expectancy: men	55.7 yrs
Pop. per sq km	44.7	women	59.3 yrs
Average annual growth in pop. 2015–20, %	0.8	Adult literacy	94.6
Pop. aged 0–24, %	48.6	Fertility rate (per woman)	2.3
Pop. aged 70 and over, %	3.2	Urban population, 2020, %	67.2
			per 1,000 pop.
No. of men per 100 women	96.8	Crude birth rate	19.8
Human Development Index	66.6	Crude death rate	12.6

The economy

GDP	$315bn	GDP per head	$5,775
GDP	R4,014bn	GDP per head in purchasing power parity (USA=100)	23.8
Av. ann. growth in real GDP 2010–15	2.1%	Economic freedom index	62.3

Origins of GDP	*% of total*	**Components of GDP**	*% of total*
Agriculture	2	Private consumption	60
Industry, of which:	29	Public consumption	21
manufacturing	13	Investment	21
Services	69	Exports	31
		Imports	-32

Structure of employment

	% of total		*% of labour force*
Agriculture	5.6	Unemployed 2015	25.2
Industry	23.9	Av. ann. rate 2005–15	24.0
Services	70.5		

Energy

	m TOE		
Total output	137.8	Net energy imports as % of energy use	-14
Total consumption	142.0		
Consumption per head kg oil equivalent	2,714		

Inflation and finance

			av. ann. increase 2011–16
Consumer price inflation 2016	6.4%	Narrow money (M1)	11.10%
Av. ann. inflation 2011–16	6.8%	Broad money	6.9%
Treasury bill rate, Dec. 2016	7.61%		

Exchange rates

	end 2016		*December 2016*
R per $	13.68	Effective rates	2010 = 100
R per sdr	18.40	– nominal	63.48
R per €	14.39	– real	80.01

Trade

Principal exports

	$bn fob
Mineral products	16.6
Precious metals	14.8
Vehicles, aircraft & vessels	10.2
Iron & steel products	9.8
Total incl. others	**81.5**

Principal imports

	$bn cif
Machinery & equipment	21.3
Mineral products	13.8
Vehicles, aircraft & vessels	8.9
Chemicals	8.8
Total incl. others	**85.7**

Main export destinations

	% of total
China	9.2
United States	7.6
Germany	6.2
Namibia	4.8

Main origins of imports

	% of total
China	19.4
Germany	11.9
United States	7.5
India	5.3

Balance of payments, reserves and debt, $bn

Visible exports fob	81.6
Visible imports fob	-84.6
Trade balance	-3.0
Invisibles inflows	23.0
Invisibles outflows	-31.2
Net transfers	-2.6
Current account balance	-13.9
– as % of GDP	-4.4
Capital balance	15.1
Overall balance	-0.8
Change in reserves	-3.2
Level of reserves end Dec.	45.9
No. months of import cover	4.8
Official gold holdings, m oz	4.0
Foreign debt	137.9
– as % of GDP	43.8
– as % of total exports	131.3
Debt service ratio	7.7

Health and education

Health spending, % of GDP	8.8
Doctors per 1,000 pop.	0.8
Hospital beds per 1,000 pop.	...
Improved-water source access, % of pop.	93.2
Education spending, % of GDP	6.1
Enrolment, %: primary	100
secondary	92
tertiary	19

Society

No. of households, m	15.3
Av. no. per household	3.6
Marriages per 1,000 pop.	...
Divorces per 1,000 pop.	...
Religion, % of pop.	
Christian	81.2
Non-religious	14.9
Muslim	1.7
Hindu	1.1
Other	0.9
Jewish	0.1
Cost of living, Dec. 2016 New York = 100	51
Cars per 1,000 pop.	120
Colour TV households, % with:	
cable	...
satellite	8.9
Telephone lines per 100 pop.	7.7
Mobile telephone subscribers per 100 pop.	164.5
Broadband subs per 100 pop.	2.6
Internet users, % of pop.	51.9

SOUTH KOREA

Area, sq km	100,266	Capital	Seoul
Arable as % of total land	15.1	Currency	Won (W)

People

Population, m	50.3	Life expectancy: men	79.5 yrs
Pop. per sq km	501.7	women	85.7 yrs
Average annual growth in pop. 2015–20, %	0.4	Adult literacy	...
Pop. aged 0–24, %	27.5	Fertility rate (per woman)	1.3
Pop. aged 70 and over, %	8.9	Urban population, 2020, %	83.1
No. of men per 100 women	98.8		*per 1,000 pop.*
Human Development Index	90.1	Crude birth rate	9.1
		Crude death rate	6.1

The economy

GDP	$1,383bn	GDP per head	$27,490
GDP	W1,564trn	GDP per head in purchasing power parity (USA=100)	65.8
Av. ann. growth in real GDP 2010–15	3.0%	Economic freedom index	74.3

Origins of GDP	*% of total*	Components of GDP	*% of total*
Agriculture	2	Private consumption	50
Industry, of which:	38	Public consumption	15
manufacturing	30	Investment	29
Services	60	Exports	46
		Imports	-39

Structure of employment

	% of total		*% of labour force*
Agriculture	5.2	Unemployed 2015	3.6
Industry	25.1	Av. ann. rate 2005–15	3.4
Services	69.7		

Energy

	m TOE		
Total output	37.6	Net energy imports as % of energy use	82
Total consumption	280.6		
Consumption per head kg oil equivalent	5,323		

Inflation and finance

			av. ann. increase 2011–16
Consumer price inflation 2016	1.0%	Narrow money (M1)	12.5%
Av. ann. inflation 2011–16	3.4%	Broad money	6.6%
Money market rate, Dec. 2016	1.23%		

Exchange rates

	end 2016		*December 2016*
W per $	1,208.50	Effective rates	2010 = 100
W per sdr	1,624.62	– nominal	...
W per €	1,271.64	– real	...

Trade

Principal exports

	$bn fob
Machinery & transport equip.	310.6
Manufactured goods	67.2
Chemicals & related products	58.9
Miscellaneous manufactured articles	44.1
Total incl. others	**526.9**

Principal imports

	$bn cif
Machinery & transport equip.	145.4
Mineral fuels & lubricants	103.4
Manufactured goods	50.4
Chemicals & related products	43.5
Total incl. others	**436.1**

Main export destinations

	% of total
China	26.0
United States	13.3
Hong Kong	5.8
Vietnam	5.3

Main origins of imports

	% of total
China	20.7
Japan	10.5
United States	10.1
Germany	4.8

Balance of payments, reserves and debt, $bn

Visible exports fob	542.9
Visible imports fob	-420.6
Trade balance	122.3
Invisibles inflows	121.6
Invisibles outflows	-132.9
Net transfers	-5.0
Current account balance	105.9
– as % of GDP	7.7
Capital balance	-94.3
Overall balance	12.1
Change in reserves	3.9
Level of reserves end Dec.	366.7
No. months of import cover	7.9
Official gold holdings, m oz	3.4
Foreign debt	376.6
– as % of GDP	27.3
– as % of total exports	56.7
Debt service ratio	6.4

Health and education

Health spending, % of GDP	7.4
Doctors per 1,000 pop.	2.1
Hospital beds per 1,000 pop.	...
Improved-water source access, % of pop.	97.6
Education spending, % of GDP	4.6
Enrolment, %: primary	99
secondary	98
tertiary	95

Society

No. of households, m	18.7
Av. no. per household	2.7
Marriages per 1,000 pop.	5.9
Divorces per 1,000 pop.	2.1
Religion, % of pop.	
Non-religious	46.4
Christian	29.4
Buddhist	22.9
Other	1.0
Muslim	0.2
Jewish	<0.1
Cost of living, Dec. 2016 New York = 100	108
Cars per 1,000 pop.	318
Colour TV households, % with:	
cable	81.8
satellite	13.5
Telephone lines per 100 pop.	58.1
Mobile telephone subscribers per 100 pop.	118.5
Broadband subs per 100 pop.	40.2
Internet users, % of pop.	89.6

SPAIN

Area, sq km	505,992	Capital	Madrid
Arable as % of total land	24.5	Currency	Euro (€)

People

Population, m	46.1	Life expectancy: men	80.5 yrs
Pop. per sq km	91.1	women	85.8 yrs
Average annual growth in pop. 2015–20, %	0.0	Adult literacy	98.1
Pop. aged 0–24, %	24.3	Fertility rate (per woman)	1.5
Pop. aged 70 and over, %	13.7	Urban population, 2020, %	80.7
No. of men per 100 women	96.3		*per 1,000 pop.*
Human Development Index	88.4	Crude birth rate	8.6
		Crude death rate	9.1

The economy

GDP	$1,194bn	GDP per head	$25,891
GDP	€1,076bn	GDP per head in purchasing power parity (USA=100)	62.4
Av. ann. growth in real GDP 2010–15	-0.2%	Economic freedom index	63.6

Origins of GDP		**Components of GDP**	
	% of total		*% of total*
Agriculture	3	Private consumption	58
Industry, of which:	24	Public consumption	19
manufacturing	14	Investment	20
Services	74	Exports	33
		Imports	-31

Structure of employment

	% of total		*% of labour force*
Agriculture	4.1	Unemployed 2015	22.1
Industry	19.9	Av. ann. rate 2005–15	17.6
Services	76.0		

Energy

	m TOE		
Total output	15.4	Net energy imports as % of energy use	69
Total consumption	136.9		
Consumption per head kg oil equivalent	2,465		

Inflation and finance

Consumer price inflation 2016	-0.3%		*av. ann. increase 2011–16*
Av. ann. inflation 2011–16	2.9%	Narrow money (M1)	8.1%
Treasury bill rate, Dec. 2016	-0.24%	Broad money	3.6%

Exchange rates

	end 2016		*December 2016*
€ per $	0.95	Effective rates	2010 = 100
€ per sdr	1.28	– nominal	97.94
		– real	92.59

Trade

Principal exports

	$bn fob
Machinery & transport equip.	96.1
Food, drink & tobacco	42.2
Chemicals & related products	38.3
Mineral fuels & lubricants	18.8
Total incl. others	**277.1**

Principal imports

	$bn cif
Machinery & transport equip.	98.6
Chemicals & related products	46.9
Mineral fuels & lubricants	42.8
Food, drink & tobacco	30.9
Total incl. others	**304.9**

Main export destinations

	% of total
France	15.9
Germany	11.1
Italy	7.5
United Kingdom	7.5
EU28	65.1

Main origins of imports

	% of total
Germany	14.8
France	12.1
China	7.2
Italy	6.6
EU28	60.7

Balance of payments, reserves and aid, $bn

Visible exports fob	277.4
Visible imports fob	-301.5
Trade balance	-24.1
Invisibles inflows	176.4
Invisibles outflows	-124.0
Net transfers	-12.1
Current account balance	16.2
– as % of GDP	1.4
Capital balance	-14.4
Overall balance	5.7
Change in reserves	3.6
Level of reserves end Dec.	54.0
No. months of import cover	1.5
Official gold holdings, m oz	9.1
Aid given	1.4
– as % of GDP	0.1

Health and education

Health spending, % of GDP	9.0
Doctors per 1,000 pop.	4.9
Hospital beds per 1,000 pop.	3.1
Improved-water source access, % of pop.	100
Education spending, % of GDP	4.3
Enrolment, %: primary	105
secondary	130
tertiary	90

Society

No. of households, m	18.8
Av. no. per household	2.5
Marriages per 1,000 pop.	3.4
Divorces per 1,000 pop.	2.2
Religion, % of pop.	
Christian	78.6
Non-religious	19.0
Muslim	2.1
Jewish	0.1
Other	0.1
Hindu	<0.1
Cost of living, Dec. 2016 New York = 100	80
Cars per 1,000 pop.	468
Colour TV households, % with:	
cable	13.9
satellite	12.7
Telephone lines per 100 pop.	41.5
Mobile telephone subscribers per 100 pop.	108.2
Broadband subs per 100 pop.	28.7
Internet users, % of pop.	78.7

SWEDEN

Area, sq km	447,000	Capital	Stockholm
Arable as % of total land	6.4	Currency	Swedish krona (Skr)

People

Population, m	9.8	Life expectancy: men	81.1 yrs
Pop. per sq km	21.9	women	84.4 yrs
Average annual growth in pop. 2015–20, %	0.7	Adult literacy	...
Pop. aged 0–24, %	29.6	Fertility rate (per woman)	1.9
Pop. aged 70 and over, %	13.4	Urban population, 2020, %	86.6
No. of men per 100 women	99.9		*per 1,000 pop.*
Human Development Index	91.3	Crude birth rate	12.2
		Crude death rate	9.0

The economy

GDP	$496bn	GDP per head	$50,581
GDP	Skr4,181bn	GDP per head in purchasing power parity (USA=100)	86.6
Av. ann. growth in real GDP 2010–15	2.0%	Economic freedom index	74.9

Origins of GDP	*% of total*	**Components of GDP**	*% of total*
Agriculture	1	Private consumption	45
Industry, of which:	26	Public consumption	26
manufacturing	17	Investment	24
Services	72	Exports	46
		Imports	-41

Structure of employment

	% of total		*% of labour force*
Agriculture	2.0	Unemployed 2015	7.4
Industry	18.2	Av. ann. rate 2005–15	7.6
Services	79.2		

Energy

	m TOE		
Total output	15.7	Net energy imports as % of energy use	28
Total consumption	52.8		
Consumption per head kg oil equivalent	5,132		

Inflation and finance

			av. ann. increase 2011–16
Consumer price inflation 2016	1.1%	Narrow money (M1)	9.2%
Av. ann. inflation 2011–16	2.8%	Broad money	3.6%
Treasury bill rate, Dec. 2016	-0.79%		

Exchange rates

	end 2016		*December 2016*
Skr per $	9.06	Effective rates	2010 = 100
Skr per sdr	12.18	– nominal	96.58
Skr per €	9.53	– real	91.29

Trade

Principal exports

	$bn fob
Machinery & transport equip.	55.1
Chemicals & related products	17.9
Mineral fuels & lubricants	9.2
Raw materials	8.9
Total incl. others	**140.0**

Principal imports

	$bn cif
Machinery & transport equip.	53.4
Chemicals & related products	16.2
Food, drink & tobacco	14.7
Mineral fuels & lubricants	13.5
Total incl. others	**138.3**

Main export destinations

	% of total
Norway	10.3
Germany	10.2
United States	7.7
United Kingdom	7.2
EU28	58.5

Main origins of imports

	% of total
Germany	17.8
Netherlands	8.1
Norway	7.8
Denmark	7.7
EU28	70.0

Balance of payments, reserves and aid, $bn

Visible exports fob	152.1
Visible imports fob	-138.5
Trade balance	13.5
Invisibles inflows	121.4
Invisibles outflows	-103.4
Net transfers	-8.2
Current account balance	23.3
– as % of GDP	4.7
Capital balance	-10.1
Overall balance	1.3
Change in reserves	-4.5
Level of reserves end Dec.	58.1
No. months of import cover	2.9
Official gold holdings, m oz	4.0
Aid given	7.1
– as % of GDP	1.4

Health and education

Health spending, % of GDP	11.9
Doctors per 1,000 pop.	3.9
Hospital beds per 1,000 pop.	2.7
Improved-water source access, % of pop.	100
Education spending, % of GDP	7.7
Enrolment, %: primary	121
secondary	133
tertiary	62

Society

No. of households, m	5.1
Av. no. per household	1.9
Marriages per 1,000 pop.	5.5
Divorces per 1,000 pop.	2.7
Religion, % of pop.	
Christian	67.2
Non-religious	27.0
Muslim	4.6
Other	0.8
Hindu	0.2
Jewish	0.1
Cost of living, Dec. 2016 New York = 100	80
Cars per 1,000 pop.	478
Colour TV households, % with:	
cable	57.5
satellite	20.1
Telephone lines per 100 pop.	36.7
Mobile telephone subscribers per 100 pop.	130.4
Broadband subs per 100 pop.	36.1
Internet users, % of pop.	90.6

SWITZERLAND

Area, sq km	41,285	Capital	Berne
Arable as % of total land	10.1	Currency	Swiss franc (SFr)

People

Population, m	8.3	Life expectancy: men	81.6 yrs
Pop. per sq km	201.0	women	85.5 yrs
Average annual growth in pop. 2015–20, %	0.8	Adult literacy	...
Pop. aged 0–24, %	26.2	Fertility rate (per woman)	1.6
Pop. aged 70 and over, %	12.7	Urban population, 2020, %	74.4
No. of men per 100 women	98.1		*per 1,000 pop.*
Human Development Index	93.9	Crude birth rate	10.5
		Crude death rate	8.0

The economy

GDP	$671bn	GDP per head	$80,802
GDP	SFr645bn	GDP per head in purchasing power parity (USA=100)	103.9
Av. ann. growth in real GDP 2010–15	1.5%	Economic freedom index	81.5

Origins of GDP	*% of total*	**Components of GDP**	*% of total*
Agriculture	1	Private consumption	54
Industry, of which:	26	Public consumption	11
manufacturing	18	Investment	23
Services	74	Exports	63
		Imports	-51

Structure of employment

	% of total		*% of labour force*
Agriculture	3.2	Unemployed 2015	4.6
Industry	19.3	Av. ann. rate 2005–15	4.2
Services	74.9		

Energy

	m TOE		
Total output	6.8	Net energy imports as % of energy use	47
Total consumption	30.9		
Consumption per head kg oil equivalent	3,060		

Inflation and finance

			av. ann. increase 2011–16
Consumer price inflation 2016	-0.4%	Narrow money (M1)	4.2%
Av. ann. inflation 2011–16	1.9%	Broad money	3.6%
Treasury bill rate, Dec. 2016	-0.91%		

Exchange rates

	end 2016		*December 2016*
SFr per $	1.02	Effective rates	2010 = 100
SFr per sdr	1.37	– nominal	124.67
SFr per €	1.07	– real	110.64

Trade

Principal exports

	$bn fob
Chemicals	88.0
Precision instruments, watches & jewellery	48.6
Machinery, equipment & electronics	32.3
Metals & metal manufactures	12.3
Total incl. others	**210.8**

Principal imports

	$bn cif
Chemicals	40.3
Machinery, equipment & electronics	29.6
Precision instruments, watches & jewellery	21.7
Motor vehicles	17.5
Total incl. others	**172.8**

Main export destinations

	% of total
Germany	19.6
United States	14.5
Hong Kong	11.9
India	10.1
EU28	43.4

Main origins of imports

	% of total
Germany	30.1
United Kingdom	18.6
United States	11.8
Italy	11.3
EU28	64.5

Balance of payments, reserves and aid, $bn

Visible exports fob	303.1
Visible imports fob	-249.5
Trade balance	53.6
Invisibles inflows	268.3
Invisibles outflows	-231.2
Net transfers	-13.3
Current account balance	77.4
– as % of GDP	11.5
Capital balance	-12.7
Overall balance	98.8
Change in reserves	56.6
Level of reserves end Dec.	602.4
No. months of import cover	15.0
Official gold holdings, m oz	33.4
Aid given	3.6
– as % of GDP	0.5

Health and education

Health spending, % of GDP	11.7
Doctors per 1,000 pop.	4.0
Hospital beds per 1,000 pop.	5.0
Improved-water source access, % of pop.	100
Education spending, % of GDP	5.1
Enrolment, %: primary	103
secondary	100
tertiary	57

Society

No. of households, m	3.7
Av. no. per household	2.2
Marriages per 1,000 pop.	5.1
Divorces per 1,000 pop.	2.1
Religion, % of pop.	
Christian	81.3
Non-religious	11.9
Muslim	5.5
Other	0.6
Hindu	0.4
Jewish	0.3
Cost of living, Dec. 2016 New York = 100	107
Cars per 1,000 pop.	535
Colour TV households, % with:	
cable	82.4
satellite	16.0
Telephone lines per 100 pop.	50.3
Mobile telephone subscribers per 100 pop.	136.5
Broadband subs per 100 pop.	45.1
Internet users, % of pop.	87.5

TAIWAN

Area, sq km	36,179	Capital	Taipei
Arable as % of total land	...	Currency	Taiwan dollar (T$)

People

Population, m	23.4	Life expectancy: men	77.0 yrs
Pop. per sq km	646.8	women	83.5 yrs
Average annual growth in pop. 2015–20, %	0.2	Adult literacy	...
Pop. aged 0–24, %	26.9	Fertility rate (per woman)	1.1
Pop. aged 70 and over, %	8.5	Urban population, 2020, %	78.0
No. of men per 100 women	99.0		*per 1,000 pop.*
Human Development Index	...	Crude birth rate	8.0
		Crude death rate	7.3

The economy

GDP	$525bn	GDP per head	$22,446
GDP	T$16,759bn	GDP per head in purchasing power parity (USA=100)	84.0
Av. ann. growth in real GDP 2010–15	2.5%	Economic freedom index	76.5

Origins of GDP	*% of total*	**Components of GDP**	*% of total*
Agriculture	2	Private consumption	51
Industry, of which:	35	Public consumption	14
manufacturing	30	Investment	23
Services	63	Exports	63
		Imports	-50

Structure of employment

	% of total		*% of labour force*
Agriculture	4.9	Unemployed 2015	3.4
Industry	35.9	Av. ann. rate 2005–15	...
Services	59.2		

Energy

	m TOE		
Total output	10.4	Net energy imports as % of energy use	...
Total consumption	115.1		
Consumption per head kg oil equivalent	...		

Inflation and finance

			av. ann. increase 2011–16
Consumer price inflation 2016	1.1%	Narrow money (M1)	6.5%
Av. ann. inflation 2011–16	3.0%	Broad money	4.9%
Treasury bill rate, Dec. 2016	...		

Exchange rates

	end 2016		*December 2016*
T$ per $	32.43	Effective rates	2010 = 100
T$ per sdr	...	– nominal	...
T$ per €	34.12	– real	...

Trade

Principal exports

	$bn fob
Machinery & electrical equip.	150.4
Basic metals & articles	25.5
Plastic & rubber articles	21.1
Chemicals	18.2
Total incl. others	**263.2**

Principal imports

	$bn cif
Machinery & electrical equip.	84.1
Minerals	41.6
Chemicals & related products	25.6
Basic metals & articles	19.2
Total incl. others	**236.4**

Main export destinations

	% of total
China	27.9
Hong Kong	14.9
United States	13.1
Japan	7.4

Main origins of imports

	% of total
China	19.1
Japan	16.4
United States	12.3
South Korea	5.7

Balance of payments, reserves and debt, $bn

Visible exports fob	284.9
Visible imports fob	-231.6
Trade balance	53.3
Invisibles inflows	86.5
Invisibles outflows	-60.3
Net transfers	-3.4
Current account balance	76.2
– as % of GDP	14.5
Capital balance	68.0
Overall balance	151.1
Change in reserves	5.1
Level of reserves end Dec.	440.5
No. months of import cover	18.1
Official gold holdings, m oz	13.6
Foreign debt	159.0
– as % of GDP	30.3
– as % of total exports	39.0
Debt service ratio	2.9

Health and education

Health spending, % of GDP	...
Doctors per 1,000 pop.	...
Hospital beds per 1,000 pop.	...
Improved-water source access, % of pop.	...
Education spending, % of GDP	...
Enrolment, %: primary	...
secondary	...
tertiary	...

Society

No. of households, m	7.8
Av. no. per household	3.0
Marriages per 1,000 pop.	...
Divorces per 1,000 pop.	...
Religion, % of pop.	
Other	60.5
Buddhist	21.3
Non-religious	12.7
Christian	5.5
Hindu	<0.1
Jewish	<0.1
Cost of living, Dec. 2016 New York = 100	75
Cars per 1,000 pop.	274
Colour TV households, % with:	
cable	84.6
satellite	0.4
Telephone lines per 100 pop.	59.7
Mobile telephone subscribers per 100 pop.	127.3
Broadband subs per 100 pop.	24.3
Internet users, % of pop.	78.0

THAILAND

Area, sq km	513,120	Capital	Bangkok
Arable as % of total land	32.9	Currency	Baht (Bt)

People

Population, m	68.0	Life expectancy: men	71.8 yrs
Pop. per sq km	132.5	women	78.5 yrs
Average annual growth in pop. 2015–20, %	0.2	Adult literacy	94.0
Pop. aged 0–24, %	30.9	Fertility rate (per woman)	1.5
Pop. aged 70 and over, %	6.7	Urban population, 2020, %	55.8
No. of men per 100 women	97.2		*per 1,000 pop.*
Human Development Index	74.0	Crude birth rate	9.9
		Crude death rate	8.4

The economy

GDP	$399bn	GDP per head	$5,871
GDP	Bt13,673bn	GDP per head in purchasing power parity (USA=100)	29.2
Av. ann. growth in real GDP 2010–15	2.9%	Economic freedom index	66.2

Origins of GDP	*% of total*	**Components of GDP**	*% of total*
Agriculture	9	Private consumption	47
Industry, of which:	36	Public consumption	17
manufacturing	27	Investment	24
Services	55	Exports	69
		Imports	-58

Structure of employment

	% of total		*% of labour force*
Agriculture	32.3	Unemployed 2015	0.7
Industry	23.7	Av. ann. rate 2005–15	1.0
Services	43.9		

Energy

	m TOE		
Total output	62.5	Net energy imports as % of energy use	42
Total consumption	129.0		
Consumption per head kg oil equivalent	1,990		

Inflation and finance

			av. ann. increase 2011–16
Consumer price inflation 2016	0.3%	Narrow money (M1)	5.7%
Av. ann. inflation 2011–16	3.5%	Broad money	6.2%
Treasury bill rate, Dec. 2016	1.50%		

Exchange rates

	end 2016		*December 2016*
Bt per $	35.83	Effective rates	2010 = 100
Bt per sdr	48.17	– nominal	...
Bt per €	37.70	– real	...

Trade

Principal exports[a]	$bn fob
Machinery, equip. & supplies	94.4
Food	26.7
Manufactured goods	26.5
Chemicals	20.5
Total incl. others	**211.0**

Principal imports[a]	$bn cif
Machinery, equip. & supplies	76.2
Manufactured goods	34.5
Fuel & lubricants	30.1
Chemicals	21.6
Total incl. others	**201.9**

Main export destinations	% of total
United States	11.2
China	11.1
Japan	9.4
Hong Kong	5.5

Main origins of imports	% of total
Japan	20.3
China	15.4
United States	6.9
Malaysia	5.9

Balance of payments, reserves and debt, $bn

Visible exports fob	214.1
Visible imports fob	-187.2
Trade balance	26.8
Invisibles inflows	66.7
Invisibles outflows	-68.0
Net transfers	6.7
Current account balance	32.1
– as % of GDP	8.1
Capital balance	-17.1
Overall balance	5.9
Change in reserves	-0.7
Level of reserves end Dec.	156.5
No. months of import cover	7.4
Official gold holdings, m oz	4.9
Foreign debt	129.7
– as % of GDP	32.8
– as % of total exports	45.2
Debt service ratio	6.7

Health and education

Health spending, % of GDP	6.5
Doctors per 1,000 pop.	0.4
Hospital beds per 1,000 pop.	2.1
Improved-water source access, % of pop.	97.8
Education spending, % of GDP	4.1
Enrolment, %: primary	103
secondary	129
tertiary	49

Society

No. of households, m	22.5
Av. no. per household	3.0
Marriages per 1,000 pop.	...
Divorces per 1,000 pop.	...
Religion, % of pop.	
Buddhist	93.2
Muslim	5.5
Christian	0.9
Non-religious	0.3
Hindu	0.1
Jewish	<0.1
Cost of living, Dec. 2016 New York = 100	77
Cars per 1,000 pop.	125
Colour TV households, % with:	
cable	9.9
satellite	4.9
Telephone lines per 100 pop.	7.9
Mobile telephone subscribers per 100 pop.	152.7
Broadband subs per 100 pop.	9.2
Internet users, % of pop.	39.3

a 2013

TURKEY

Area, sq km	785,000	Capital	Ankara
Arable as % of total land	26.9	Currency	Turkish Lira (YTL)

People

Population, m	78.7	Life expectancy: men	73.0 yrs
Pop. per sq km	100.3	women	79.3 yrs
Average annual growth in pop. 2015–20, %	0.9	Adult literacy	95.7
Pop. aged 0–24, %	42.3	Fertility rate (per woman)	2.1
Pop. aged 70 and over, %	4.9	Urban population, 2020, %	75.7
No. of men per 100 women	96.7		*per 1,000 pop.*
Human Development Index	76.7	Crude birth rate	15.7
		Crude death rate	5.8

The economy

GDP	$859bn	GDP per head	$10,915
GDP	YTL2,338bn	GDP per head in purchasing power parity (USA=100)	43.2
Av. ann. growth in real GDP 2010–15	4.4%	Economic freedom index	65.2

Origins of GDP	*% of total*	**Components of GDP**	*% of total*
Agriculture	9	Private consumption	69
Industry, of which:	27	Public consumption	16
manufacturing	18	Investment	18
Services	65	Exports	28
		Imports	-31

Structure of employment

	% of total		*% of labour force*
Agriculture	20.4	Unemployed 2015	10.2
Industry	27.2	Av. ann. rate 2005–15	9.7
Services	52.4		

Energy

	m TOE		
Total output	15.6	Net energy imports as % of energy use	74
Total consumption	131.3		
Consumption per head kg oil equivalent	1,568		

Inflation and finance

			av. ann. increase 2011–16
Consumer price inflation 2016	9.0%	Narrow money (M1)	18.9%
Av. ann. inflation 2011–16	8.4%	Broad money	15.3%
Treasury bill rate, Dec. 2016	14.00%		

Exchange rates

	end 2016		*December 2016*
YTL per $	3.52	Effective rates	2010 = 100
YTL per sdr	4.74	– nominal	...
YTL per €	3.70	– real	...

Trade

Principal exports	$bn fob
Agricultural products	26.3
Transport equipment	18.6
Textiles & clothing	15.6
Iron & steel	13.6
Total incl. others	**143.8**

Principal imports	$bn cif
Fuels	37.8
Chemicals	29.0
Mechanical equipment	24.4
Transport equipment	21.8
Total incl. others	**207.2**

Main export destinations	% of total
Germany	9.3
Iraq	5.9
United Kingdom	7.3
Italy	4.8
EU28	44.5

Main origins of imports	% of total
China	12.0
Germany	10.3
Russia	9.8
United States	5.4
EU28	38.0

Balance of payments, reserves and debt, $bn

Visible exports fob	152.0
Visible imports fob	-200.1
Trade balance	-48.1
Invisibles inflows	51.4
Invisibles outflows	-36.8
Net transfers	1.4
Current account balance	-32.1
– as % of GDP	-3.7
Capital balance	10.1
Overall balance	-11.8
Change in reserves	-16.9
Level of reserves end Dec.	110.5
No. months of import cover	5.6
Official gold holdings, m oz	16.6
Foreign debt	397.7
– as % of GDP	46.4
– as % of total exports	195.0
Debt service ratio	26.9

Health and education

Health spending, % of GDP	5.4
Doctors per 1,000 pop.	1.7
Hospital beds per 1,000 pop.	2.5
Improved-water source access, % of pop.	100
Education spending, % of GDP	4.8
Enrolment, %: primary	107
secondary	100
tertiary	86

Society

No. of households, m	21.2
Av. no. per household	3.7
Marriages per 1,000 pop.	7.8
Divorces per 1,000 pop.	1.7
Religion, % of pop.	
Muslim	98.0
Non-religious	1.2
Christian	0.4
Other	0.3
Hindu	<0.1
Jewish	<0.1
Cost of living, Dec. 2016 New York = 100	72
Cars per 1,000 pop.	130
Colour TV households, % with:	
cable	7.0
satellite	51.0
Telephone lines per 100 pop.	15.0
Mobile telephone subscribers per 100 pop.	96.0
Broadband subs per 100 pop.	12.4
Internet users, % of pop.	53.7

UKRAINE

Area, sq km	603,500	Capital	Kiev
Arable as % of total land	56.2	Currency	Hryvnya (UAH)

People

Population, m	44.8	Life expectancy: men	66.2 yrs
Pop. per sq km	74.2	women	76.1 yrs
Average annual growth in pop. 2015–20, %	-0.5	Adult literacy	99.8
Pop. aged 0–24, %	25.8	Fertility rate (per woman)	1.5
Pop. aged 70 and over, %	11.3	Urban population, 2020, %	70.8
No. of men per 100 women	86.3		*per 1,000 pop.*
Human Development Index	74.3	Crude birth rate	10.7
		Crude death rate	15.7

The economy

GDP	$91bn	GDP per head	$2,030
GDP	UAH1,989bn	GDP per head in purchasing power parity (USA=100)	13.6
Av. ann. growth in real GDP 2010–15	-2.3%	Economic freedom index	48.1

Origins of GDP	*% of total*	**Components of GDP**	*% of total*
Agriculture	14	Private consumption	67
Industry, of which:	26	Public consumption	20
manufacturing	14	Investment	15
Services	60	Exports	53
		Imports	-55

Structure of employment

	% of total		*% of labour force*
Agriculture	15.3	Unemployed 2015	9.1
Industry	24.7	Av. ann. rate 2005–15	7.7
Services	60.1		

Energy

	m TOE		
Total output	68.0	Net energy imports as % of energy use	27
Total consumption	105.5		
Consumption per head kg oil equivalent	2,334		

Inflation and finance

			av. ann. increase 2011–16
Consumer price inflation 2016	15.1%	Narrow money (M1)	11.2%
Av. ann. inflation 2011–16	13.4%	Broad money	10.0%
Money market rate, Dec. 2016	13.63%		

Exchange rates

	end 2016		*December 2016*
UAH per $	27.19	Effective rates	2010 = 100
UAH per sdr	36.55	– nominal	44.97
UAH per €	28.61	– real	76.01

Trade

Principal exports

	$bn fob
Food & beverages	14.6
Non-precious metals	9.5
Machinery & equipment	4.6
Fuels	3.1
Total incl. others	**37.9**

Principal imports

	$bn cif
Fuels	11.7
Machinery & equipment	8.0
Chemicals	5.0
Food & beverages	3.5
Total incl. others	**36.3**

Main export destinations

	% of total
Russia	12.8
Turkey	7.3
China	6.3
Egypt	5.5
EU28	34.1

Main origins of imports

	% of total
Russia	19.3
Germany	10.0
China	9.7
Belarus	6.3
EU28	40.9

Balance of payments, reserves and debt, $bn

Visible exports fob	35.4
Visible imports fob	-38.9
Trade balance	-3.5
Invisibles inflows	16.7
Invisibles outflows	-16.1
Net transfers	2.6
Current account balance	-0.2
– as % of GDP	-0.2
Capital balance	1.2
Overall balance	0.8
Change in reserves	5.8
Level of reserves end Dec.	13.3
No. months of import cover	2.9
Official gold holdings, m oz	0.9
Foreign debt	122.8
– as % of GDP	135.5
– as % of total exports	211.3
Debt service ratio	56.9

Health and education

Health spending, % of GDP	7.1
Doctors per 1,000 pop.	3.5
Hospital beds per 1,000 pop.	9.0
Improved-water source access, % of pop.	96.2
Education spending, % of GDP	5.9
Enrolment, %: primary	104
secondary	99
tertiary	82

Society

No. of households, m	17.7
Av. no. per household	2.5
Marriages per 1,000 pop.	6.9
Divorces per 1,000 pop.	3.0
Religion, % of pop.	
Christian	83.8
Non-religious	14.7
Muslim	1.2
Jewish	0.1
Other	0.1
Hindu	<0.1
Cost of living, Dec. 2016 New York = 100	47
Cars per 1,000 pop.	163
Colour TV households, % with:	
cable	23.2
satellite	15.5
Telephone lines per 100 pop.	21.6
Mobile telephone subscribers per 100 pop.	144.0
Broadband subs per 100 pop.	11.8
Internet users, % of pop.	48.9

UNITED ARAB EMIRATES

Area, sq km	83,600	Capital	Abu Dhabi
Arable as % of total land	0.4	Currency	Dirham (AED)

People

Population, m	9.2	Life expectancy: men	76.9 yrs
Pop. per sq km	110.0	women	79.1 yrs
Average annual growth in pop. 2015–20, %	1.4	Adult literacy	93.0
Pop. aged 0–24, %	26.6	Fertility rate (per woman)	2.4
Pop. aged 70 and over, %	0.5	Urban population, 2020, %	86.8
No. of men per 100 women	274.0		*per 1,000 pop.*
Human Development Index	84.0	Crude birth rate	10.0
		Crude death rate	1.8

The economy

GDP	$370bn	GDP per head	$40,250
GDP	AED1,360bn	GDP per head in purchasing power parity (USA=100)	124.6
Av. ann. growth in real GDP 2010–15	4.7%	Economic freedom index	76.9

Origins of GDP	*% of total*	**Components of GDP**	% of total
Agriculture	1	Private consumption	45
Industry, of which:	48	Public consumption	13
manufacturing	...	Investment	28
Services	52	Exports	97
		Imports	-83

Structure of employment

	% of total		*% of labour force*
Agriculture	...	Unemployed 2015	3.8
Industry	...	Av. ann. rate 2005–15	3.8
Services	...		

Energy

	m TOE		
Total output	229.5	Net energy imports as % of energy use	-184
Total consumption	106.5		
Consumption per head kg oil equivalent	7,756		

Inflation and finance

			av. ann. increase 2011–16
Consumer price inflation 2016	3.6%	Narrow money (M1)	11.5%
Av. ann. inflation 2011–16	4.0%	Broad money	8.5%
Treasury bill rate, Dec. 2016	...		

Exchange rates

	end 2016		*December 2016*
AED per $	3.67	Effective rates	2010 = 100
AED per sdr	4.94	– nominal	129.72
AED per €	3.86	– real	...

Trade

Principal exports

	$bn fob
Re-exports	134.8
Crude oil	31.6
Gas	7.7
Total incl. others	**300.4**

Principal imports

	$bn cif
Precious stones & metals	45.2
Machinery & electrical equip.	39.3
Vehicles & other transport equipment	28.8
Base metals & related products	13.2
Total incl. others	**263.4**

Main export destinations

	% of total
Oman	13.3
Japan	10.8
India	9.4
Iran	7.4

Main origins of imports

	% of total
China	7.9
United States	6.7
India	6.2
Germany	4.1

Balance of payments, reserves and debt, $bn

Visible exports fob	300.4
Visible imports fob	-223.9
Trade balance	76.6
Invisibles inflows	60.7
Invisibles outflows	-80.9
Net transfers	-39.6
Current account balance	16.7
– as % of GDP	4.5
Capital balance	-3.2
Overall balance	15.3
Change in reserves	15.5
Level of reserves end Dec.	93.9
No. months of import cover	3.7
Official gold holdings, m oz	0.2
Foreign debt	203.3
– as % of GDP	54.9
– as % of total exports	53.6
Debt service ratio	5.3

Health and education

Health spending, % of GDP	3.6
Doctors per 1,000 pop.	2.5
Hospital beds per 1,000 pop.	1.1
Improved-water source access, % of pop.	99.6
Education spending, % of GDP	...
Enrolment, %: primary	116
secondary	...
tertiary	...

Society

No. of households, m	1.7
Av. no. per household	5.4
Marriages per 1,000 pop.	...
Divorces per 1,000 pop.	...
Religion, % of pop.	
Muslim	76.9
Christian	12.6
Hindu	6.6
Other	2.8
Non-religious	1.1
Jewish	<0.1
Cost of living, Dec. 2016 New York = 100	72
Cars per 1,000 pop.	195
Colour TV households, % with:	
cable	1.0
satellite	98.4
Telephone lines per 100 pop.	23.6
Mobile telephone subscribers per 100 pop.	187.3
Broadband subs per 100 pop.	12.9
Internet users, % of pop.	91.2

UNITED KINGDOM

Area, sq km	244,000	Capital	London
Arable as % of total land	25.8	Currency	Pound (£)

People

Population, m	64.7	Life expectancy: men	79.4 yrs
Pop. per sq km	265.2	women	83.1 yrs
Average annual growth in pop. 2015–20, %	0.6	Adult literacy	...
Pop. aged 0–24, %	30.1	Fertility rate (per woman)	1.9
Pop. aged 70 and over, %	12.1	Urban population, 2020, %	83.8
No. of men per 100 women	97.2		*per 1,000 pop.*
Human Development Index	90.9	Crude birth rate	12.4
		Crude death rate	9.1

The economy

GDP	$2,863bn	GDP per head	$44,255
GDP	£1,873bn	GDP per head in purchasing power parity (USA=100)	74.5
Av. ann. growth in real GDP 2010–15	2.0%	Economic freedom index	76.4

Origins of GDP	*% of total*	**Components of GDP**	*% of total*
Agriculture	1	Private consumption	65
Industry, of which:	19	Public consumption	19
manufacturing	10	Investment	17
Services	80	Exports	28
		Imports	-29

Structure of employment

	% of total		*% of labour force*
Agriculture	1.1	Unemployed 2015	5.3
Industry	18.5	Av. ann. rate 2005–15	6.5
Services	79.7		

Energy

	m TOE		
Total output	99.9	Net energy imports as % of energy use	40
Total consumption	200.8		
Consumption per head kg oil equivalent	2,777		

Inflation and finance

			av. ann. increase 2011–16
Consumer price inflation 2016	0.7%	Narrow money (M1)	...
Av. ann. inflation 2011–16	3.7%	Broad money	5.1%
Treasury bill rate, Dec. 2016	0.05%		

Exchange rates

	end 2016		*December 2016*
£ per $	0.81	Effective rates	2010 = 100
£ per sdr	1.09	– nominal	97.97
£ per €	0.85	– real	105.96

Trade

Principal exports

	$bn fob
Machinery & transport equip.	163.7
Chemicals & related products	79.8
Mineral fuels & lubricants	33.2
Food, drink & tobacco	28.0
Total incl. others	**439.4**

Principal imports

	$bn cif
Machinery & transport equip.	237.4
Chemicals & related products	76.9
Food, drink & tobacco	59.5
Mineral fuels & lubricants	50.8
Total incl. others	**622.3**

Main export destinations

	% of total
United States	15.2
Germany	10.6
Switzerland	7.3
China	6.2
EU28	44.4

Main origins of imports

	% of total
Germany	14.9
China	9.8
United States	9.3
Netherlands	7.6
EU28	53.6

Balance of payments, reserves and aid, $bn

Visible exports fob	439.3
Visible imports fob	-622.2
Trade balance	-182.9
Invisibles inflows	555.5
Invisibles outflows	-457.6
Net transfers	-37.7
Current account balance	-122.6
– as % of GDP	-4.3
Capital balance	132.7
Overall balance	31.3
Change in reserves	21.9
Level of reserves end Dec.	129.6
No. months of import cover	1.4
Official gold holdings, m oz	10.0
Aid given	18.6
– as % of GDP	0.7

Health and education

Health spending, % of GDP	9.1
Doctors per 1,000 pop.	2.8
Hospital beds per 1,000 pop.	2.9
Improved-water source access, % of pop.	100
Education spending, % of GDP	5.8
Enrolment, %: primary	108
secondary	128
tertiary	57

Society

No. of households, m	27.2
Av. no. per household	2.4
Marriages per 1,000 pop.	4.5
Divorces per 1,000 pop.	2.0
Religion, % of pop.	
Christian	71.1
Non-religious	21.3
Muslim	4.4
Other	1.4
Hindu	1.3
Jewish	0.5
Cost of living, Dec. 2016 New York = 100	89
Cars per 1,000 pop.	514
Colour TV households, % with:	
cable	14.4
satellite	41.7
Telephone lines per 100 pop.	52.0
Mobile telephone subscribers per 100 pop.	124.1
Broadband subs per 100 pop.	38.6
Internet users, % of pop.	92.0

UNITED STATES

Area, sq km	9,832,000	Capital	Washington DC
Arable as % of total land	16.9	Currency	US dollar ($)

People

Population, m	321.8	Life expectancy: men	77.3 yrs
Pop. per sq km	32.7	women	81.9 yrs
Average annual growth in pop. 2015–20, %	0.7	Adult literacy	...
Pop. aged 0–24, %	32.6	Fertility rate (per woman)	1.9
Pop. aged 70 and over, %	9.8	Urban population, 2020, %	82.5
No. of men per 100 women	98.3		*per 1,000 pop.*
Human Development Index	92.0	Crude birth rate	12.6
		Crude death rate	8.4

The economy

GDP	$18,037bn	GDP per head	$56,049
Av. ann. growth in real GDP 2010–15	2.1%	GDP per head in purchasing power parity (USA=100)	100.0
		Economic freedom index	75.1

Origins of GDP	*% of total*	**Components of GDP**	*% of total*
Agriculture	1	Private consumption	68
Industry, of which:	20	Public consumption	14
manufacturing	12	Investment	20
Services	80	Exports	13
		Imports	-15

Structure of employment

	% of total		*% of labour force*
Agriculture	1.6	Unemployed 2015	5.3
Industry	18.5	Av. ann. rate 2005–15	6.8
Services	79.9		

Energy

	m TOE		
Total output	2,050.5	Net energy imports as % of energy use	9
Total consumption	2,451.1		
Consumption per head kg oil equivalent	6,949		

Inflation and finance

			av. ann. increase 2011–16
Consumer price inflation 2016	1.2%	Narrow money (M1)	8.9%
Av. ann. inflation 2011–16	3.4%	Broad money	4.3%
Treasury bill rate, Dec. 2016	0.52%		

Exchange rates

	end 2016		*December 2016*
$ per sdr	1.34	Effective rates	2010 = 100
$ per €	1.05	– nominal	125.44
		– real	123.11

Trade

Principal exports

	$bn fob
Capital goods, excl. vehicles	539.4
Industrial supplies	426.0
Consumer goods, excl. vehicles	197.7
Vehicles & products	151.9
Total incl. others	**1,502.6**

Principal imports

	$bn fob
Industrial supplies	485.8
Capital goods, excl. vehicles	602.0
Consumer goods, excl. vehicles	594.3
Vehicles & products	349.2
Total incl. others	**2,248.2**

Main export destinations

	% of total
Canada	18.6
Mexico	15.7
China	7.7
Japan	4.2
EU28	18.2

Main origins of imports

	% of total
China	21.4
Canada	13.1
Mexico	13.1
Japan	5.8
EU28	18.9

Balance of payments, reserves and aid, $bn

Visible exports fob	1,510.3
Visible imports fob	-2,272.9
Trade balance	-762.6
Invisibles inflows	1,533.8
Invisibles outflows	-1,089.2
Net transfers	-145.0
Current account balance	-463.0
– as % of GDP	-2.6
Capital balance	188.9
Overall balance	-6.3
Change in reserves	-50.7
Level of reserves end Dec.	383.7
No. months of import cover	1.4
Official gold holdings, m oz	261.5
Aid given	31.0
– as % of GDP	0.2

Health and education

Health spending, % of GDP	17.1
Doctors per 1,000 pop.	2.5
Hospital beds per 1,000 pop.	2.9
Improved-water source access, % of pop.	99.2
Education spending, % of GDP	4.9
Enrolment, %: primary	100
secondary	98
tertiary	86

Society

No. of households, m	124.5
Av. no. per household	2.6
Marriages per 1,000 pop.	6.8
Divorces per 1,000 pop.	2.8
Religion, % of pop.	
Christian	78.3
Non-religious	16.4
Other	2.0
Jewish	1.8
Muslim	0.9
Hindu	0.6
Cost of living, Dec. 2016 New York = 100	100
Cars per 1,000 pop.	375
Colour TV households, % with:	
cable	56.6
satellite	29.5
Telephone lines per 100 pop.	38.4
Mobile telephone subscribers per 100 pop.	117.6
Broadband subs per 100 pop.	31.0
Internet users, % of pop.	74.5

VENEZUELA

Area, sq km	912,050	Capital	Caracas
Arable as % of total land	2.9	Currency	Bolivar (Bs)

People

Population, m	31.1	Life expectancy: men	70.9 yrs
Pop. per sq km	34.1	women	79.0 yrs
Average annual growth in pop. 2015–20, %	1.3	Adult literacy	95.4
Pop. aged 0–24, %	45.8	Fertility rate (per woman)	2.3
Pop. aged 70 and over, %	3.9	Urban population, 2020, %	89.3
No. of men per 100 women	99.1		*per 1,000 pop.*
Human Development Index	76.7	Crude birth rate	18.5
		Crude death rate	5.7

The economy

GDP	$260bn	GDP per head	$8,363
GDP	Bs6,025bn	GDP per head in purchasing power parity (USA=100)	29.5
Av. ann. growth in real GDP 2010–15	0.1%	Economic freedom index	27.0

Origins of GDP[a]	*% of total*	**Components of GDP[a]**	*% of total*
Agriculture	6	Private consumption	75
Industry, of which:	42	Public consumption	15
manufacturing	14	Investment	25
Services	53	Exports	17
		Imports	-31

Structure of employment

	% of total		*% of labour force*
Agriculture	7.4	Unemployed 2015	6.8
Industry	21.3	Av. ann. rate 2005–15	8.0
Services	71.1		

Energy

	m TOE		
Total output	169.5	Net energy imports as % of energy use	...
Total consumption	82.7		
Consumption per head kg oil equivalent	...		

Inflation and finance

			av. ann. increase 2011–16
Consumer price inflation 2016	475.8%	Narrow money (M1)	89.0%
Av. ann. inflation 2011–16	46.9%	Broad money	61.3%
Money market rate, Dec. 2016	0.35%		

Exchange rates

	end 2016		*December 2016*
Bs per $	9.98	Effective rates	2010 = 100
Bs per sdr	13.41	– nominal	32.36
Bs per €	10.50	– real	...

Trade

Principal exports[b]	$bn fob
Oil	85.6
Non-oil	3.2
Total	**88.8**

Principal imports[b]	$bn cif
Intermediate goods	25.9
Capital goods	11.1
Consumer goods	8.9
Total incl. others	**49.4**

Main export destinations	% of total
United States	35.4
India	16.6
China	12.9
Netherlands Antilles	8.2

Main origins of imports	% of total
United States	23.4
China	19.5
Brazil	12.4
Colombia	7.5

Balance of payments, reserves and debt, $bn

Visible exports fob	37.2
Visible imports fob	-36.5
Trade balance	0.8
Invisibles inflows	2.4
Invisibles outflows	-23.4
Net transfers	-0.2
Current account balance	-20.4
– as % of GDP	-7.8
Capital balance	18.5
Overall balance	-4.5
Change in reserves	-5.8
Level of reserves end Dec.	15.6
No. months of import cover	3.1
Official gold holdings, m oz	8.8
Foreign debt	123.7
– as % of GDP	26.0
– as % of total exports	310.8
Debt service ratio	60.3

Health and education

Health spending, % of GDP	5.3
Doctors per 1,000 pop.	...
Hospital beds per 1,000 pop.	0.9
Improved-water source access, % of pop.	93.1
Education spending, % of GDP	...
Enrolment, %: primary	100
secondary	90
tertiary	...

Society

No. of households, m	7.9
Av. no. per household	3.9
Marriages per 1,000 pop.	3.0
Divorces per 1,000 pop.	...
Religion, % of pop.	
Christian	89.3
Non-religious	10.0
Muslim	0.3
Other	0.3
Hindu	<0.1
Jewish	<0.1
Cost of living, Dec. 2016 New York = 100	50
Cars per 1,000 pop.	114
Colour TV households, % with:	
cable	29.3
satellite	5.7
Telephone lines per 100 pop.	24.9
Mobile telephone subscribers per 100 pop.	93.0
Broadband subs per 100 pop.	8.2
Internet users, % of pop.	61.9

a 2014 b 2013

VIETNAM

Area, sq km	330,967	Capital	Hanoi
Arable as % of total land	20.7	Currency	Dong (D)

People

Population, m	93.4	Life expectancy: men	71.7 yrs
Pop. per sq km	282.2	women	80.8 yrs
Average annual growth in pop. 2015–20, %	1.0	Adult literacy	94.5
Pop. aged 0–24, %	40.0	Fertility rate (per woman)	1.8
Pop. aged 70 and over, %	4.7	Urban population, 2020, %	36.8
No. of men per 100 women	97.9		*per 1,000 pop.*
Human Development Index	68.3	Crude birth rate	16.2
		Crude death rate	5.9

The economy

GDP	$191bn	GDP per head	$2,048
GDP	D4,192trn	GDP per head in purchasing power parity (USA=100)	10.6
Av. ann. growth in real GDP 2010–15	5.9%	Economic freedom index	52.4

Origins of GDP	*% of total*	**Components of GDP**	*% of total*
Agriculture	19	Private consumption	65
Industry, of which:	37	Public consumption	6
manufacturing	15	Investment	28
Services	44	Exports	90
		Imports	-89

Structure of employment

	% of total		*% of labour force*
Agriculture	43.6	Unemployed 2015	2.1
Industry	23.1	Av. ann. rate 2005–15	2.2
Services	33.3		

Energy

	m TOE		
Total output	43.5	Net energy imports as % of energy use	...
Total consumption	57.2		
Consumption per head kg oil equivalent	...		

Inflation and finance

			av. ann. increase 2011–16
Consumer price inflation 2016	2.0%	Narrow money (M1)	17.1%
Av. ann. inflation 2011–16	6.4%	Broad money	18.9%
Deposit rate, Oct. 2016	4.80%		

Exchange rates

	end 2016		*December 2016*
D per $	22,159.00	Effective rates	2010 = 100
D per sdr	29,789.01	– nominal	...
D per €	23,316.81	– real	...

Trade

Principal exports

	$bn fob
Telephones & mobile phones	30.2
Textiles & garments	22.8
Computers & electronic products	15.6
Footwear	12.0
Total incl. others	**162.0**

Principal imports

	$bn cif
Machinery & equipment	27.6
Electronics, computers & parts	23.2
Telephones & mobile phones	11.0
Textiles	10.2
Total incl. others	**165.8**

Main export destinations

	% of total
United States	20.9
China	10.4
Japan	8.8
South Korea	5.6

Main origins of imports

	% of total
China	28.1
South Korea	15.7
Japan	8.1
Taiwan	6.0

Balance of payments, reserves and debt, $bn

Visible exports fob	162.1
Visible imports fob	-154.7
Trade balance	7.4
Invisibles inflows	11.6
Invisibles outflows	-25.8
Net transfers	7.7
Current account balance	0.9
– as % of GDP	0.5
Capital balance	1.6
Overall balance	-6.0
Change in reserves	-5.9
Level of reserves end Dec.	28.3
No. months of import cover	1.9
Official gold holdings, m oz	0.0
Foreign debt	77.8
– as % of GDP	40.7
– as % of total exports	41.6
Debt service ratio	3.5

Health and education

Health spending, % of GDP	7.1
Doctors per 1,000 pop.	1.2
Hospital beds per 1,000 pop.	2.0
Improved-water source access, % of pop.	97.6
Education spending, % of GDP	5.7
Enrolment, %: primary	109
secondary	...
tertiary	29

Society

No. of households, m	27.1
Av. no. per household	3.4
Marriages per 1,000 pop.	...
Divorces per 1,000 pop.	...
Religion, % of pop.	
Other	45.6
Non-religious	29.6
Buddhist	16.4
Christian	8.2
Muslim	0.2
Jewish	<0.1
Cost of living, Dec. 2016 New York = 100	73
Cars per 1,000 pop.	21
Colour TV households, % with:	
cable	17.8
satellite	19.5
Telephone lines per 100 pop.	6.3
Mobile telephone subscribers per 100 pop.	130.6
Broadband subs per 100 pop.	8.1
Internet users, % of pop.	52.7

ZIMBABWE

Area, sq km	390,757	Capital	Harare
Arable as % of total land	10.3	Currency	Zimbabwe dollar (Z$)[a]

People

Population, m	15.6	Life expectancy: men	60.8 yrs
Pop. per sq km	37.4	women	64.0 yrs
Average annual growth in pop. 2015–20, %	2.3	Adult literacy	86.9
Pop. aged 0–24, %	62.5	Fertility rate (per woman)	3.5
Pop. aged 70 and over, %	2.0	Urban population, 2020, %	32.2
No. of men per 100 women	97.1		*per 1,000 pop.*
Human Development Index	51.6	Crude birth rate	32.4
		Crude death rate	7.8

The economy

GDP	$14bn	GDP per head	$908
Av. ann. growth in real GDP 2010–15	6.3%	GDP per head in purchasing power parity (USA=100)	3.2
		Economic freedom index	44.0

Origins of GDP	*% of total*	**Components of GDP**	*% of total*
Agriculture	13	Private consumption	86
Industry, of which:	28	Public consumption	23
manufacturing	11	Investment	14
Services	59	Exports	26
		Imports	-50

Structure of employment

	% of total		*% of labour force*
Agriculture	67.2	Unemployed 2015	5.1
Industry	7.4	Av. ann. rate 2005–15	5.4
Services	25.4		

Energy

	m TOE		
Total output	3.2	Net energy imports as % of energy use	...
Total consumption	4.0		
Consumption per head kg oil equivalent	...		

Inflation and finance

			av. ann. increase 2011–16
Consumer price inflation 2016	-1.6%	Narrow money (M1)	...
Av. ann. inflation 2011–16	2.8%	Broad money	...
Treasury bill rate, Dec. 2016	...		

Exchange rates

	end 2016		*December 2016*
Z$ per $	...	Effective rates	2010 = 100
Z$ per SDR	...	– nominal	...
Z$ per €	...	– real	...

Trade

Principal exports[b]	$bn fob
Gold	0.8
Platinum	0.8
Tobacco	0.5
Ferro-alloys	0.4
Total incl. others	**3.4**

Principal imports[b]	$bn cif
Machinery & transport equip.	0.5
Fuels & lubricants	0.4
Manufactures	0.3
Chemicals	0.2
Total incl. others	**4.7**

Main export destinations	% of total
South Africa	70.8
Mozambique	15.1
United Arab Emirates	5.4
Zambia	3.4

Main origins of imports	% of total
South Africa	46.1
Zambia	24.5
China	3.9
Botswana	3.7

Balance of payments, reserves and debt, $bn

Visible exports fob	3.6
Visible imports fob	-6.0
Trade balance	-2.4
Invisibles inflows	0.6
Invisibles outflows	-1.9
Net transfers	2.1
Current account balance	-1.5
– as % of GDP	-10.7
Capital balance	1.3
Overall balance	-0.2
Change in reserves	0.1
Level of reserves end Dec.	0.4
No. months of import cover	0.7
Official gold holdings, m oz	0.0
Foreign debt	8.7
– as % of GDP	60.6
– as % of total exports	154.6
Debt service ratio	10.9

Health and education

Health spending, % of GDP	6.4
Doctors per 1,000 pop.	0.1
Hospital beds per 1,000 pop.	1.7
Improved-water source access, % of pop.	76.9
Education spending, % of GDP	8.4
Enrolment, %: primary	100
secondary	48
tertiary	8

Society

No. of households, m	3.1
Av. no. per household	5.0
Marriages per 1,000 pop.	...
Divorces per 1,000 pop.	...
Religion, % of pop.	
Christian	87.0
Non-religious	7.9
Other	4.2
Muslim	0.9
Hindu	<0.1
Jewish	<0.1
Cost of living, Dec. 2016 New York = 100	...
Cars per 1,000 pop.	54
Colour TV households, % with:	
cable	...
satellite	...
Telephone lines per 100 pop.	2.2
Mobile telephone subscribers per 100 pop.	84.8
Broadband subs per 100 pop.	1.1
Internet users, % of pop.	16.4

a Zimbabwe adopted a multi-currency system in 2009. Its dollar was decommissioned in mid-2015.

b 2014

EURO AREA[a]

Area, sq km	2,678,181	Capital	–
Arable as % of total land	24.4	Currency	Euro (€)

People

Population, m	335.2	Life expectancy: men	79.8 yrs
Pop. per sq km	125.2	women	84.8 yrs
Average annual growth in pop. 2015–20, %	0.1	Adult literacy	...
Pop. aged 0–24, %	25.7	Fertility rate (per woman)	1.6
Pop. aged 70 and over, %	14.4	Urban population, 2020, %	76.9
No. of men per 100 women	95.6		*per 1,000 pop.*
Human Development Index	89.7	Crude birth rate	9.5
		Crude death rate	10.1

The economy

GDP	$11,606bn	GDP per head	$34,624
GDP	€10,459bn	GDP per head in purchasing power parity (USA=100)	75.2
Av. ann. growth in real GDP 2010–15	0.7%	Economic freedom index	67.1

Origins of GDP	*% of total*	**Components of GDP**	*% of total*
Agriculture	2	Private consumption	55
Industry, of which:	25	Public consumption	21
manufacturing	17	Investment	20
Services	72	Exports	46
		Imports	-42

Structure of employment

	% of total		*% of labour force*
Agriculture	3.2	Unemployed 2015	10.8
Industry	23.6	Av. ann. rate 2005–15	9.8
Services	72.5		

Energy

	m TOE		
Total output	...	Net energy imports as % of energy use	...
Total consumption	1,077.4		
Consumption per head kg oil equivalent	3,267		

Inflation and finance

			av. ann. increase 2011–16
Consumer price inflation 2016	0.2%	Narrow money (M1)	8.1%
Av. ann. inflation 2011–16	3.3%	Broad money	3.6%
Interbank rate, Dec. 2016	-0.35%		

Exchange rates

	end 2016		*December 2016*
€ per $	0.95	Effective rates	2010 = 100
€ per SDR	1.28	– nominal	97.25
		– real	90.63

Trade[b]

Principal exports

	$bn fob
Machinery & transport equip.	678.3
Other manufactured goods	363.2
Chemicals & related products	284.1
Food, drink & tobacco	102.0
Mineral fuels & lubricants	77.1
Total incl. others	**1,612.6**

Principal imports

	$bn cif
Machinery & transport equip.	483.8
Other manufactured goods	407.0
Mineral fuels & lubricants	296.1
Chemicals & related products	167.2
Food, drink & tobacco	97.9
Total incl. others	**1,558.5**

Main export destinations

	% of total
United States	20.8
China	9.5
Switzerland	8.4
Turkey	4.4

Main origins of imports

	% of total
China	20.3
United States	14.4
Russia	7.9
Switzerland	5.9

Balance of payments, reserves and aid, $bn

Visible exports fob	2,339.9
Visible imports fob	-1,951.9
Trade balance	388.0
Invisibles inflows	1,570.8
Invisibles outflows	-1,437.6
Net transfers	-148.7
Current account balance	372.4
– as % of GDP	3.2
Capital balance	-303.4
Overall balance	42.1
Change in reserves	-44.2
Level of reserves end Dec.	701.6
No. months of import cover	2.5
Official gold holdings, m oz	346.9
Aid given – as % of GDP	

Health and education

Health spending, % of GDP	10.4
Doctors per 1,000 pop.	3.9
Hospital beds per 1,000 pop.	5.6
Improved-water source access, % of pop.	99.9
Education spending, % of GDP	5.3
Enrolment, %: primary	...
secondary	...
tertiary	...

Society

No. of households, m, m	152.2
Av. no. per household	2.2
Marriages per 1,000 pop.	3.5
Divorces per 1,000 pop.	1.8
Cost of living, Dec. 2016 New York = 100	...
Cars per 1,000 pop.	516
Colour TV households, % with: cable	41.0
satellite	25.4
Telephone lines per 100 pop.	31.0
Mobile telephone subscribers per 100 pop.	123.8
Broadband subs per 100 pop.	37.2
Internet users, % of pop.	78.3

a Data generally refer to the 18 EU members that had adopted the euro as at December 31 2014: Austria, Belgium, Cyprus, Estonia, Finland, France, Germany, Greece, Ireland, Italy, Latvia, Luxembourg, Malta, Netherlands, Portugal, Slovakia, Slovenia and Spain.

b EU28, excluding intra-trade.

WORLD

Area, sq km	129,733,173	Capital	...
Arable as % of total land	10.9	Currency	...

People

Population, m	7,349.5	Life expectancy: men	69.5 yrs
Pop. per sq km	49.4	women	73.9 yrs
Average annual growth in pop. 2015–20	1.1	Adult literacy	86.2
Pop. aged 0–24, %	42.3	Fertility rate (per woman)	2.5
Pop. aged 70 and over, %	5.3	Urban population, 2020, %	56.2
No. of men per 100 women	101.8		*per 1,000 pop.*
Human Development Index	71.7	Crude birth rate	18.6
		Crude death rate	7.8

The economy

GDP	$74.2trn	GDP per head	$10,095
Av. ann. growth in real GDP 2010–15	2.6%	GDP per head in purchasing power parity (USA=100)	29.3
		Economic freedom index	58.4

Origins of GDP	*% of total*	**Components of GDP**	*% of total*
Agriculture	4	Private consumption	58
Industry, of which:	28	Public consumption	17
manufacturing	15	Investment	24
Services	68	Exports	30
		Imports	-29

Structure of employment

	% of total		*% of labour force*
Agriculture	19.8	Unemployed 2015	5.7
Industry	28.8	Av. ann. rate 2005–15	5.9
Services	51.4		

Energy

	m TOE		
Total output	12,546.5	Net energy imports as % of energy use	-2.5
Total consumption	13,643.0		
Consumption per head kg oil equivalent	1,929		

Inflation and finance

			av. ann. increase 2011–16
Consumer price inflation 2016	2.8%	Narrow money (M1)	
Av. ann. inflation 2011–16	2.8%	Broad money	
LIBOR $ rate, 3-month, Dec. 2016	0.98%		

Trade

World exports

	$bn fob
Manufactures	11,404.3
Fuels	2,105.2
Food	1,508.4
Ores & minerals	729.3
Agricutural raw materials	248.6
Total incl. others	**16,576.1**

Main export destinations

	% of total
United States	13.1
China	8.7
Germany	6.4
United Kingdom	3.9
Japan	3.6

Main origins of imports

	% of total
China	13.9
United States	8.7
Germany	7.9
Japan	4.2
France	3.2

Balance of payments, reserves and aid, $bn

Visible exports fob	16,082
Visible imports fob	-15,648
Trade balance	434
Invisibles inflows	8,413
Invisibles outflows	-8,296
Net transfers	-231
Current account balance	320
– as % of GDP	0.4
Capital balance	...
Overall balance	...
Change in reserves	-839
Level of reserves end Dec.	12,383
No. months of import cover	6.2
Official gold holdings, m oz	1,053
Aid given – as % of GDP	

Health and education

Health spending, % of GDP	10
Doctors per 1,000 pop.	1.5
Hospital beds per 1,000 pop.	...
Improved-water source access, % of pop.	91.0
Education spending, % of GDP	4.7
Enrolment, %: primary	105
secondary	75
tertiary	35

Society

No. of households, m, m	2,012.2
Av. no. per household	3.7
Marriages per 1,000 pop.	...
Divorces per 1,000 pop.	...
Religion, % of pop.	
Christian	31.5
Muslim	23.2
Non-religious	16.3
Hindu	15.0
Other	13.8
Jewish	0.2
Cost of living, Dec. 2016 New York = 100	...
Cars per 1,000 pop.	132
Colour TV households, % with:	
cable	...
satellite	...
Telephone lines per 100 pop.	12.6
Mobile telephone subscribers per 100 pop.	106.6
Broadband subs per 100 pop.	18.0
Internet users, % of pop.	48.0

a OECD countries.

WORLD RANKINGS QUIZ

Test your knowledge with our new world rankings quiz. Answers can be found on the pages indicated.

Geography and demographics

1 Which country is the largest (by land area)?
a Brazil **b** China **c** United States **d** Australia *page 12*

2 France's marine territory is 20 times its land area, true or false?
a True **b** False *page 12*

3 Over half the world's mountains higher than 8,000m are in Nepal.
a True **b** False *page 13*

4 Which river is longest?
a Yangtze **b** Amazon **c** Mississippi *page 13*

5 Which desert is the largest?
a Syrian **b** Great Basin **c** Patagonian *page 13*

6 Which is the largest of the Great Lakes?
a Michigan **b** Superior **c** Huron *page 13*

7 Which of these has a population under 50m?
a Colombia **b** South Korea **c** Tanzania **d** Turkey *page 14*

8 Afghanistan has a faster-growing population than Nigeria.
a True **b** False *page 15*

9 Out of these, which has the most total births?
a Angola **b** Germany **c** Japan **d** United Kingdom *page 16*

10 Ukraine has a lower fertility rate than Germany.
a True **b** False *page 17*

11 Which of these has the highest proportion of people over the age of 70?
a Austria **b** Italy **c** Japan **d** Spain *page 18*

12 Which city in Latin America has the biggest population?
a Buenos Aires **b** Lima **c** Mexico City **d** São Paulo *page 19*

13 Out of these, which has the fastest rate of urban growth?
a Nigeria **b** Russia **c** Uganda **d** Ukraine *page 20*

14 This country is the world's biggest source of migrants.
a Mexico **b** India **c** Afghanistan **d** Bangladesh *page 22*

Economics and business

1 How many of the top ten fastest-growing economies in 1995–2005 remained so over the next decade?
a One **b** Three **c** Five **d** Eight *pages 30–1*

2 Which country experienced the biggest decline in services output over 2007–15?
a Bahamas **b** Greece **c** Italy **d** Japan *page 32*

3 Which country scores lowest on the United Nations Development Programme's Human Development Index?
a Yemen **b** Central African Rep. **c** South Sudan **d** Afghanistan *page 28*

4 On the Human Development Index, Iceland ranks ninth, but adjusted for inequality, its ranking rises to:
a First **b** Sixth **c** Second **d** Fourth *page 29*

5 Which non-Asian country receives the highest level of remittances from workers in foreign countries?
a Mexico **b** Egypt **c** Germany **d** France *page 36*

6 Which currency was most undervalued against the dollar in 2016?
a Hong Kong **b** China **c** India *page 37*

7 Out of these, which has the highest foreign debt?
a Indonesia **b** Malaysia **c** South Korea **d** Taiwan *page 40*

8 Which of these has the highest proportional household debt?
a Finland **b** Ireland **c** Sweden **d** United Kingdom *page 41*

9 Which country received the most foreign aid per person?
a Jordan **b** Lebanon **c** Syria **d** West Bank & Gaza *page 42*

10 Ethiopia had the highest growth in industrial output between 2007–15.
a True **b** False *page 44*

11 Which country depends most on agriculture?
a Mali **b** Liberia **c** Chad **d** Kenya *page 46*

12 Which country produces the most coffee?
a Brazil **b** Colombia **c** Vietnam **d** Indonesia *page 49*

13 Germany accounts for more than a fifth of zinc consumption in the EU28.
a True **b** False

14 Which country produces most energy?
a Canada **b** Indonesia **c** Australia **d** India

15 Japan is a bigger net energy importer than Iraq.
a True **b** False

16 Which country has the highest labour-force participation rate?
a Qatar **b** Rwanda **c** Greece **d** Italy

17 A higher proportion of women are working in Latvia than in Lithuania.
a True **b** False

18 The average working week is longest in:
a Turkey **b** Peru **c** Egypt **d** Hong Kong

19 A greater proportion of workers in Mali earn less than $2 per day than in Zimbabwe.
a True **b** False

20 Over half of the world's 20 most expensive cities for office rents are in Asia.
a True **b** False *page 59*

21 Which country has the highest foreign direct investment inflows?
a Germany **b** United Kingdom **c** Ireland
d Netherlands *page 59*

22 Which European country tied with Venezuela for the highest brain-drain score?
a Romania **b** Moldova **c** Macedonia **d** Serbia *page 60*

23 Which country spends the highest percentage of GDP on research and development?
a United States **b** Israel **c** South Korea **d** Japan *page 61*

24 On an index of innovation, which country scores highest?
a Sweden **b** Hong Kong **c** United States
d Switzerland *page 61*

25 Amazon's market capitalisation is bigger than Microsoft's.
a True **b** False *page 62*

Politics and society

1 Where is primary school enrolment lowest?
a Senegal **b** Mali **c** Syria **d** Sudan *page 68*

2 Which country has the lowest adult literacy rate?
a Chad **b** Afghanistan **c** Nigeria **d** Benin *page 69*

3 Which country has the lowest marriage rate?
a Iceland **b** Kuwait **c** Netherlands **d** Qatar *page 70*

4 Which country has the highest divorce rate?
a Cuba **b** Denmark **c** Russia **d** United States *page 71*

5 In years, what is the mean age of marriage in India?
a 16.7 **b** 17.8 **c** 18.2 **d** 19.5 *page 71*

6 Where is the biggest average household size?
a Iraq **b** Libya **c** Pakistan **d** Oman *page 72*

7 The cost of living is higher in Norway than in France.
a True **b** False *page 73*

8 Which country is the most generous?
a United States **b** Myanmar **c** Sweden
d Sri Lanka *page 73*

9 Car use has grown most in the past 20 years in:
a Argentina **b** Belarus **c** Canada **d** Kuwait *page 76*

10 Germany has a bigger merchant fleet than the United States.
a True **b** False *page 80*

11 Which country had the most terrorist incidents in 2015?
a Syria **b** Libya **c** India **d** Egypt *page 83*

12 Which country emits the most carbon dioxide per person?
a Poland **b** Qatar **c** Russia **d** United States *page 85*

13 Which of these countries has the most forested land?
a Bolivia **b** Colombia **c** Mexico **d** Peru *page 87*

14 Which country has the most dams?
a China **b** India **c** Spain **d** United States *page 88*

15 The UK has a better environmental ranking than Denmark.
a True **b** False *page 89*

Health and welfare

1 Which of these countries has the highest life expectancy?
a Andorra **b** Finland **c** Hong Kong **d** Israel *page 90*

2 People in the United States live longer than people in the US Virgin Islands.
a True **b** False *page 90*

3 In Swaziland life expectancy is lower for women than men.
a True **b** False *page 91*

4 Which of these countries has the highest death rate?
a Belarus **b** Hungary **c** Romania **d** Russia *page 92*

5 Which country has the highest infant mortality rate?
a Angola **b** Burundi **c** Chad **d** Mali *page 93*

6 Diabetes prevalence is highest in:
a Qatar **b** Kuwait **c** Mauritius **d** Malaysia *page 94*

7 Which country has the higher incidence of cardiovascular disease?
a Belarus **b** Georgia **c** Russia **d** Ukraine *page 94*

8 Which country has the highest rate of deaths caused by respiratory disease?
a Bangladesh **b** China **c** India **d** Pakistan *page 94*

9 HIV/AIDS is most prevalent in which country?
a Botswana **b** Lesotho **c** South Africa
d Swaziland *page 95*

10 Zimbabwe has a higher death rate from AIDS than South Africa.
a True **b** False *page 95*

11 Health spending is lower in South Sudan than in Congo-Kinshasa.
a True **b** False *page 96*

12 Where has obesity grown most?
a United States **b** South Africa **c** Oman **d** Egypt *page 97*

13 Which country has the greatest food deficit?
a Haiti **b** North Korea **c** Zimbabwe **d** Ethiopia *page 97*

Culture and entertainment

1 Germany has more landline telephones per person than France.
a True **b** False *page 98*

2 Which country publishes the most new books per person?
a Spain **b** France **c** Denmark **d** Italy *page 100*

3 Which of these has the most total visits to the cinema?
a Brazil **b** Japan **c** Russia **d** South Korea *page 101*

4 The French make more visits to the cinema than the British.
a True **b** False *page 101*

5 Which country has the least-free press?
a China **b** Eritrea **c** North Korea **d** Saudi Arabia *page 102*

6 Which country has produced most Nobel prize winners?
a Canada **b** Russia **c** Sweden **d** France *page 103*

7 Tennis's Davis Cup has been won most by:
a Germany **b** Argentina **c** France **d** Sweden *page 104*

8 Which country has been the more efficient gold medal winner at summer Olympic games?
a United States **b** China **c** Soviet Union
d East Germany *page 105*

9 Which country consumes the most beer per person?
a Austria **b** Czech Republic **c** Germany **d** Poland *page 106*

10 Americans are bigger tourist spenders than the Chinese.
a True **b** False *page 107*

11 Which of these has more smokers per person?
a Belarus **b** China **c** Lebanon **d** Russia *page 106*

12 Which of these saw the most tourist arrivals?
a Germany **b** Russia **c** Turkey **d** United Kingdom *page 107*

13 Australia saw the most gambling losses per person.
a True **b** False *page 106*

14 The United States has a higher circulation of newspapers than Japan.
a True **b** False *page 102*

Glossary

Balance of payments The record of a country's transactions with the rest of the world. The **current account** of the balance of payments consists of: visible trade (goods); "invisible" trade (services and income); private transfer payments (eg, remittances from those working abroad); official transfers (eg, payments to international organisations, famine relief). Visible imports and exports are normally compiled on rather different definitions to those used in the trade statistics (shown in principal imports and exports) and therefore the statistics do not match. The **capital account** consists of long- and short-term transactions relating to a country's assets and liabilities (eg, loans and borrowings). The **current and capital accounts**, plus an errors and omissions item, make up the **overall balance**. **Changes in reserves** include gold at market prices and are shown without the practice often followed in balance of payments presentations of reversing the sign.

Big Mac index A light-hearted way of looking at exchange rates. If the dollar price of a burger at McDonald's in any country is higher than the price in the United States, converting at market exchange rates, then that country's currency could be thought to be over-valued against the dollar and vice versa.

Body-mass index A measure for assessing obesity – weight in kilograms divided by height in metres squared. An index of 30 or more is regarded as an indicator of obesity; 25 to 29.9 as over-weight. Guidelines vary for men and for women and may be adjusted for age.

CFA Communauté Financière Africaine. Its members, most of the francophone African nations, share a common currency, the CFA franc, pegged to the euro.

Cif/fob Measures of the value of merchandise trade. Imports include the cost of "carriage, insurance and freight" (cif) from the exporting country to the importing. The value of exports does not include these elements and is recorded "free on board" (fob). Balance of payments statistics are generally adjusted so that both exports and imports are shown fob; the cif elements are included in invisibles.

CIS is the Commonwealth of Independent States, including Georgia, Turkmenistan and Ukraine.

Crude birth rate The number of live births in a year per 1,000 population. The crude rate will automatically be relatively high if a large proportion of the population is of childbearing age.

Crude death rate The number of deaths in a year per 1,000 population. Also affected by the population's age structure.

Debt, foreign Financial obligations owed by a country to the rest of the world and repayable in foreign currency. The **debt service ratio** is debt service (principal repayments plus interest payments) expressed as a percentage of the country's earnings from exports of goods and services.

Debt, household All liabilities that require payment of interest or principal in the future.

Economic Freedom Index The ranking includes data on labour and business freedom as well as trade policy, taxation, monetary policy, the banking system, foreign-investment rules, property rights, government spending, regulation policy, the level of corruption and the extent of wage and price controls.

Effective exchange rate The nominal index measures a currency's depreciation (figures below 100) or appreciation (figures over 100) from a base date against a trade-weighted basket of the currencies of the country's main trading partners. The real effective exchange rate reflects adjustments for relative movements in prices or costs.

EU European Union. Members are: Austria, Belgium, Bulgaria, Croatia, Cyprus, Czech Republic, Denmark, Estonia, Finland, France, Germany, Greece, Hungary, Ireland, Italy, Latvia, Lithuania, Luxembourg, Malta, Netherlands, Poland,

Portugal, Romania, Slovakia, Slovenia, Spain, Sweden and the United Kingdom.

Euro area The 19 euro area members of the EU are Austria, Belgium, Cyprus, Estonia, Finland, France, Germany, Greece, Ireland, Italy, Latvia, Lithuania, Luxembourg, Malta, Netherlands, Portugal, Slovakia, Slovenia and Spain. Their common currency is the euro.

Fertility rate The average number of children born to a woman who completes her childbearing years.

G7 Group of seven countries: United States, Japan, Germany, United Kingdom, France, Italy and Canada.

GDP Gross domestic product. The sum of all output produced by economic activity within a country. GNP (gross national product) and GNI (gross national income) include net income from abroad, eg, rent, profits.

Import cover The number of months of imports covered by reserves, ie, reserves ÷ 1/12 annual imports (visibles and invisibles).

Inflation The annual rate at which prices are increasing. The most common measure and the one shown here is the increase in the consumer price index.

Life expectancy The average length of time a baby born today can expect to live.

Literacy is defined by UNESCO as the ability to read and write a simple sentence, but definitions can vary from country to country.

Median age Divides the age distribution into two halves. Half of the population is above and half below the median age.

Money supply A measure of the "money" available to buy goods and services. Various definitions exist. The measures shown here are based on definitions used by the IMF and may differ from measures used nationally. Narrow money (M1) consists of cash in circulation and demand deposits (bank deposits that can be withdrawn on demand). "Quasi-money" (time, savings and foreign currency deposits) is added to this to create broad money.

OECD Organisation for Economic Co-operation and Development. The "rich countries" club was established in 1961 to promote economic growth and the expansion of world trade. It is based in Paris and now has 35 members from July 1st 2016, when Latvia joined.

Official reserves The stock of gold and foreign currency held by a country to finance any calls that may be made for the settlement of foreign debt.

Opec Set up in 1960 and based in Vienna, Opec is mainly concerned with oil pricing and production issues. The current members (2017) are: Algeria, Angola, Ecuador, Equatorial Guinea, Gabon, Iran, Iraq, Kuwait, Libya, Nigeria, Qatar, Saudi Arabia, United Arab Emirates and Venezuela.

PPP Purchasing power parity. PPP statistics adjust for cost of living differences by replacing normal exchange rates with rates designed to equalise the prices of a standard "basket" of goods and services. These are used to obtain PPP estimates of GDP per head. PPP estimates are shown on an index, taking the United States as 100.

Real terms Figures adjusted to exclude the effect of inflation.

SDR Special drawing right. The reserve currency, introduced by the IMF in 1970, was intended to replace gold and national currencies in settling international transactions. The IMF uses SDRs for book-keeping purposes and issues them to member countries. Their value is based on a basket of the US dollar (with a weight of 41.73%), the euro (30.93%), the Chinese renminbi (10.92%), the Japanese yen (8.33%), and the pound sterling (8.09%).

List of countries

	Population	GDP	GDP per head	Area	Median age
	m, 2015	*$bn, 2015*	*$PPP, 2015*	*'000 sq km*	*yrs, 2015*
Afghanistan	32.5	19.7	1,908	653	17.5
Albania	2.9	11.4	11,242	29	34.3
Algeria	39.7	164.8	14,614	2,382	27.6
Andorra	0.07	2.8	45,186	0.0	41.6
Angola	25.0	103.0	7,393	1,247	16.1
Argentina	43.4	631.6	20,346	2,780	30.8
Armenia	3.0	10.5	8,465	30	34.6
Australia	24.0	1,229.7	47,652	7,741	37.5
Austria	8.6	377.2	47,186	84	43.2
Azerbaijan	9.8	50.8	17,325	87	30.9
Bahamas	0.4	8.9	22,313	14	32.4
Bahrain	1.4	31.1	45,829	1	30.3
Bangladesh	161.0	206.7	3,603	148	25.6
Barbados	0.3	4.4	15,523	0.0	38.5
Belarus	9.5	56.3	18,311	208	39.6
Belgium	11.3	455.3	43,961	31	41.5
Benin	10.9	8.3	2,053	115	18.6
Bermuda	0.06	5.9	56,807	0.0	39.0
Bolivia	10.7	33.2	6,970	1,099	24.1
Bosnia & Herz.	3.8	16.3	10,702	51	41.5
Botswana	2.3	14.4	15,314	582	24.2
Brazil	207.8	1,801.5	15,477	8,516	31.3
Brunei	0.4	12.9	82,913	6	30.6
Bulgaria	7.1	50.2	19,433	111	43.5
Burkina Faso	18.1	11.1	1,698	274	17.0
Burundi	11.2	3.0	699	28	17.6
Cambodia	15.6	17.8	3,485	181	23.9
Cameroon	23.3	28.4	3,121	475	18.5
Canada	35.9	1,552.8	45,601	9,985	40.6
Central African Rep.	4.9	1.6	614	623	20.0
Chad	14.0	11.0	2,183	1,284	16.0
Channel Islands	0.2	9.2	57,500[ab]	0.0	42.6
Chile	17.9	242.5	23,823	756	34.4
China	1,376.0	11,226.2	14,314	9,563	37.0
Colombia	48.2	291.5	13,834	1,142	30.0
Congo-Brazzaville	4.6	8.6	6,568	342	18.7
Congo-Kinshasa	77.3	38.5	811	2,345	16.9
Costa Rica	4.8	55.5	15,906	51	31.4
Croatia	4.2	48.7	21,704	57	42.8
Cuba	11.4	87.1	22,357	110	41.2
Cyprus	1.2	19.6	23,728	9	35.9
Czech Republic	10.5	185.2	32,193	79	41.5
Denmark	5.7	301.3	46,890	43	41.6
Dominican Rep.	10.5	68.2	14,276	49	26.1
Ecuador	16.1	100.2	11,506	256	26.6
Egypt	91.5	332.1	11,712	1,001	24.7
El Salvador	6.1	25.9	8,657	21	26.7

	Population	GDP	GDP per head	Area	Median age
	m, 2015	*$bn, 2015*	*$PPP, 2015*	*'000 sq km*	*yrs, 2015*
Equatorial Guinea	0.8	13.8	43,488	28	20.5
Eritrea	5.3	4.7	1,647	118	18.6
Estonia	1.3	22.5	28,742	45	41.7
Ethiopia	99.4	64.7	1,632	1,104	18.6
Fiji	0.9	4.4	8,924	18	27.6
Finland	5.5	232.5	40,953	338	42.5
France	64.4	2,420.2	41,395[c]	549	41.2
French Guiana	0.3	5.0	16,667[ab]	84	24.5
French Polynesia	0.3	5.1	23,833	4	31.5
Gabon	1.7	14.4	20,354	268	21.4
Gambia, The	2.0	0.9	1,651	11	16.8
Georgia	4.0	14.0	8,930	70	37.5
Germany	80.7	3,365.3	47,833	357	46.2
Ghana	27.4	37.4	4,212	239	20.6
Greece	11.0	195.0	25,964	132	43.6
Guadeloupe	0.5	12.0	25,532[ab]	2	39.4
Guam	0.2	5.7	24,410	1	30.1
Guatemala	16.3	63.8	7,743	109	21.2
Guinea	12.6	6.7	1,191	246	18.5
Guinea-Bissau	1.8	1.0	1,501	36	19.4
Guyana	0.8	3.2	7,221	215	24.7
Haiti	10.7	8.7	1,760	28	23.0
Honduras	8.1	20.7	5,078	112	23.4
Hong Kong	7.3	309.4	56,983	1	43.2
Hungary	9.9	121.7	26,419	93	41.3
Iceland	0.3	16.8	50,700	103	36.0
India	1,311.1	2,088.2	6,104	3,287	26.6
Indonesia	257.6	861.1	11,063	1,911	28.4
Iran	79.1	374.3	17,035	1,745	29.5
Iraq	36.4	179.8	15,941	435	19.3
Ireland	4.7	283.4	64,844	70	36.9
Israel	8.1	299.4	35,217	22	30.3
Italy	59.8	1,825.8	36,559	301	45.9
Ivory Coast	22.7	32.8	3,551	322	18.4
Jamaica	2.8	14.2	8,816	11	29.1
Japan	126.6	4,382.4	40,432	378	46.5
Jordan	7.6	37.6	10,895	89	22.5
Kazakhstan	17.6	184.4	25,037	2,725	29.3
Kenya	46.1	63.6	3,085	580	18.9
Kosovo	1.9	6.4	3,390	11	24.0
Kuwait	3.9	114.1	75,015	18	31.0
Kyrgyzstan	5.9	6.7	3,467	200	25.1
Laos	6.8	12.6	5,551	237	21.9
Latvia	2.0	27.0	24,504	64	42.9
Lebanon	5.9	50.8	14,106	10	28.5
Lesotho	2.1	2.4	3,187	30	21.0
Liberia	4.5	2.0	835	111	18.6

	Population	GDP	GDP per head	Area	Median age
	m, 2015	*$bn, 2015*	*$PPP, 2015*	*'000 sq km*	*yrs, 2015*
Libya	6.3	29.8	9,083	1,760	27.5
Liechtenstein	0.04	6.4	80,000	0.2	42.0
Lithuania	2.9	41.4	28,636	65	43.1
Luxembourg	0.6	56.8	94,815	3	39.2
Macau	0.6	46.2	107,192	0	37.9
Macedonia	2.1	10.1	13,891	26	37.5
Madagascar	24.2	9.7	1,468	587	18.7
Malawi	17.2	6.4	1,186	118	17.2
Malaysia	30.3	296.3	26,978	331	28.5
Maldives	0.4	3.2	15,014	0.3	26.4
Mali	17.6	13.1	2,028	1,240	16.2
Malta	0.4	10.3	40,650	0.3	41.5
Martinique	0.4	12.0	31,579[ab]	1	46.1
Mauritania	4.1	4.8	3,893	1,031	19.8
Mauritius	1.3	11.5	18,976	2	35.2
Mexico	127.0	1,151.0	17,592	1,964	27.4
Moldova	4.1	6.5	4,379	34	35.6
Monaco	0.04	6.3	169,750	0	56.0
Mongolia	3.0	11.7	12,054	1,564	27.3
Montenegro	0.6	4.0	16,652	14	37.6
Morocco	34.4	100.6	7,967	447	28.0
Mozambique	28.0	14.8	1,191	799	17.1
Myanmar	53.9	59.5	5,249	677	27.9
Namibia	2.5	11.5	10,240	824	21.2
Nepal	28.5	21.3	2,463	147	23.1
Netherlands	16.9	750.7	49,732	42	42.7
New Caledonia	0.3	8.9	29,211	19	33.1
New Zealand	4.5	173.3	37,346	268	38.0
Nicaragua	6.1	12.7	5,185	130	25.2
Niger	19.9	7.2	955	1,267	14.8
Nigeria	182.2	493.8	6,004	924	17.9
North Korea	25.2	16.3	1,587	121	33.9
Norway	5.2	386.6	68,473	385	39.1
Oman	4.5	69.8	39,329	310	29.0
Pakistan	188.9	271.1	4,931	796	22.5
Panama	3.9	52.1	22,403	75	28.7
Papua New Guinea	7.6	21.2	3,549	463	21.2
Paraguay	6.6	27.3	9,253	407	24.9
Peru	31.4	192.4	12,290	1,285	27.5
Philippines	100.7	292.5	7,387	300	24.2
Poland	38.6	477.1	26,213	313	39.6
Portugal	10.3	199.2	28,223	92	44.0
Puerto Rico	3.7	102.9	35,578	9	36.3
Qatar	2.2	164.6	143,817	12	30.7
Réunion	0.9	22.0	24,444[ab]	3	34.3
Romania	19.5	177.5	21,332	238	42.1
Russia	143.5	1,365.9	26,200	17,098	38.7

	Population	GDP	GDP per head	Area	Median age
	m, 2015	*$bn, 2015*	*$PPP, 2015*	*'000 sq km*	*yrs, 2015*
Rwanda	11.6	8.3	1,831	26	19.2
Saudi Arabia	31.5	651.8	54,105	2,150	28.3
Senegal	15.1	13.7	2,435	197	18.0
Serbia	8.9	37.2	10,979	88	40.6
Sierra Leone	6.5	4.5	1,558	72	18.5
Singapore	5.6	296.8	85,128	1	40.0
Slovakia	5.4	87.3	30,094	49	39.1
Slovenia	2.1	42.8	30,371	20	43.1
Somalia	10.8	5.9	410	638	16.5
South Africa	54.5	314.7	13,354	1,219	25.7
South Korea	50.3	1,382.8	36,907	100	40.6
South Sudan	12.4	12.5	1,913	644	18.6
Spain	46.1	1,193.6	34,985	506	43.2
Sri Lanka	20.7	81.2	11,914	66	32.3
Sudan	40.2	81.4	4,195	1,879	19.4
Suriname	0.5	4.9	17,396	164	29.0
Swaziland	1.3	3.9	8,441	17	20.5
Sweden	9.8	495.7	48,561	447	41.0
Switzerland	8.3	670.7	58,216	41	42.3
Syria	18.5	28.4	3,016	185	20.8
Taiwan	23.4	525.2	47,094	36	37.5
Tajikistan	8.5	7.9	2,827	141	22.5
Tanzania	53.5	45.6	2,593	947	17.3
Thailand	68.0	399.2	16,380	513	38.0
Timor-Leste	1.2	2.9	4,589	15	18.5
Togo	7.3	4.2	1,499	57	18.7
Trinidad & Tobago	1.4	23.6	32,359	5	33.8
Tunisia	11.3	43.2	11,292	164	31.2
Turkey	78.7	859.0	24,239	785	29.8
Turkmenistan	5.4	36.0	16,438	488	26.4
Uganda	39.0	25.1	2,055	242	15.9
Ukraine	44.8	90.9	7,601	604	40.3
United Arab Emirates	9.2	370.3	69,858	84	33.3
United Kingdom	64.7	2,863.3	41,741	244	40.0
United States	321.8	18,036.7	56,049	9,832	38.0
Uruguay	3.4	53.1	21,441	176	34.9
Uzbekistan	29.9	65.4	6,299	447	26.3
Venezuela	31.1	260.1	16,525	912	27.4
Vietnam	93.4	191.3	5,925	331	30.4
Virgin Islands (US)	0.1	3.8	37,920[ab]	0.4	41.0
West Bank & Gaza	4.7	13.4	2,850	6	19.3
Yemen	26.8	37.7	2,824	528	19.3
Zambia	16.2	21.2	3,838	753	16.9
Zimbabwe	15.6	14.2	1,798	391	18.9
Euro area (19)	335.2	11,606.0	40,580	2,759	43.8
World	7,349.5	74,196.0	15,630	129,733	29.6

a Latest available year. b Estimate.
c Including French Guiana, Guadeloupe, Martinique and Réunion.

Sources

Academy of Motion Pictures
AFM Research
Airports Council International, *Worldwide Airport Traffic Report*

Bank of East Asia
Bloomberg
BP, *Statistical Review of World Energy*

CAF, *The World Giving Index*
CBRE, *Global Prime Office Occupancy Costs*
Central banks
Central Intelligence Agency, *The World Factbook*
Company reports
Cornell University
Council of Tall Buildings and Urban Habitat

The Economist, www.economist.com
Economist Intelligence Unit, *Cost of Living Survey; Country Forecasts; Country Reports; Liveability Index*
Encyclopaedia Britannica
Euromonitor International
Eurostat, *Statistics in Focus*

FIFA
Finance ministries
Food and Agriculture Organisation

Global Democracy Ranking
Global Entrepreneurship Monitor
Global Terrorism Database, University of Maryland
Government statistics

H2 Gambling Capital
The Heritage Foundation, *Index of Economic Freedom*
Holman Fenwick Willan

IFPI
IMD, *World Competitiveness Yearbook*
IMF, *International Financial Statistics; World Economic Outlook*
INSEAD
Institute for Criminal Policy Research
International Civil Aviation Organisation
International Cocoa Organisation, *Quarterly Bulletin of Cocoa Statistics*
International Coffee Organisation
International Commission on Large Dams
International Cotton Advisory Committee, *March Bulletin*
International Cricket Council
International Diabetes Federation, *Diabetes Atlas*
International Grains Council
International Institute for Strategic Studies, *Military Balance*
International Labour Organisation
International Olympic Committee
International Organisation of Motor Vehicle Manufacturers
International Publishers Association
International Rubber Study Group, *Rubber Statistical Bulletin*
International Sugar Organisation, *Statistical Bulletin*
International Telecommunication Union, *ITU Indicators*
International Union of Railways
Inter-Parliamentary Union

Johnson Matthey

McDonald's

National Institute of Statistics and Economic Studies

National statistics offices
Nobel Foundation

OECD, *Development Assistance Committee Report; Economic Outlook; Government at a Glance; OECD.Stat; Revenue Statistics*

Pew Research Centre, *The Global Religious Landscape*
Population Reference Bureau
Progressive Media

Reporters Without Borders, *Press Freedom Index*

Sovereign Wealth Fund Institute
Stockholm International Peace Research Institute
Swiss Re

Taiwan Statistical Data Book
The Times, *Atlas of the World*
Thomson Reuters

UN, *Demographic Yearbook; National Accounts; State of World Population Report; World Fertility Report*
UNCTAD, *Review of Maritime Transport; World Investment Report*
UNCTAD/WTO International Trade Centre
UN Development Programme, *Human Development Report*
UNESCO Institute for Statistics
UN High Commissioner for Refugees
UN Office on Drugs and Crime
UN, Population Division
UNAIDS
US Department of Agriculture
US Energy Information Administration
US Federal Aviation Administration

Visionofhumanity.org

WHO, *Global Health Observatory; Global Immunisation Data; World Health Statistics*
World Anti-Doping Agency
World Bank, *Doing Business; Global Development Finance; Migration and Remittances Data; World Development Indicators; World Development Report*
World Bureau of Metal Statistics, *World Metal Statistics*
World Economic Forum, *Global Competitiveness Report*
World Federation of Exchanges
World Health Organisation
World Intellectual Property Organization
World Tourism Organisation, *Yearbook of Tourism Statistics*
World Trade Organisation, *Annual Report*

Yale University